Soldiering On –
Finding My Homes

Memoir of an Army Brat

Christine Kriha Kastner

authorHOUSE®

AuthorHouse™
1663 Liberty Drive
Bloomington, IN 47403
www.authorhouse.com
Phone: 1-800-839-8640

First published by AuthorHouse 4/22/2011

ISBN: 978-1-4567-4183-9 (e)
ISBN: 978-1-4567-4184-6 (dj)
ISBN: 978-1-4567-4185-3 (sc)

Library of Congress Control Number: 2011903223

Printed in the United States of America

Any people depicted in stock imagery provided by Thinkstock are models, and such images are being used for illustrative purposes only. Certain stock imagery © Thinkstock.

This book is printed on acid-free paper.

For Aunt Mary, who helped verify what I had long suspected.

"In all literature there are only two plots: someone takes a journey or someone returns home." —Alix Kates Shulman, "A Good Enough Daughter"

Contents

Prologue ix

Out of Cyberspace. 1

My Mother Wore Combat Boots 6

Moving On 16

Orders from Headquarters 18

The Royal DeLuxe 22

Resourceful 25

Making Myself Over. 30

"We Shall Return"...Like the General 34

Coming Home 56

Our First Day 77

Good to Go! 86

Himeyuri. 89

Battlefields Tour 97

Yamada-san's Buddha 104

Kokusai Dori. 110

Shujiro Castle 120

Cape Hedo 123

Behold: The Power of eBay 129

School Days. 143

Whisky Tango Foxtrot! 156

Sam's By The Sea. 164

So These Are My Siblings? 169

Frank Lloyd Wrong. 175

But Wait, There's More! 181

Colorblind 186

Army Nurse 191

Flubber 206

SOS 211

Army Slang 215

Last Days 218

Addicted 220

The Mess Kit 223

Hotei 226

Closing Ceremony 228

Drawing Down 231

Back Where We Started 240

Reconnecting 251

Dad's Military Records 260

Epilogue 267

Prologue

I'm around five years old. I'm staring up at an oven door. It's rounded at the top and set into a brick wall. I'm standing next to my father, with my hand in his. We're in a large, cold building, and the floors must be cement. And I hear someone talking about people being put into ovens . . .

That's my earliest memory, and I remember looking up at Dad and asking if this was the oven for Hansel and Gretel? And where was the Wicked Witch?

But all that Dad said to me back then was, "Not for Hansel and Gretel."

Stationed in Munich, Germany, Dad was in the U.S. Army. We were on a family outing, and my family was touring Dachau—the concentration camp.

That early image stuck with me and through the years, I thought of the large oven in the brick wall. Eventually, when I grew older and learned the history behind Dachau, I realized where we had been, and what I had seen. I finally understood how terrible that place was.

"*Plus Jamais.*" For a long time I never knew what those two words meant or what the language was, but they were printed on the cover of a booklet that my parents received in 1956 when we were touring Dachau. I was probably nine or ten years old when I came across it in a drawer, and I stared at the horrifying black-and-white photographs…piles of dead people tossed into mass graves and corpses being pushed into ovens…I couldn't stop looking at those images. They were burned into my memory.

As I grew older and learned more about what took place there, I didn't want to see those ghastly pictures again. I almost forgot about that little booklet.

Twenty years later I returned to Germany. As I talked about my trip, Dad pulled that same little booklet from somewhere in his desk, and handed it over—as though he had come across an old Michelin Guide to Germany.

"Here. You might want to take a look at this," he said. "You don't remember, but we went to Dachau when we were stationed in Munich."

I have that little booklet now. And I know that those French words translate into *"Never Again."* I *do* remember it, Dad.

I traveled with my friends to Munich for the Oktoberfest in 1976, and I convinced them that we should take an eighteen-kilometer train ride to the small town of Dachau to visit what has now become a memorial and a museum.

Something drew me back to Dachau. It was overcast, and gray and solemn, as it should be.

At the concentration camp now, there is a large bronze sculpture designed by a survivor of the camp. It depicts skeletons hanging against a barbed-wire fence background and symbolizes the emaciated bodies of the prisoners.

I found that building, the *Krematorium*. I stood in front of what must have been the same oven where I once stood as a little girl. My friends and I walked along the gravel pathways around what is now an elaborate memorial site—with a museum where graphic black-and-white photographs and glass cases full of artifacts document the unspeakable horrors that took place.

Now, I appreciate and understand Dachau's somber history. How could my mother and father have brought me to this place when I was a little girl, assuming that I would not pay any attention? That I would remember nothing? That it required no explanation?

Later that afternoon, while on the train returning to Munich, one of my friends exclaimed, "So whose idea was this anyway? What a depressing way to spend the day. I'll be drinking lots of beer tonight."

Clearly, my friends wished we had not gone to Dachau and wondered why I would have even suggested it.

I remember telling them that it was an important part of history and should not be forgotten. We needed to see Dachau. Actually, *I* needed to see Dachau once more for myself, but could not explain why to my friends. I was beginning my return to places where I had been. I wanted to revisit places that I remembered. I wanted to make sense of my memories. I once was an army brat.

I created a list back when I was in high school—with fifteen specific addresses—places that I could call "home" and ten schools that I attended—many of them named after war heroes like General George C. "Old Blood and Guts" Patton and General "Vinegar Joe" Stilwell—in places scattered all over the globe.

Any military brat can tell you how many homes they lived in and how many schools they attended.

I would often think about many of the places we lived and wonder what they were like now. When we left a post, I wondered what the next family would be like that moved into our quarters. Who would live in our house? Who would sleep in my bedroom? I even wondered who would be sitting at my old desk, in my old classroom, in my old school.

I daydreamed about going back to some of those places I remembered. I was at just the right age to remember the most about our years living in California: Fort Ord, Seaside and the Monterey Bay area, Mission San Juan Bautista. And then as a teenager, I remembered even more from the tiny Pacific island of Okinawa. I was twelve when we moved overseas, and the four years we spent on that island seemed to be the happiest years for my family.

While living in California, we'd pile into the Plymouth on Sundays to go for long rides. It was a family thing. We just drove. Dad headed down the coast highway, through Pacific Grove, Carmel, and into Big Sur, to Point Lobos, where we'd pull over to let our dachshund go for a run along the beach. (Back then, beaches weren't private. You just pulled over and found a spot to park the car.) Tina Marie would dart wildly across the sand like a "slinky-dog" and bite the waves as they rolled onto shore, determined to catch them. She would get tangled, rolling in piles of kelp that washed up onto the beach. There were caves along the beach that flooded when the tide swept in. Wooden steps led to cliffs above those caves, and we walked along narrow pathways atop windswept cliffs high above the beach, with only staked ropes to hold onto. It was a challenge when you met someone walking from the opposite direction and had to squeeze past one another. But it was exhilarating. It felt like we could blow right off those rocky cliffs.

We drove through the city, past the Monterey Presidio, past the marina, into the cannery area, beneath connecting walkways that made up John Steinbeck's Cannery Row. I knew who Steinbeck was and was reading his newest book, *Travels with Charley*.

We drove past lettuce fields in Salinas and artichoke fields in Castroville. We drove through Pacific Grove one autumn to see for ourselves the cypress and eucalyptus trees covered in millions of orange-and-black-and-white butterflies. It was time for the monarchs to spend their winter in California. The bark on the trees along historic 17-Mile-Drive, were covered with the fluttering butterflies.

There was an airport somewhere nearby and when Mom worked on weekends, we would park outside a fence and watch the planes take off. Dad and my brothers sat on top of the car hood, staring up at the sky. I sat inside, reading a book. Watching planes was not what I cared about. I couldn't wait to go home.

It seems as though there is always one child in a family who has the ability to stand back and observe. That child is the one who often ends up writing about the family. I'm that child in our family. As the oldest, I saw and remembered the most. I observed my family's life, and these are my memories.

So much of life is fate. My independence started when my family's military life ended. It happened when I graduated from high school and found my first job.

Through the years, whenever people would ask where I was from, I would tell them that I was born in Cleveland, but never lived there until we retired from the army after twenty-one years of service. It's how many of us military brats explain our origins. It's a question that cannot be answered easily. It's complicated. Some brats simply go with the city where they were born. Others pick the place that they liked the best. There's no one simple answer.

But when I started that first job out of high school and a co-worker asked me where I was from—I responded as always and told him that I lived in many places before we retired from the army. He laughed and said, "You mean *your father* retired from the army!"

No. I know for sure that *we* retired from the army. It was a family effort. We were all behind the scenes for Dad—his army wife and his three little army brats. All of us followed the chain of command. Everything we did reflected on Dad and his military record.

Many army wives feel that they enlist for duty when they marry a soldier and follow him wherever the U.S. Army orders him. In my mother's case, she was wearing her own combat boots and was already enlisted when she met my father. Mom was an army nurse stationed at Camp Cooke, California when she met Dad. She already had an idea of what military life was like.

Mom and Dad chose their army. We three kids were born into our parents' army and made the best of the situation. We never knew anything else. Army life was our "normal."

Six photo albums document my family's life—assorted photographs of the five of us in the many places we've lived. Often out-of-focus, some with the tops of heads chopped off, most are black-and-white, with a few faded color snapshots. Some of the photos have identification on the back—written in Mom's slanted skinny cursive handwriting, in green fountain pen ink. Everything was neatly organized by Mom after we finally stopped moving around and ended up in a house of our own in Ohio. After all those years, she finally found time to neatly organize our life into those six albums. Those albums hold the clues to finding out about my family.

As a little girl, I liked to peer closely at the black-and-white snapshots of my mother's early life, asking questions about the people in the pictures—especially the little dog that Mom told me was named "Tossie." It was the only dog she had as a girl. She loved that dog. I looked through those albums often. Mom told me many stories about growing up with her brothers in a little house along Hale Avenue. I liked hearing Mom tell those old stories about relatives that I never really knew.

Mom told me about her grandmother, my great-grandmother Mary Koik, who lived well into her nineties. I learned that she once worked in a Cleveland chewing gum factory as a young girl, packaging sticks of gum by hand. I also discovered that great-grandma once had been "courted" by Dr. Scholl. (Yes, *that* Dr. Scholl!) When I learned this, I knew his name from the exercise sandals I was wearing! If my great-grandmother had ended up with the "King of Corns," the gene pool would certainly have been altered!

Mom told me about her father—my grandfather—Ralph Weber, who named me.

She said, "When I was trying to think of a good name for you, he suggested 'Christine,' and it sounded good to me."

When I look through those old albums, I see life highlighted by photos of our houses and pets—signifying milestones. Most of the photos include our many dachshunds—which help to identify times and places. And it's the sentiment associated with those locations that compels me to return to some of them. I have this desire to revisit and recapture those memories. Who says you can't go home again? I don't believe that. I'm making serious progress in my quest to return to places I've been.

The six photo albums are mine now. The chain of custody ends with me. I'm convinced I'm the only one with any sense of history, so I'm in charge of preserving our family's photographic record.

When you're a military brat, you don't have one house that you can always call home. No lifelong pets. No neighbors that always lived next-door. You've always on the move. Your family is your only constant connection to the past.

We lived in strange places just long enough…long enough to make them familiar. And then we moved on.

Out of Cyberspace

A late-night e-mail rolled in from John "Dub" Bauer, a Kubasaki High School alumnus from the Class of '68. I could just picture some guy named "Dub" trolling the Internet, locating people all around the world with a past connection to the Okinawa school, encouraging them to join the alumni association. That's how he snagged me.

Surely "Dub" was single-handedly responsible for increasing the membership of the Kubasaki alumni group.

The Kubasaki High School Alumni Association (KHSAA) was open to anyone who had ever attended, taught or worked at the Department of Defense Dependent Schools (DoDDS) high school, and with Internet visibility, was growing rapidly.

Back to my computer. I read and then re-read his message. Amazing! This was an incredible opportunity to actually return to the island of Okinawa! It was a trip that I was not likely to ever plan on my own. I had put the small Pacific island out of my mind long ago. Costing $2500 total, this was something I couldn't pass up. I'd never have another chance like this!

It wasn't too far past midnight, so I woke my sleeping husband to tell him this exciting news. Don mumbled something incoherent and rolled over, burying his face into the pillow.

Being a "night-owl," I returned to my cyber-basement. I responded that I was definitely interested in the trip and would immediately contact the trip's organizer. But all Dub mentioned in the e-mail was a Washington D.C. phone number and address. For some reason, our trip organizer, Larry Laurion, was just not reachable like the rest of us.

The next morning, I phoned Larry and left a message on his answering machine. A few hours later I left another. I ended up leaving several messages throughout the weekend, because Dub warned that there would be a cutoff for the trip, and I definitely wanted to be included. I just had to be on that trip!

Around noon, my husband called me from the office and said that the trip probably was something that I should go ahead and check out. Obviously he had just been experiencing one of his "Fred Mertz" moments the night before.

Don actually said, "You will regret it forever if you don't go." (Translation: "I will never hear the end of this if you don't go.")

I told Don that I would definitely try to find out more details about the trip. (Translation: "I'm already going—so it's a good thing that you're coming around.")

Specifics for the trip involved five payments of five hundred dollars that were to be mailed off to Larry Laurion in Washington, D.C. over the next six months. I was a bit wary about simply mailing personal checks off to some guy in Washington D.C. At one point, when I spoke to Larry over the phone, I inquired if the checks should be made payable to the Kubasaki High School Alumni Association. He told me to "just make them payable to Larry Laurion."

"Shouldn't they be made out to the 'Larry Laurion 401-K Account'?" I joked. I had no idea yet if "low-tech Larry" even possessed a sense of humor. At least he laughed. That was a good sign.

All apparently was legit; after the final payment hit the mail, I received a handwritten itinerary, along with a handwritten list of the names and addresses of the attendees from Larry, "the Luddite."

When I joined the alumni association and received a membership roster, I came across many names that I remembered from the past. There was some serious alumni activity taking place on a regular basis, with reunion events happening throughout the year in places like Honolulu and Las Vegas. I never seriously considered going though because I figured that no one would remember me. I was such a quiet, shy student, and I always considered myself "invisible," a phenomenon that I had discovered was common among "fortress daughters," girls who grew up in the military patriarchy as "daughters of warriors."

But this was different. This would not be just another party reunion. This would be a return trip all the way back to Okinawa. It wasn't important who might or might not remember me. This was my chance of a lifetime—to return to another place where I once had lived. I would do it. I would go.

Researching the military brat phenomenon has helped me to understand my own family. Years ago, I wandered into a book store to browse the new titles and stared at a book entitled *Military Brats, Legacies of Childhood Inside the Fortress,* by Mary Edwards Wertsch. I hung out in many bookstores and had never encountered anything that specifically addressed me and how I'd lived. I bought it immediately and began to read.

I read it back in 1991. And then I read it again, just recently.

A sociological phenomenon has emerged among military families in which wives are referred to as "fortress mothers" —performing a supportive role in the family unit by offering a source of emotional warmth. The author refers to boys as "warrior-sons" and girls as "invisible daughters of warriors." And of course the "warrior" is the husband/father. Being female in a military man's world takes a toll on mothers and daughters. That book explained so much about how I felt.

I always had this feeling that people would not remember me—that I was "invisible" among those around me. Because I was shy and quiet, I did not make a lasting impression on the people around me—my classmates and neighbors—and they would never remember me. I didn't stand out. When I began to research the life of a military brat and the dynamic of the military family, I discovered that many daughters really *do* feel invisible—especially to their fathers! To learn that what I have always felt is so commonplace among many daughters of military men explains so much.

I never got to know my father very well. Dad was not communicative and didn't know what to make of me. I don't think he knew what to do with any of us kids, but especially me, his daughter.

Early the next morning, I called my mother to tell her about the trip. I was so excited. Mom was also excited and happy for me. She encouraged me to go, stressing that I'd probably never get another opportunity like this.

After I signed on for the trip, Mom called Julia Gillion, down in South Carolina—her best friend and the mother of one of my girlfriends on Okinawa, to tell her the big news. In touch through the years, Mom and Julia exchanged Christmas cards and kept each other up to date on family milestones.

A unique bond exists among military families. Isolated in remote locations for long stretches of time, those friends and neighbors become very close. Military families remain strongly connected through shared experiences. And they stay connected, sometimes only through Christmas cards.

Only when we retired and moved back to Cleveland, did we finally get to know our relatives. Military families often spend the holidays far away from home. As a result, Christmas traditions include an array of holiday items acquired from around the world. Mom displayed a carved bamboo nativity set from Okinawa, along with Christmas candles from Germany. The aluminum Christmas tree came from California with little *Schuco* motorized cars from Munich, zooming around a track beneath the tree.

Christmas cards reflected where we were stationed. While on Okinawa, the cards we sent depicted a geisha standing against a snowy backdrop of Mount Fuji. We received cards from people we knew who lived in Germany—"*Frohliche Weihnachten*"—and I learned early on that "*Mele Kalikimaka*" more or less translated into "Merry Christmas" when we received cards from friends in Hawaii. Cards arrived from people all around the world, and they continued until we lost track of one another.

(By the way, I discovered years later that "*Mele Kalikimaka*" didn't even mean "Merry Christmas" and was just pure Hawaiianization for *haoles* (tourists) who missed their mainland holiday.)

There's an unwritten rule among military families: *Addresses should only be written in pencil.*

Julia became so excited while talking to Mom, that she proclaimed, "I just have to go along! I have to! Is there some way I can hide in Chris' suitcase?"

Maybe Julia was just joking, but I took her remark seriously enough to track down Larry Laurion, who said that Julia could go along with the group—if there was room for her. She had a strong connection to Okinawa. She could come! Taking Julia along was definitely the best thing I could have done.

My Mother Wore Combat Boots

"Grace, what have you done?" Grandma must have responded with an anguished tone to her voice when Mom broke the news to her in a long-distance phone call from California early in 1951. Mom was serving as a nurse in the Women's Army Corps (WAC). She'd wrapped up basic training in Fort Lee, Virginia and trained as a med-tech in Fort Sam Houston, Texas when she got orders for Camp Cooke.

And now she was all the way out there, over a thousand miles from home—and pregnant. That wasn't good. Back in those days, if you got pregnant while serving in the U.S. Army, you went home—immediately. Mom actually told me this significant fact of army life at one point when I was a young girl. And then she mentioned it several times more through the years. Now that I think back on it, she was clearly trying to make me aware of something.

"You couldn't stay in the army and have your baby. There was no way to care for a baby. You had to just get out," she mentioned more than once.

"Your mother wears combat boots!" Remember that childhood taunt? Well, *my* mom really *did* wear combat boots! She told us kids about how she had served as a WAC and how she had worn a gas mask

during basic training. She described how she had to go into a gas-filled chamber and pick up her gas mask and pull it over her head, fasten the strap securely and then breathe through the filter. It had to be done calmly and without panic. My brothers and I listened in awe as *our mother* told us this tale. She must have even held a gun in her hands. She could have fired that gun! Mom must have been pretty confident that she could actually do all of this to become a soldier. But, why? Why on earth would she want to become a soldier?

Mom told us how she graduated from Jane Addams Vocational High School in Cleveland where she was a member of the very first class of licensed practical nurses. She got her first nursing job at Huron Road Hospital in East Cleveland and then decided to join the WACs and was sent off to Fort Lee, Virginia for eight weeks of basic training

Our mother in a tent? Our mother wearing a helmet? Wearing combat boots? The mother we knew would never even consider camping!

Trying to solve the mystery of Mom and why on earth she decided to enlist in the army, I tracked down her best friend since fifth grade, Mary Muster. Mary and Mom grew up near each other and walked to St. Jerome's Catholic school until eighth grade. After that, they rode the streetcar together from their homes on the east side of Cleveland to Jane Addams High School along Carnegie Avenue near downtown. Both graduated in 1947—Mary trained to operate power machines, and Mom trained in licensed practical nursing.

Mary explained matter-of-factly, "Grace was determined to join the army, but she couldn't meet the weight requirement. She needed a few extra pounds on her, so she wrapped a chain around her waist and hid it beneath her clothes for the weigh-in."

I couldn't conceal my surprise at this disclosure, and immediately an episode of *Andy Griffith* came to mind: Barney Fife, with a chain wrapped around him, to add weight so that he could qualify for a promotion to detective. (Like my husband says, "You can't make this stuff up!")

When I realized that I hadn't been listening, Mary hadn't even noticed.

Now she was saying something about her sister Roseann wanting to become a WAC. Mary rambled on that her sister Roseann also joined the army, but had to wait until she turned eighteen because their mother wouldn't give permission for her to enlist before she was of age.

It was 1950 and the Korean conflict was heating up. There was some serious recruiting activity taking place back then…so all I can imagine now is that Mom was caught up in the old slogan, "Join the Army and See the World!" Mom was looking for adventure…and she ended up…with Dad.

But to wear a chain for added weight! Long ago, Mom told me about how she always was skinny and underweight as a girl. She talked about how someone decided to send her off to a "fresh-air camp" to try to put some weight on her. Both Mom and Grandma referred to it as a summer camp where city children went back in the 1930s and 1940s. But to me, "fresh-air camp" sounded like a punishment. I discovered that the camps had something to do with low-income families and an opportunity for better nutrition and obviously "fresh air" because they were far away from the city.

As she grew up, Mom remained skinny. Food was not the issue. Apparently body type was. Mom was just your basic "ectomorph." Nothing could change her body type. She could never evolve into an endomorph. She would remain skinny.

Anyway, I'm more and more convinced now that only a handful of people knew that Mom was not married when she came home pregnant. And perhaps it was only her parents who really knew, because she had the perfect cover! Who wouldn't believe that she got married while stationed out at Camp Cooke? And now it was becoming clear to me that even her closest friend Mary didn't have a clue.

Mary had planned a baby shower for the end of August. We talked about it when I visited. I brought along the old photo album, full of black-and-white snapshots. Everyone was gathered in Grandma's living room, opening baby gifts. Even my grandfather was proudly holding up a little satin comforter.

But Mom was not in any of the snapshots.

Mary said, "We all arrived at the house and expected to surprise Grace…but suddenly your grandmother announced to us that she had a big surprise of her own—Grace was in the hospital, and you had been born!"

I've decided to simply accept that my mother wanted to get away from home to change her life—and joining the army was a way to do that. That's all I can come up with. And the fact that she ended up getting pregnant isn't even an issue today. I know how upset Grandma and Grandpa Weber must have been back then in 1951. It was supposed to be marriage before the baby carriage! The story was that my parents got married out in California, Mom became pregnant, Dad got orders for Korea, and Mom came home to have me! Something tells me they covered it up very well and no one was the wiser—except for Dad's side of the family, all those "cheese-heads" up in Wisconsin.

I visited with my Aunt Mary in Dad's hometown of Oshkosh and decided to find out what she knew about the past. When I told her that I needed to talk to her about when my parents got married, she turned and looked at me slyly, and said, "You tell me what *you* know—and I'll tell you what *I* know." I was definitely onto something.

It turned out that Dad's entire family was aware of his indiscretion. Everyone knew the truth back then, but they were amazingly good at keeping secrets. They knew all along, but wanted to protect my feelings.

Dad arrived in Oshkosh without warning in early September of 1951. He told the family he was a father—but there was even some confusion about what I was—a boy or a girl? How could he not know that? The army shipped Dad home from overseas and he was supposed to be headed to Cleveland to get hitched. He didn't have a lot of details, but clearly he was having second thoughts about getting married.

Dad's visit home was cut short in the middle of the night—around the time he set fire to Grandma's living room sofa.

Aunt Mary was the only girl, clearly outnumbered in a household full of older brothers, six boys who stormed in and out, leaving trails of dirty laundry and always looking for something to eat. Grandma certainly had her hands full, but got a break as each of her sons went off and joined various branches of the military and then made their way in the world. She was lucky. Amazingly, all of her boys returned home safely after the war ended.

Edward, the oldest boy, a cook in the U.S. Army Air Corps, was stationed on Tinian Island in the Marianas and had the best war story of all.

After he was discharged, Ed revealed that something top-secret had been under way. "It was all hush-hush," he said. "Planes kept taking off and landing from the island. And then came August 6th and a B-29 with the name '*Enola Gay*' painted on her nose, took off with what we later learned was something code-named '*Little Boy.*'"

"Little Boy," the 9000-pound atomic bomb, had been stashed right there on Tinian Island, and went through intensive target-testing before it was dropped on Hiroshima on August 6th, 1945. Everyone finally learned what had been under way. And if "Little Boy" was there, "Fat Man" must have been close by.

Alois ("Ollie") enlisted in the U.S. Navy, served on PT Boat 186, and saw combat as a gunner's mate, sinking at least one Japanese warship in the Pacific.

Raymond served in the U.S. Marines aboard the USS Grant, a transport ship that ferried troops along the coast from San Francisco to Seattle to Kodiak to Honolulu. Uncle Ray was always out for a good time and smuggled booze onto the ship…and apparently never got caught.

Albert signed up with the Merchant Marines and served on board an oil tanker based out of Long Beach.

John was in the U.S. Army, stationed aboard a hospital ship, the USS Dogwood, that sailed from England to New Zealand.

And Joe, the youngest son, ended up making a career out of the U.S. Army, learning to make excellent false teeth in military dental labs, serving in Japan and Korea, and getting his "rite-of-passage" tattoos—JAPAN on one arm and KOREA on the other—in simple block letters. (Those must have been the first words I learned to read!)

Back to that blaze! Aunt Mary recalled how her youngest brother came home from Korea unexpectedly and went out drinking with his buddies. Dad's buddies were guys with nicknames—like "Bounce" and "Punky"—youthful nicknames that stuck. So even when they became balding men with beer bellies, they seemed eternally young because they were still called by those nicknames and would be until the day they died.

The blaze! Grandma woke up in the middle of the night, smelled the smoke and beat out the flames on the sofa. Then she sent Dad packing. He was on the next train to Cleveland, following orders from Grandma and the U.S. Army—to make an honest woman out of my mother. "Bad-Boy Joe" most certainly was my mother's downfall.

Hearing the stories from Aunt Mary made me realize there was so much I didn't know about my father. Everything she told me became more and more fascinating.

That courthouse wedding on September 12, 1951 in downtown Cleveland was my parents' first official wedding date.

As I looked through Mom's old photo album, I peered closely at several snapshots which were taken out in California in March of 1951. Mom was wearing a loose tweed "swing coat." Apparently I was the slight bulge beneath that loose coat. What was going through her mind back then? She had her whole future ahead of her, and she couldn't have known for sure that she and my father would get married. She must have been worried.

And then I looked closely at pictures of my parents standing beside Grandma and Grandpa in the back yard of the little house on Hale Avenue, the ones taken on September 12, 1951. That's the date that Mom wrote on the photos in green ink, in skinny cursive writing, with her fountain pen. She wasn't worried any longer. She was married.

It all made so much sense now. I was a "love child" for seventeen days!

That date appeared on the marriage certificate that I came across one day when I was simply rummaging through the desk—the marriage certificate from the courthouse in Cleveland. When I was sixteen years old, I discovered that I was born illegitimate. It was on my mind for a long time after that, but I never could bring myself to question Mom about my discovery.

As the years went by, it became less important, and I really didn't even think about the date of my parents' marriage any more. At least they got married.

No wonder there was so much confusion through the years about their wedding anniversary. Obviously, the September courthouse ceremony was not mentioned. Mom always said that their real anniversary was in December, when they got married out in California, but Grandma always claimed that the *real* wedding was the ceremony in an army chapel—the one that I attended as a two-year-old.

That ceremony took place in Camp Crowder, Missouri. Mom's younger brother Herb took the train from Cleveland with Grandma to visit. While down there in Missouri, Grandma insisted that a ceremony take place in the chapel. So we all went off to the nearby army chapel for a wedding. Mom wore her plaid wedding suit and Dad wore his uniform. I wore a white cardigan sweater and black-and-white saddle shoes.

I'm in those wedding snapshots—the little girl hanging onto my mother's hands and poking my shoe into the grass.

Now there were three dates—the fictitious California wedding date that Mom always vaguely referred to, so that my birth on August 27th appeared legitimate; the September 12th date in the courthouse; and finally, the army chapel ceremony in Missouri on May 14, 1953.

I bought cards for two anniversaries because Grandma would remind me of the May anniversary and then Mom would mention the December anniversary! Dad got away with the confusion and I don't remember him ever getting Mom a card or flowers, except for her birthday.

Just before Mom died, my brother Dan uncovered the Cleveland courthouse marriage certificate among my parents' papers. Mom's deepest secret was uncovered for the second time, and Dan couldn't wait to tell me the big news. He gleefully announced his discovery that I was a "bastard," right there in the hospital waiting room.

"I already knew," I responded.

I'm sure Dan didn't believe me. He thought he was dropping a bombshell. Sister-in-law Paula stood by Dan's side, probably expecting me to break down in tears. If I hadn't already known, I might have. But what was shocking to me once, long ago, had now lost its significance.

Mom's secret was responsible for my existence. I urged my brother Dan *not* to say anything to either Mom or Dad. Now near the end of her life, it was important to let Mom take her secret with her.

More than fifty years have gone by, and what might have been scandalous back then, is commonplace now. Girls got pregnant before marriage back then. Girls still get pregnant. But back in Mom's time, girls went off for a "visit" with relatives and ended up in homes for unwed mothers. They either put up the babies for adoption or kept them and hastily got married. I'm glad I'm here. I wasn't planned, but all these wedding ceremonies were! And I was around for all of them!

I would never have asked Mom about her secret. It was obvious what must have happened, and it seemed easier to go along with Mom's story that Dad was overseas when I was born and that he didn't come home again until I was around two years old.

But what was it about Dad? And what was it that attracted Mom to him? What attracted them to each other? Every child wonders about that and hardly ever finds out. But I did.

Mom was tall and thin. And apparently Dad had a thing for tall, thin women.

Before we shipped out for Germany in 1955, we drove north from Missouri to Oshkosh, Wisconsin to meet all of Dad's relatives. By then, I was three years old, and it was the first time that Dad's family had laid eyes on Mom and me.

Aunt Mary told me, "When Grace walked into the room, we were struck by her resemblance to someone that Joe knew before he left town to join the army. He really liked her and they went on a few dates, but she didn't pay attention to him. She was tall and thin… with brown hair…your mother looked so much like her."

The thing I remember most about Mom is how long and slender her fingers were. But they simply matched the rest of her. She was tall. Mom usually wore flat or low-heeled shoes because she was five feet, ten inches tall—to Dad's average height of five-six. Another thing about her was that she never wore makeup—only lipstick. She wore Revlon's "Love That Red" bright movie-star-red lipstick and never left the house without it! Years later, when she was getting dressed up to go with Dad to a party, she would ask me to come over and put eye makeup on her. That never went well. I could not suddenly glamorize Mom for an evening out.

And somehow, her brown hair never turned gray! Well into her seventies, Mom still had that brown hair of hers, with only random gray hairs scattered throughout. I'm counting on those good hair genes. And forget about red lipstick!

Aunt Mary also remembered that she made some comment about Mom's skinny legs…something about "Olive-Oyl" and that she was sure my mother took it the wrong way.

"But Mom really *did* have legs like Olive-Oyl," I laughed. "When we were kids, I'm sure we must have told her that when we looked at those pictures in the old albums.

She had long skinny legs and wore white socks with penny loafers."

Olive-Oyl. Definitely Olive-Oyl.

Moving On

After Mom and Dad went downtown to the courthouse for that first wedding ceremony, Dad returned to active duty in Korea. Mom went back to her nursing job at Huron Road Hospital while assorted relatives took care of me. Mom had a strong support system.

Grandma worked in a Fisher Foods grocery store and Grandpa worked nearby at the Collinwood Railroad yard. Back in those days, your world was smaller and everything seemed to be within walking distance—work and shopping and school. You got around easily by streetcar or bus. My grandparents didn't drive.

I don't know why Grandpa didn't meet my father with a shotgun, but for some amazing reason, the two of them hit it off well enough that they went out and got drunk together!

Mom told me that Dad came home on leave after I was born. She said that was the first time he saw me. She said that he and Grandpa put a fence around the front porch railing so that I couldn't wander away once I started walking. And she told me how the two of them walked down East 152nd Street to the Sylvia Café, where all the railroad workers hung out. They had a great time. Years later, every time I drove past the old Sylvia Café, I thought about how they "tied one on."

I was ten months old when my grandfather dropped dead from a heart attack. He was fifty-one years old. Mom told me many times how Grandpa was so proud to be a home owner, but was determined to pay off the mortgage as soon as possible. She told me how he worked all the overtime he could at the railroad yard, how he had chest pains and the only thing doctors could do back then was to prescribe nitroglycerine tablets and rest. But instead of resting, Grandpa kept working. One day, he walked home from work and was lying on the bed until dinner was ready. Mom said she went in the bedroom to tell him that dinner was on the table and found him dead.

Mom spoke about that day often and how there was nothing that could be done. When Grandpa felt chest pains, he simply took a few nitro tablets and tried to ignore it. All he wanted to do was to put in extra hours.

Mom was so sad that her father didn't live very long after I was born. She said that he loved me so much and she reminded me often that he was responsible for selecting my name.

"Paying off that mortgage was the most important goal in his life, and it was just about impossible to do," Mom said many times over. "Debt bothered him. It killed him. He didn't like owing money."

It was sad. If only he had not worked himself to death. If only Grandpa had spent more time enjoying me—his first grandchild. He was so proud of me, and yet I have absolutely no memory of the person who loved me that much and was responsible for selecting my name.

After Grandpa Weber's death on June 22, 1952, it was another eight months before my father came home from Korea and our little family drove off in a used Dodge to Camp Crowder, Missouri, our first PCS (Permanent Change of Station). Our military family odyssey was just beginning.

Orders from Headquarters

As I look at old black-and-white snapshots in the photo albums, I can see now that we lived in some pretty ramshackle dwellings—some real shacks. There I was, a little girl sitting on one of those front porches, perched upon open wooden planks, at one of four addresses in Missouri. And then there I was, sitting on another porch that looked pretty much the same, but at a different address.

There's no one left now to tell me why we lived on-post for a short time in 1953, in two sets of quarters, only to move two more times in 1954, into a rented house on Delaware Street and then another rented house on Murphy Street. If Mom and Dad thought they were "trading up," it didn't look that way. There were cyclone fences and clotheslines in the back yards of both little shacks.

While in Missouri, the most memorable event besides my parents' second wedding ceremony, was baby brother Raymond's birth on July 13, 1954. Now there were two little army brats.

Dad must have decided by then to make the army a career, so he reenlisted for another three-year hitch. Every three years, he could "re-up" or get discharged. While in Missouri, we got orders to go overseas to Munich, Germany. We left the port of New York on February 23, 1955, aboard the USNS General William O. Darby and docked in Bremerhaven on March 4, 1955. We were traveling by ship because Mom had claustrophobia. She liked to tell people how she traveled all over the world—and never once flew in an airplane.

In Munich, we lived in the *Perlacher Forst* housing complex. All I can remember is climbing lots of steps to get to a playroom on the top floor of our building. My best friend was a girl named Renee. That was where I started school—kindergarten in Munich, Germany.

Mom always liked to tell the story about how she took me off to my first day of kindergarten, and how I walked home later that morning because I wanted a drink of water! Apparently I didn't catch on that I was supposed to stay there.

And it was in 1956, while in Munich, that Mom received a letter from her mother. Grandma got married! She married an old railroad friend of my grandfather's, a long-time acquaintance named Oscar Jepson. It was on June 16, 1956. Mom was in tears. How could Grandma have remarried? Just like that?

It's not like I remember her tears, but I do remember Mom telling me about this. Mom told me a lot. She said that she was so hurt that Grandma had remarried. Mom wanted her father's memory preserved.

All I knew was that my new grandfather went by two nicknames—"Popeye" and "Red"—and was someone whom Mom could only vaguely remember. Soon after they married, my grandparents moved out west, to Klamath Falls, Oregon where "Red" got a job with the Southern Pacific Railroad as a brakeman. Grandma was off to a new life in a place that she always referred to as "God's Country."

That expression really irritated my mother. Grandma was excited about a new beginning and Mom could only think about what had been in the past in Cleveland.

When we returned from Germany, we had orders for Fort Lewis, Washington and that put us out on the west coast. We spent a lot of time driving down to Klamath Falls and we kids got to know our grandparents.

We called Grandma's new husband "Grampa." And we kids liked him. I couldn't wait to learn why he was called "Popeye." He put up with three instant grandchildren and walked us over to the local newsstand to let us pick out "funny-books." He introduced me to stamp collecting and bought me my first stamp album. He showed me how to soak off the adhesive from the backs of used stamps and fasten them with stamp hinges into the album. Grampa collected first-day-issue covers and walked to the post office to buy them as they were released. He took me along.

He had an old black cocker spaniel that couldn't be trusted not to snap at us. "Wimpy" was the dog's name, and it fit perfectly with "Popeye," which was the nickname he got because of the time he spent sailing the world with the merchant marines. As a teenager, he joined the merchant marines with his brother Roy. The two brothers signed up together and were assured that they would sail on the same ship—and rarely saw each other again until they got back on dry land. I treasure a photo taken of the two of them at Sloppy Joe's Bar in Havana in 1929—dressed in three-piece suits, leaning back against the bar, wine glasses in hand, holding cigars.

Grampa puffed away on stinky cigars, but also used Skoal chewing tobacco. I remember how he called it "snoose." I think he came up with some story about how kids wouldn't like the taste and finally offered us a tiny bit because we kept pestering him. Once Ray and Danny began spitting all over the ground, I didn't need to give it a try.

He rode the rails from Klamath Falls down through southern California and back, often returning home with bags of walnuts. He would sit out in the back yard, shelling them on an old tree stump. My brothers thought it was great fun to help him and pound away at those walnuts. In that back yard was a shed with an alley behind it. Wild cats lived in that shed. Grampa fed them, but drowned any newborn kittens by placing them into a burlap bag in a bucket of water. He said it had to be done. No, it didn't. But he wouldn't listen to me. Their eyes hadn't even opened yet. I wanted to save them all.

He *was* the only real grandfather we kids ever knew, and he was good to us. It was clear though that Mom felt betrayed. I never realized this until years later when I was older. Now I realize how it must have broken Mom's heart to see us having fun with him.

The Royal DeLuxe

While Mom suffered through the years with claustrophobia, I craved small cozy spaces and sought them out—the snuggier the better!

I crawled onto the bottom mattress of a trundle bed when I had to share a room with my brothers in California. They were in a bunk bed across from me. I hid out from my brothers and spied on them while they played with their friends.

In a ramshackle rental in Seaside with worn linoleum floors and a noisy, clattering print shop right next door, I claimed a tiny bedroom closet for my own and hid myself away from everyone. That little closet became "my space" and with clothes hanging above my head, I sat on an upended pink metal doll trunk in front of a small wooden dresser that my grandfather made for Mom when she was a little girl. I played with my dolls and was able to avoid my annoying brothers. I ran a cord for a little dresser lamp with a ruffled shade under the door—so I wasn't totally in the dark.

I hated having to share a room with my brothers, but it was just temporary until we got quarters on post. So I would spend hours hidden away. I could go into my closet, shut out the real world and create my own. If only the back of my closet had a secret door that opened up...like the back of the wardrobe to the land of Narnia.

There was a small metal swing set out in the back yard that was surrounded by a fence on one side, the print shop building on the other and an alley behind it. The yard was so tiny that the only other thing in it was a wooden picnic table pushed up alongside the print shop. When I was all by myself, I would swing and sing at the top of my lungs.

Other children—civilian kids—were singing songs like "On Top of Old Smokey" and "Waltzing Matilda" in elementary school, but I knew all of the words to the anthems for each branch of the military. That's what I was singing.

"From the halls of Montezuma, to the shores of Tripoli, oh those caissons go rolling along," and then I probably changed to "Anchors Aweigh." The next selection was probably "Over hill, over dale, we will hit the dusty trail," and then "Off we go…into the wild blue yonder," my favorite anthem, despite that it was not army, but air force.

Grandma took the train down from Klamath Falls to visit with us in California, and had a birthday surprise for me. She carried what appeared to be a small black suitcase.

"Here. This is for you. Aunt Margaret wanted you to have it."

I didn't really know Aunt Margaret, Grandma's sister, but Aunt Margaret knew me when I was a toddler in Cleveland while Dad was overseas.

I flipped open the twin latches on the front of that small black case. When I lifted the lid, there was a black typewriter inside, a 1935 portable Royal DeLuxe, with glass-covered keys. There was a manual clipped beneath the lid that showed a secretary with a bobbed-hair style on the cover. A small stiff-bristled cleaning brush was tucked along the side and there were two keys on a string. I could lock it. I loved it. I couldn't wait to type.

I turned a fresh sheet of three-ring notebook paper into the typewriter and began to peck out words on those glass keys. I didn't know how to "touch-type," but I would learn. Until then, I could pretend.

I liked to pretend I was writing stories… and then I pretended I was writing a diary…I liked to peck out stories. I remember typing passages from *The Diary of Anne Frank*, pretending it was my own diary. I typed letters to Aunt Margaret and to Grandma. Learning to type was the best thing ever.

Aunt Margaret lived in Cleveland and Grandma had been visiting with her. Grandma could travel anywhere by train for free because her husband worked for the railroad. That rail pass got her back and forth to Cleveland.

I don't know what made Aunt Margaret think that I would like that typewriter, but it was the best gift I ever received from anyone.

I used that little typewriter all through school for my reports and papers. It typed in twelve-point Elite. I still have it.

Resourceful

Like other army wives, Mom gathered familiar things around us every time we moved. She could make any house a home. She was good at that.

Armed with drapery hooks, pleater-tape, and her treasured Pfaff sewing machine from Munich, Mom would whip up window coverings wherever we lived. Other people ordered curtains from the Sears or J.C. Penney catalogs, but Mom bought sheets—simple flat white sheets. She used to tell people, "With sheets, there's a ready-made hem along one edge, and when you cut them down to fit the windows and stitch the pleater-tape in place, you insert drapery hooks…and your windows are covered!"

Mom was going through a pastel period while we were stationed at Fort Ord, California—and the hot new color in sheets at the time was a cool, minty green.

The afternoon sun shining through those drapes provided our living room with an air of phosphorescence. The room definitely took on a cool, rather "nuclear" tinge.

It was around then that the three of us kids got our own dog tags. Just like Dad's.

That little metal plate was embossed with my name and my religion. And probably Dad's serial number was on there too.

I wore my tag proudly beneath my undershirt. I liked the sound the tag made when I ran it up and down the silver steel ball chain.

Now I know why we got those dog tags. Now I know that it was not for fun. It was for identification. We were soldiers' kids and those tags could be used to identify us, like real soldiers in battle

In October of 1962, the world came closest to nuclear war. I remember a high level of anxiety and tension. Our country was on the verge of something big. Military personnel were "on alert" and "combat-ready." The Cuban Missile Crisis was under way. All I heard at the time was that the Bay of Pigs had been invaded and President Kennedy was in charge.

We lived in a duplex at the bottom of a steep hill. The family in the other half of our house was a colored family with five or six kids. I remember the night my family and our neighbors were standing around, talking to one another in hushed tones about President Kennedy and Fidel Castro, and Premier Nikita Khrushchev. I listened as adults whispered about what was happening. I was a sixth grader at Joseph Stilwell Elementary School and I knew something serious was under way—that there could be a nuclear war.

A standoff was under way in the Atlantic Ocean around Communist Cuba. The Soviets were building up their missile bases in Cuba and President Kennedy called for a blockade of Cuban ports by U.S. Navy vessels. The Soviet ships headed toward Cuba finally turned around and retreated with their missiles.

We were protected. What could be safer than living on an army post, surrounded by barbed-wire fencing? And by check-point gates guarded by armed MPs?

Streets in the housing areas were often named for famous battles—we lived on Carentan Road in Fort Ord, California. That street was named for a battle site in France during World War II. Our schools were named for famous military leaders—Joseph W. Stilwell Elementary and George C. Patton Junior High. General Stilwell had a home in Carmel, California and was famous for creation of the first soldiers' home at Fort Ord in 1943 on the bluffs overlooking Monterey Bay. (Not all schools were named for war heroes or generals though. I discovered that kids on Okinawa stationed at Kadena Air Base attended Bob Hope Elementary School.)

Our quarters at Fort Ord were a duplex unit, ranch style with a storage room, which was subtly intended as a "bomb shelter" because it was an interior room with no outside windows—a place to hide out during an attack.

It was where we kept the Christmas decorations and our photo albums. There were extra boxes of cereal and canned goods stacked on the shelves in that storage room. Combat rations (C-rations) also were stashed upon the shelves of our "bomb shelter."

That was when I broke into Dad's stash of C-rations.

Whenever I was left home alone, I flipped off the little metal keys that were soldered onto the lids and cranked open the olive-drab green cans—after making sure they were labeled "cookies, crackers or pudding." Those were the only things worth eating. It was my covert operation and dangerous. I can remember cutting my fingers a few times on the edges of those razor-sharp lids. But I never cut myself badly enough that I had to ask Mom for a bandage.

It wasn't like I had to worry about "lock-jaw," with all the shots I got. Army brats were fully-immunized at all times for almost anything.

C-rations were created to provide meals in battlefield conditions when it wasn't possible to set up a mess tent. C-rations were provisioned in 1938 and packaged to last forever, adding a lot of weight to a soldier's pack. C-rations probably would have gotten us through Y2K—if we had truly been in peril.

Production of C-rations was modified and ended in 1958, but stockpiles continued to be issued to soldiers serving in Vietnam. So what I consumed in 1962 was not so seriously outdated after all.

Underground bomb shelters were in vogue back then, but our "closet" was in no way close to a bomb shelter. There wasn't even a first aid kit around from what I can remember. It's a good thing those warheads didn't come our way. How would we have all fit into that one little room? All five of us? With our dachshund, Tina?

In the early 1950s test bombs were exploding all around the globe. Hydrogen bombs, not atomic bombs, became the issue. The Soviets and America were in a race to build up arms. Annihilation was rapidly becoming a goal. Tests took place on islands far away in the Pacific Ocean and on deserts in Nevada.

The U.S. detonated the first H-bomb on November 1, 1952 on an island in an atoll of the Pacific Ocean. Nine months later, the U.S.S.R. tested its own H-bomb. The largest peacetime arms buildup was under way. We kids were pretty much unaware of all this testing—until we began to take cover beneath our sturdy school desks in those "duck-and-cover" drills.

With the Cold War under way, I can remember Mr. Lichti (my first "man-teacher") at Stilwell Elementary instructing us in those "duck and cover" drills in case of a nuclear attack—the ones documented in grainy black-and-white film footage, where schoolchildren were shown taking cover, hunkering down underneath indestructible school desks! We were told to crouch beneath the windows of our classrooms, so shattering glass could pass right over us.

I thought about those Soviets a lot.

Once a week, I remained after school to attend Catechism classes with the other Catholic kids. I remember our religion teacher passing out comic books that depicted those Commies—the Soviets—the Red Menace—shutting down churches, closing down libraries, burning books, limiting freedom, and encouraging ordinary people to spy upon one another and report everything to the Secret Police. Even if you weren't doing anything suspicious, you could be branded a spy. The Secret Police could knock on your door at any time and take you away. You were guilty. Forget about pleading innocent. You were guilty.

People secretly tuned in to Radio Free Europe on hidden radios. And if your radio was discovered, it was confiscated and you were arrested. Everyone was an informant. You couldn't trust anyone, not even your closest friend or neighbor.

We were taught to fear those "Commies." I was afraid of them. I thought a lot about Secret Police and losing my freedom to read. Research proves the accuracy of my childhood memories. Comic books entitled *This Godless Communism* were produced by Treasure Chest Comics in the early sixties! And who was responsible for that comic propaganda? Apparently the Catholic Church!

And what I learned about the Iron Curtain and the Cold War haunted me. I thought about girls my age living behind the Berlin Wall under Communism. How freedom didn't exist, how they couldn't read what they wanted, how books weren't available like they were to me. I'd already identified with Anne Frank, reading her diary long before it became required in school. There was a lot for me to think about.

Making Myself Over

Each time we moved there was another first day at another school, and it meant another opportunity to reinvent myself.

Once again I found myself the "new girl of the week," but this time maybe it could be different. Maybe *I* could be different, I thought. This time, in this new school, I would raise my hand and speak up. I would provide witty answers. I would let my sparkling personality emerge and show my true sense of humor. This time I would be popular.

It never worked. I still was shy and quiet, buried myself in books, and rarely raised my hand, even when I knew the answers. It's not like I expected to become a cheerleader. I couldn't transform myself into anything other than what I was. Before I knew it, I was back in the library, back in my sanctuary.

The best thing about the dependent school system was that you were never the "new girl" for long. There was another fresh face arriving to take the attention away from you.

The boldest move I ever made was to join the high school choir at Fort Campbell, Kentucky where my low-pitched alto voice placed me near the tenors, alongside the boys. There were no tryouts required. A good thing, because shy girls don't sing solos. I was excited to be in the choir and enjoyed it, but it only lasted a few months—ending when Dad retired in October of my senior year, and I transferred to North High School in Eastlake, Ohio.

One last school. One last chance to transform myself. Could it still happen?

I remember back when we were standing around beneath some trees to watch the Okinawa Soap Box Derby at Kadena Air Base in 1965. The boys had been taking their runs down the slope to determine the grand champion from Okinawa who would compete in the National Soap Box Derby competition in Akron.

Standing there, in pretty dresses, one wearing a crown on her head, was the Soap Box Derby queen and her attendants—and there was Phyllis Simmons from my fifth grade class at Fort Ord! One of the attendants!

But now she was known as "Jeannie." And now she had become blonder than I could remember! More important to me, "Phyllis/Jeannie" was popular now. If "Phyllis/Jeannie" could do it, maybe I could too.

It wasn't until I encountered brat author Pat Conroy at a book signing event that I realized just how much we military brats all had in common.

When I read *The Great Santini*, I knew exactly what those Meecham kids went through. I knew how the lonely outcasts at each new school approached and befriended them, how Ben and Mary Anne Meecham accepted them as friends—but only until they could "trade up."

I knew what Conroy was talking about. It happened to me when I ended up at North High School when Dad retired.

Dad insisted that he didn't want the retirement parade he was entitled to after twenty-one years of service! We could have been there in the reviewing stand, along with other retirees and their families, and the military band and soldiers would have paraded past…instead, we just drove off early one morning, and my parents never looked back.

I rode backwards in the "jump-seat" of our Chevy Bel Air station wagon. I looked back all the way, staring out at the twinkling lights of Fort Campbell in the early morning darkness. As we turned north on Route 41 toward Ohio, my eyes filled with tears.

Mom reassured me that this would be my last new school, and as soon as I graduated, I could get a job. But being the new girl at this school lasted way too long. I was an outsider among students who'd known one another most of their lives.

As I sat shyly on the sidelines in the cafeteria of my last new school, it was another shy and lonely girl who befriended me. She apparently didn't have many friends, and it was an opportunity to claim me because I had none.

Unlike the Meecham kids, I didn't "trade up." This civilian school was tough on outsiders. This was the first time I didn't make any friends at all. I absolutely hated it there.

Some days it seemed like no one spoke to me. And for the first time, I encountered prejudice against the military. These were all civilians. There was no one like me at North High. Most of these kids clearly had been friends with each other since they had started kindergarten! I was an outsider. With the situation escalating in Vietnam and American support for the war dwindling, hostility toward anything military was rampant. "Going to 'Nam" was on the minds of the guys at North. Identifying myself as an army brat in a civilian school was not well-received. But it soon would be over. Graduation was a few months away.

I found a part-time job while in my senior year—working at a bakery near home. I remember a group of girls from high school coming in one evening, and I overheard their comments about me being an "army brat." I had the feeling they looked down on me. I couldn't wait until June.

Mom was my ally when it came to skipping school. She knew how much I hated each day there and let me stay home often; she wrote notes for me.

I graduated with a group of strangers, after deliberately letting myself become invisible.

I still receive notices about reunions for the Class of '69, the "Finest of the Fine."

Who *are* these people? Some of the names sound familiar, but I don't know them at all. So many people carry their high school experience with them for the rest of their lives, but for me, my real life began as soon as high school ended.

"We Shall Return"...Like the General

As I eagerly planned my return to Okinawa, I couldn't help but think of the words of General MacArthur. This was not the first return of Kubasaki alumni to the island. When I watched a videotape about a trip that took place five years earlier, I understood the feelings those old students had when they discovered the places that meant so much to them.

Larry (Class of '58) Laurion was responsible for arranging that first-ever historic Kubasaki alumni trip to Okinawa in 2001. A group of twenty Kubasaki High School Dragons from the 1950s traveled back to the island. *Real* Dragons, they were the first kids to attend classes in the "Quonset huts down by the East China Sea." Kubasaki High School on Okinawa was the first of the Department of Defense Dependents Schools (DoDDS) established after victory in the Pacific.

I discovered that other military brats shared my desire to find their homes and familiar places. I was not unique. Searching for the original site of the Kubasaki they attended, the Kubasaki that they remembered, the group anxiously peered from the windows of the bus for a landmark rock along the highway that marked the turnoff, but to no avail.

While riding that bus through the old housing areas, several Dragons located their old quarters. Some walked up to the front doors to have their pictures taken—while curious housewives and children watched from the windows. Amy (Class of '59) Nitahara burst into tears when she found a small grove of broad-leafed banana trees still growing in the back yard—trees that were descendants of those that her father had planted years before.

That 2001 reunion trip coincided with the Third International Uchinanchu Festival—a worldwide cultural event that brings together people of Okinawan heritage from all over the globe every five years. The people of Okinawa have a saying, "*ichariba-chode*" which translates to "Once we meet, we are like brothers and sisters." Okinawans have a well-earned reputation for hospitality.

Physically different from mainland Japanese, Okinawans have darker skin, wavy hair and some of the physical characteristics of the Ainu people of Northern Japan. Okinawans refer to themselves as "*uchinanchu.*"

Our trip coincided with the Fourth International Uchinanchu Festival, so I found myself in Chicago, in the International Concourse, of O'Hare International Airport. I was on the lookout for a lady I hadn't seen in years—an old friend whom I had gotten to know very well again through the past five months via e-mails and phone calls who told me that I would spot her because she would be carrying a pink flamingo tote bag—the one that her kids gave her as a "bon voyage" gift.

I approached Gate 59 and there was Julia—engaged in animated conversation with the uniformed man behind the United Airlines counter.

"Julia, I'm really here! We actually managed to pull this thing off!"

"Girl-san, we did it, all right," responded Julia with a hug. "We're going home."

Proud of our success, we'd cautioned each other throughout the past five months not to attempt anything foolish that could jeopardize our travel plans. And so far, only one of us had evidence of injury, and it was not me. Julia wore a wrist brace on her left arm. (She managed to do a "tumble and roll" down the driveway while going to the mailbox—and as a result, was wearing a brace.)

Worse things could have happened. We were careful when driving...and I didn't fall out of the attic while fetching suitcases. We managed to deflect all manner of potential problems—because there would be no second chance for a trip of this magnitude.

Seventy-three-year-old Julia Gillion was my mother's best friend, my friend Cathy's mother. Our two families were friends back on Okinawa. Settling down in South Carolina, our families remained in touch through the years with Christmas cards. Julia's a "hoot" with her "Minnie-Pearl" voice and had a youthful outlook on life. We ended up as roommates for this trip. I kept assuring Julia how well I got along with "old ladies," and Julia kept calling me "girl-san." This would work out great.

We were to meet up with four other Kubasaki Dragons who would share the flight from Chicago to Osaka. Plans called for all of the Dragons to converge upon Osaka from three hubs—Dulles, O'Hare and LAX—eventually meeting up with our leader, Larry, in the Kansai Airport hotel for the night. The next morning, the group would embark on a two-hour flight south to Naha, Okinawa for eleven days—on a mission to recapture happy memories from our shared past. Julia and I were on a mission all right, following our bliss.

While at O'Hare, Julia and I scanned the crowd, trying to find four more people who looked like they could be headed for a high school reunion on Okinawa—but everyone looked pretty Japanese to us! It wasn't until we were on the plane that we located the two Kellys, Larry and Betty, with their granddaughter, Anna, sitting just across the aisle! Larry Kelly had been busy sending eager e-mails for weeks. And it helped that they were wearing Kubasaki alumnae t-shirts. How'd we miss them?

Another alum, David (Class of '69) Knowles, was seated on the other side of the plane. The flight was at capacity and so was our excitement. We had about fourteen hours ahead of us…and no flight plan. We weren't pacing ourselves. We would do everything wrong.

Shortly after takeoff, two little Japanese women in front of us pushed back their seats and reclined! I don't know what I was expecting, but this wasn't it. With the seats in front of us fully-reclined, and the back seat pocket loaded with magazines and headphones and personal clutter, there wasn't any legroom at all. I stowed items above and stuffed items below, and made the best of it. But we failed to plan to sleep.

The stewardesses explained everything bilingually—in English and in Japanese—and were incredibly attentive. They were on a hydration mission with green tea, water and soda—and offered even more as we got closer and closer to Asia.

I tuned to a new release, *The Devil Wears Prada,* and Julia and I tried to calm down, stop our intense chatter, and watch the movie.

When the films ended, the stewardesses started them all over again. Since there was nothing else I was particularly interested in, I again watched *The Devil Wears Prada*—this time in Japanese. Several seats ahead of me, I saw someone tuned to a map and I located that option on my console. This was amazing—a map grid of our flight path—and I could see a tiny little airplane icon moving ever so slowly…heading north to Canada. We were flying at an altitude of 34,000 feet and the outside air temperature was freezing. Eventually our plane neared Juneau, Alaska and swung out over the Beaufort Sea. I kept switching from the flight path screen over to the *Devil*. I had a book with me but was too excited to read.

Julia and I laughed and talked—and reminisced about how our families found one another in 1963 while traveling to Okinawa from San Francisco aboard a navy transport ship on an eighteen-day crossing.

We left America when everyone remembers where they were. For me, it was just another of many last days of school, when I once again gathered up my belongings and moved to another new place.

Friday, November 22, 1963: the final day in my seventh grade class at Marina Del Rey School in Marina, California, before my transfer to a DoDDS junior high school located on Okinawa.

An announcement came over the school's public address system. Our principal said that something terrible had happened—then he told us that President Kennedy had been assassinated in Dallas. School was dismissed early, and I walked home to our rented California house in a new subdivision just north of Fort Ord. Mom was waiting for me and my brothers. The house was empty. Our household goods were already on the move to Okinawa, our other furniture was sent off to permanent storage, and now we were finally moving out on our own.

While stationed at Fort Ord, I remembered Dad coming home one day with news that he was up for another PCS to the Far East—and that meant orders for Hawaii, Japan, or Okinawa. We'd heard of Hawaii and Japan, but not Okinawa. We got Okinawa.

A small paperback book was our only introduction to Okinawa, the tiny Pacific island that we would call home for almost four years. Okinawa was a tour of duty where concurrent travel was not available. GIs had to travel ahead of their families and arrange for civilian rental housing before their families could join them. Dad found an off-post rental that was approved for army housing, so he made arrangements for us to join him.

Mom had been thoroughly briefed by Dad before he left to go overseas—and I remember all of us driving north to Oakland to the terminal where our Plymouth would be loaded onto the ship. That was the "dry-run" to familiarize Mom with the labyrinth of bay area underpasses and overpasses—a drive that was not without a lot of tension and several arguments. You see, Dad had to teach Mom how to drive a car while we lived in California (and you can imagine how well that went).

We took Dad to the airfield to leave for Okinawa. It was very early in the morning and still dark. It seemed like the army always made Dad leave in the dark. He was gone and Mom was in charge again. She had to take responsibility for all the details surrounding the big overseas move—even sending our dachshund off to live with Aunt Mary and Grandma in Wisconsin. Now this was the "real thing" with Mom behind the wheel. She must have been a nervous wreck, but we couldn't tell. Someone had to get us to our next home. She was responsible for getting the three of us—me at twelve, Ray at nine and Danny at six, safely across the Pacific Ocean to our father and the next tour of duty.

Like other army wives, Mom handled all the travel details—she was responsible for making sure that our passports and shot records were in order. For months, she had been taking the three of us to the dispensary for the required inoculations. I remembered getting shots for typhoid, tetanus, Japanese encephalitis, yellow fever, cholera and probably even bubonic plague. The shots were spaced out, but some of them really made our arms stiff and sore. I can remember getting our records stamped and dated for each of the shots. Not fun. And nowadays not necessary!

So here was Mom, driving our 1957 two-tone, Plymouth Belvedere V-8 with the push-button TorqueFlite three-speed automatic transmission and cool aerodynamic tailfins. Clearly, this was way too much car for Mom.

(Flash-forward twenty years to Stephen King's classic 1983 novel… about the demonic two-tone Plymouth named CHRISTINE—oh, how I would appreciate that book one day.)

On the day of the assassination, we drove north along the Pacific Coast highway and reported to the Oakland Terminal where we awaited the departure of the USNS Barrett. Mom turned in our car at the dock, and we checked into a military transient hotel close by. There was one black-

and-white television set in the day room of the transient quarters, and a crowd of mothers and children gathered in front of it.

Now when I think back to those vague images on that black-and-white television set—that we saw then for the first time and have now viewed over and over through the years—it's as though our own trip across the ocean took on historical significance as well.

Julia remembered that time as well. "We were staying with my parents because Bay was already on Okinawa. Mama and I were getting dinner ready and Daddy was in the living room, watching TV. All of a sudden Daddy yelled that someone had just shot Lee Harvey Oswald!"

Julia missed it. We missed it too. We missed witnessing history that weekend because we were so far removed from everything normal. We were following orders. That was our priority.

San Francisco, like the rest of the nation, was at a standstill. Everything was closed to show respect for President Kennedy. The nation was in mourning. Dad's brother, our Uncle Ray, owned a small shoe-repair shop in nearby Sausalito. On Sunday afternoon, Uncle Ray picked us up and drove us around Oakland and San Francisco. Everything was closed. Everywhere, there were signs in the windows of restaurants and stores, proclaiming respect for the President.

On November 25, 1963, we boarded the USNS Barrett, a navy vessel with a full crew, troops and cargo, and assorted military dependent families to transport to Honolulu, Yokohama and Okinawa. Part of the Military Sea Transport Services (MSTS), the Barrett constantly transported personnel and cargo while crisscrossing the Pacific Ocean from San Francisco to Honolulu to Yokohama to Okinawa to Manila, Guam and Hong Kong.

When I see those grainy black-and-white images on television now, they are unfamiliar. We weren't in front of the television then as many people were. Soon after the assassination, we left the foggy Bay area, passed Alcatraz, which was still a prison and a source of fascination for us kids, *passed beneath the Golden Gate Bridge—and were on the Pacific Ocean while a whole lot of history was taking place behind us.*

We didn't see Jack Ruby shoot Oswald. We never saw the funeral and didn't see John-John salute his father. We were removed from everything for eighteen days.

Julia recalled how her family learned that they were going to Okinawa. Her husband, Bay, came home from work and announced, "I got orders for Okinawa."

"Well, I knew where Okinawa was," said Julia. "And I couldn't see myself on a little bitty island with water all around, but there was no choice. You go where the army sends you."

The Gillions sold their house in South Carolina, and Julia and the kids moved in with her family until Bay could find an approved rental unit and send for them. Julia drove their 1958 Ford Galaxie to Charleston for transport by ship and then flew out to San Francisco with her three children, Cathy, eleven, Jim, eight and Gary, two. After landing in San Francisco, they immediately boarded a helicopter and were "choppered" across the bay to the Oakland Terminal. Another adventurous military wife on a mission, she was simply following orders and shepherding her brood across the country.

That's one thing we never got to do—fly in a helicopter! How'd we miss out on that? Army brats got to do a lot of things that civilian kids never did, like climbing around inside tanks and walking through monstrous C-130 Hercules turboprops during displays of military might. I remember sitting in the seats along the sides of that huge plane—where the soldiers sat. The straps and the canvas smelled old and dirty.

We stood and watched parades at Armed Forces Day festivities; we watched fighter jets roar through the skies over our homes, leaving white contrails behind them; from our school bus windows, we saw fresh recruits jogging along the streets; and the background noise in some of the places we lived was gunfire from nearby artillery ranges.

Patriotism was bred into us. Retreat came each day at 1700 hours. The flags were lowered, the sound of a single bugle could be heard from loudspeakers around post and everything came to a halt. You stopped your car if you were driving and if you were a kid riding a bike, you stopped and stood beside it.

Julia remembered, "When we finally got into the Transient Quarters in the Staging-Out Area, it was late at night and the sheets on the beds had not been changed! I first met your mother when I was trying to find someone to give us fresh sheets. Grace just shrugged and said she had no idea where to find clean linens, so I remember telling the kids to just 'pretend that the sheets were clean' and go to sleep! What else could I do? Your mother was absolutely no help that night. Who knew that we would end up becoming best friends?"

Aboard the Barrett, our family of four had shared a small stateroom— austere navy style, with bunks and a tiny stainless steel sink. The bathroom was a large one down the hall, used by the dependent families, without any privacy.

The Barrett was scheduled to dock in Honolulu but that stop was cancelled because a typhoon was churning away nearby in the Pacific. The captain avoided the storm by sailing around it, but that added several more days to our travel time and we still had half an ocean to cross.

I remember how rough it was. Whitecaps surrounded us. The ship was pitching and rolling. When you were lying in your bunk, you could feel the ship drop down, down, down and then it seemed to shudder, like it was going to break apart. Then your body would be lifted upwards, under the power of the ship. It was the strangest out-of-control feeling, and I've never forgotten it.

We all experienced some serious seasickness—especially six-year-old Danny. I remember that Mom took him to the ship's dispensary and he finally got a shot for nausea. I felt queasy too, and spent a lot of time eating saltines and drinking some type of lemon soda. (This was back in the days when Dramamine came in little yellow pills. It was way before pressure-

point wristbands and Dramamine patches. You had to just swallow that little yellow pill and hope you didn't barf it back up.)

Someone told us that we should get out of our staterooms and up on deck for some fresh ocean air. I can remember standing out on deck, but when I saw those waves crash up and over that deck, all I wanted to do was go below, lay back in my bunk and moan. Forget fresh air. Misery was our steady companion.

Eventually when things grew calmer, we spent time in the day-room, where old movies were shown over and over.

There was a grand piano there, and I remember some type of impromptu musical combo made up of servicemen and a dependent wife with a good voice and platinum blonde bouffant hair. She sang "I Left My Heart in San Francisco," which was a big hit at the time.

When we crossed the International Dateline—that imaginary line on the globe at 180 degrees longitude that separates two calendar days and keeps the Eastern Hemisphere one day ahead of the Western Hemisphere—a celebration took place on board the Barrett. It was an excuse for a party that involved walking the plank—a board set out across the floor of the day room. We had to walk without falling off and upon completion, were presented with certificates from King Neptune and Davy Jones' Locker. I still have my certificate.

There wasn't a lot of activity aboard the ship—it wasn't like a cruise ship—and the main purpose of the voyage was to move people and cargo across the ocean. No frills.

We finally docked in Yokohama Bay in mid-December and those going ashore for Japan disembarked. With the Barrett docked in Japan for most of the day, several families decided to leave the ship for a few hours. By then, we had made some friends and I remember we took several taxis to the Yokohama Navy Base, where we went bowling and ate at the snack bar.

Somehow, we ended up at the base exchange, and my first purchase was a small Japanese doll in a wooden box, with six assorted wigs—a katsura-ningyo. I now have little ningyos everywhere…The very first Japanese doll

I ever received was the ichimatsu (fully-jointed) doll that Dad mailed to Cleveland from Japan, when he was overseas.

Julia recalled, "We didn't get off the ship! The kids wanted to go somewhere, but I was too cautious. I thought y'all were crazy, taking off for hours like that. And it was getting late that night. I was worried. Y'all finally showed up around ten o'clock."

To this day, I can't believe my mother was so adventurous. The excursion had to be someone else's idea. Mom was a follower, definitely not a leader. Several small sukoshi cabs were involved just to get all of us to the base, and at one point, I remember we were trying to get back to the ship—even drawing a picture of an ocean liner and showing it to the taxi driver, who would just nod and then take us to the wrong dock!

And who had the yen anyway?

Who could have imagined? Two families from opposite ends of the United States thrown together on a navy ship crossing the Pacific Ocean, who ended up becoming lifelong friends while living upon a small island only sixty miles long and two miles wide at its narrowest point. There was a spot on Okinawa where you could stand high on a hill and see the Pacific Ocean on one side and the East China Sea on the other.

These occurrences took place all the time with military families.

While aboard the Barrett, the families were segregated from the rest of the military personnel aboard. That dependent wife singing with the combo apparently got a little too friendly with some of the GIs, and by the time the Barrett docked in Naha, her husband had been contacted and the woman was not even allowed to disembark! Her behavior on the ship was considered inappropriate and reflected upon her husband. She was very upset and was kept on the ship for a return trip back to San Francisco.

Maybe her heart really was there. She kept on singing that song!

It was quite a scandal. I remember Mom and Julia whispering about her. (I always listened in on Mom and Julia. I was a snoop, and eavesdropping on their conversations was an education.)

Everything we did as dependents served as an extension of our husbands and fathers and became part of his military record. There were rules of comportment: simple things like not wearing shorts to the PX or going out in public with rollers in your hair. If we kids got into trouble, Dad would have been called up by his CO (commanding officer). (It's a good thing Dad retired before my brothers could really stir things up as teenagers.)

The Barrett finally docked in Naha Port on December 18, 1963, and as the tugs pushed the ship into position by the dock, we three kids actually recognized Dad by his familiar gait, slowly walking, far away along the dock. You see, Dad was bowlegged—and we were all laughing—even Mom—because of how we spotted him. He stood out from the crowd and he would not have been amused at how we knew it was him. I don't know if Mom ever told Dad.

Julia remembered talking with a master sergeant who was standing beside her at the ship's railing—he was scanning the island and remarked, "The last time I saw this place, it was all blown to hell."

Several hours away from Osaka, everything suddenly seemed five times funnier. Julia and I both developed a case of the giggles. Those two Japanese women in front of us (still fully-reclined, with their short little legs stretched out in total comfort) turned around to look at us and Julia heard them remark, "Those ladies—they laugh all the time!" And later we learned from Anna (sandwiched into one of those "five-across" middle seating sections) that she had heard us laughing and wondered what was up with us. Anna later told us that she thought to herself, "At least someone's having fun on this flight!"

Every time I glanced across the aisle, Betty Kelly was still out cold. At least she didn't snore! When we questioned her later about her ability to sleep through the entire flight, she insisted that she wasn't really sleeping—she just had her eyes closed.

As I sat in that plane bound for Osaka, I pulled out my steno book. I had to capture details. I wasn't sure where I was going with my story, but I felt compelled to scribble. So I sat, strapped into a jet, thirty-four thousand feet up over the Pacific Ocean, taking notes while flying back to a small island that I lived on more than forty years ago. It seemed like light-years. I let the events unfold, figuring I'd make sense out of it later and turn it into something.

There were twenty-three of us on the trip, ranging in age from fifty-five to eighty-six—fifteen Kubasaki alumni and eight friends and family members—each with different stories and reasons for wanting to return to a tiny little island that all of us once called home.

Eager e-mails had been arriving for days from Larry Kelly about the possibility of a typhoon—a tropical storm named *"Bebinca"* that was churning around the Philippines—a storm that could pick up steam and develop into a typhoon that would affect our time on the island. That's not what I wanted.

Larry was actually excited that we might experience a typhoon when we arrived on the sixth of October. I checked the tropical weather site on the Internet, and *Bebinca* had been downgraded to a tropical depression and disappeared—although another storm soon appeared on the horizon, and also disappeared. We didn't need that much excitement. Our days on Okinawa were going to be limited, and I certainly didn't want to be holed up in a hotel.

I remember a plastic-covered map of Okinawa thumb-tacked to the back of my bedroom door. I used a black marker to chart typhoons as they approached. There were three levels of typhoon conditions, with condition one being the most serious. I remember swimming at the Sukiran Pool when a typhoon condition was announced, the pool was closed, and we were sent home. It was a bright sunny day. It didn't seem possible that a typhoon could have been anywhere nearby. There was no weather channel back then. We listened to AM radio. We scanned the sky. A Doppler could have been a dessert for all we knew.

I remember a story from an army wife who could see several navy ships anchored down below in a Pacific inlet when she looked out from her kitchen window. It could have been the same view of the Pacific Ocean that Julia had. That woman said that if she saw those ships moving out—or gone—she knew a typhoon was on the way. Those ships were her early warning.

While we were stationed on Okinawa, Typhoon Cora, classed as a "super-typhoon" with winds peaking at 175 miles-per-hour, hit near the island. It struck near the end of August in 1966, and I can remember falling asleep to the sounds of howling winds. When I swung my feet down to the floor in the morning, I was standing in about two inches of storm water!

Our quarters on post had tropical-style louvered windows with screens, and apparently the blowing rain seeped in during the night. Everything on the floor was soaked and floating. Dad went to the Sukiran Dental Lab and borrowed some type of wet-vac machine to suck up all the standing water.

Typhoons commonly formed in the Pacific region from June into October. Sometimes school was cancelled if a storm was approaching. When the eye, or the center of the typhoon, passed over the island, depending on the width of that eye, it could become sunny and dry—but only for a short time—before the other side of the swirling storm struck with equal vengeance.

Julia was still fretting because she didn't have Yoshiko's photograph; she had the black-and-white snapshot of her maid in her hand just a few weeks before. She was showing it to her grandchildren when it was misplaced. Julia was absolutely certain that she could locate the woman who had worked as her maid the entire time her family lived on the island—especially if she had that snapshot in hand. But it wouldn't be easy.

"I can't believe I lost it. After all this planning," said Julia. "I'm going to find it after I get home. I just know it will jump right out at me!"

Julia's Yoshiko was first of all her friend; second the family babysitter; and then her maid. And I'm sure that Julia was just as gracious to her Yoshiko as Mom was to our Yoko.

I reminded Julia that finding her Yoshiko was more than likely an impossible task. How could we? With no last name? How could we possibly locate a woman who would now be well into her seventies? A woman with one of the most common first names in Japan?

I wanted to find the places I remembered; Julia wanted to bring back memories of family life when she was a young wife and mother. There were many people working to make this trip memorable. E-mails flew back and forth from Kubasaki alumni who had remained on the island, many of them planning dinners and entertainment for us.

Once again I found myself tuned to the most popular channel on the flight and saw that the airplane icon was now positioned in the Sea of Okhotsk somewhere over Siberia and the Gulf of Anadyr, what once was a certain "shoot-down area," except that today we're sort of friendly with that former "Red Menace." We began a loop around the islands of Japan in order to approach Osaka from the south. The Osaka Kansai airport was built in a harbor upon a man-made island called Airport Island. It's the only twenty-four-hour airport operating in Japan.

Most passengers had finished watching the movies and were getting restless. As we neared our destination, it seemed that everyone was staring at the four-by-six-inch monitors—proving that anything on a screen will keep most people mesmerized. Our last feeding and watering by the flight crew was scheduled for one-and-a-half hours before landing. With that completed, we knew we were getting close.

As we neared the end of our fourteen-hour flight that had taken us through eleven time zones and across the International Dateline, we couldn't take our eyes off that tiny airplane! We watched eagerly as the little icon turned south and looped around to make a final approach, landing on the causeway. Julia and I had not slept a wink during the flight. We'd flown west, halfway around the globe, toward the sun. Even though the shades had been pulled and the lights turned down, we didn't sleep. We were now far from home—fourteen hours into the future—and wired.

I never considered myself claustrophobic—but now I understand the feeling. Several days later, Julia admitted to me that she was about ready to just "open up that door and walk off that plane!" I know now that I will never attempt such a lengthy flight without seriously preparing for relaxation and sleep.

We landed in Osaka around four o'clock p.m. Larry Kelly, wife Betty, and granddaughter, Anna Geffert, became our leaders by default. The Kellys were part of that first Kubasaki reunion trip back in 2001, and Larry certainly knew his way around the Osaka Kansai airport. Julia and I were willing followers as Larry steered us through the customs area, passport control, and over to the currency exchange line. We endorsed our travelers checks and the clerk placed them into a plastic basket. Each basket disappeared behind a curtain where our dollars were transformed into *yen*. Another clerk brought the money back to us with an official exchange form and counted out the *yen* and presented it to us with a polite bow. Already the politeness of Japan was overwhelming.

Julia and I mumbled, "*domo arigato.*" It was time to start remembering to bow.

We proceeded to check in at the Hotel Nikko, adjacent to the airport. It was so exciting to finally be upon Japanese soil. The hotel was lavish, with huge stone sculptures throughout the lobby that actually *did* resemble phallic symbols—(haven't done the research, but for some reason, those symbols are very, very big in Japan) and artistic *ikebana* flower arrangements positioned in *tokonomo* alcoves on the way to the elevators—as well as on each floor of the hotel.

Familiar with the expression "falling into a stupor," Julia and I were falling—fast into just that. We kept going, but exhaustion overtook us. We got to the hotel room and unloaded our bags. We used airport luggage carts to get our suitcases into the room—very convenient. Then we simply pushed them back into the hotel lobby. There was no bellboy to tip—and we were again reminded that there is "no tipping in Japan."

When we finally caught up with Larry Laurion in Osaka, he wasn't at all what I had pictured. Slightly balding, "Class of '58 Larry" was friendly and easy-going. The "likable old Luddite" had sounded so formal and stuffy over the phone. Several others shared my opinion.

Plans called for all of the Dragons to meet for drinks in the hotel bar that evening. Drinks! That's all we needed! Julia and I located the bar and greeted the rest of the trekkers, but were so tired that we could think only of getting back to the room and falling into bed. Politely, Julia asked me if I wanted to stay and meet the rest of the group. I asked her the same thing. Then we looked at one another and realized neither of us would be awake much longer, and the rest of the group would just have to think what they wanted.

Sound asleep by eight o'clock—one of us was snoring—and I was too tired to pay any attention to her.

Our hotel bathroom had one of those high-tech Japanese *TOTO* toilets that I'd read about—with a control panel along the side that enabled you to do much more than simply go and flush. You could spray-rinse your posterior and then blow-dry it with warm air. The lid lifted and lowered at the push of a button as well. It's all a blur now. Because I was so wiped out, I didn't fully appreciate my first encounter with a *TOTO*.

Some *TOTOs* located in public restrooms even feature a "flushing" sound effect so that shy women may pee, while the sound effects cover up what they're doing! High-tech *TOTOs* are pricey, can run into thousands of dollars, and are the rage among Japanese, who now have the most sophisticated bathrooms in the world.

The *TOTO* Company began to make bathroom fixtures back in 1917 and was an offshoot of the Noritake China Company. Porcelain *is* fully-functional.

I wondered where we would encounter the traditional Japanese trench toilets—because I had not practiced squatting enough (well, not at all if you want the truth)—and I knew I'd never get Julia near one of them—let alone back up on her feet!

Around four a.m., wide awake in Osaka, I found myself staring out of the window down at a bright red neon line of huge *kanji* symbols beyond an eerily deserted street. There was no traffic. We were in a hotel at the airport and it was far too quiet, probably due to extreme soundproofing. Soon Julia was also wide awake. We ended up talking for about an hour before finally falling asleep again. This was serious jet lag. We didn't worry about waking up in time for breakfast because in another few hours we were once again wide awake.

Breakfast in the dining room was buffet style, with tables of Japanese and Western food. I sampled a bowl of rice porridge, fish and fresh fruit, with a few more unfamiliar items, before finally settling on some basic toast, orange juice and coffee. I planned to sample as much Japanese food as I could. We soon located familiar faces—the Kellys and granddaughter Anna, whom we discovered had studied in Japan. Part of a language-immersion curriculum that involved living with a Japanese family in Arita, Anna was fluent in Japanese and couldn't wait to take a train into Osaka to explore the area. With a few hours before our departure on an Air Nippon Airways (ANA) flight south to Okinawa, we really didn't have anything to do and with a new best friend like Anna, we couldn't pass up the opportunity to explore!

After breakfast, I went into the hotel business center to use one of the computers to send off an e-mail to Don. I wanted to let him know that we had arrived safely in Osaka. (If we hadn't arrived safely, I'm sure we would have been "Breaking News" on CNN.)

I struggled with the keyboard—which was the standard QWERTY, but also equipped with many *kanji* character keys in all the familiar places. For a while I tried to "hunt and peck," but finally gave up and just typed the damn thing! The alphabet letters were mostly in the right places.

That message home to Don went right into the "JUNK" folder because of its suspicious subject line. Don had been searching for a message from me and retrieved the "suspicious" e-mail.

"What did you expect? It resembled a sloppy ransom note!" Don said later. "It's a good thing I always check that folder before I empty it."

Yeah, yeah, yeah. I've heard it all before. Always scan the "JUNK folder" before you delete the contents. I do...I do... sometimes. That's why Don's the home I.T. guy.

Anyway, what follows is the actual unaltered e-mail, retrieved from "JUNK" and saved for posterity:

```
-----Original Message-----
From: Christine Kastner
[mailto:optllc@operamail.com]
    Sent: Friday, October 06, 2006 10:43 PM
    To: kastner@stratos.net
    Subject: In Osak a  and headi n g OUTINaAN h  o  u  r
```

\ t h i s i s someTYPEofstrangekanjikeyboardandIsimply can : tTYPEon I t. MaybeIshouldbringonefor y o u. I : LLcatc hupthiseveningandfillyouIN. \weA R E INosakaandleavingso onfor n a h a. Y i k e s !

In Japan, stand-up computer kiosks appear in strategic places—ready to provide ten minutes' use when three 100-*yen* coins are deposited. Whenever I used a hotel computer, my messages appeared unreadable because I just had to simply ignore punctuation. I don't think I ever located an apostrophe! Things finally improved on Okinawa when I was able to connect my own laptop in the room and use my familiar keyboard.

We piled our luggage onto handy airport push carts once more and stowed it with one of the hotel employees. Soon Julia and I were following Anna down the steps into the Osaka train station, past a bank of bright chartreuse pay phones. We let Anna figure out the purchase of metro passes from a vending machine and slid them into a gated turnstile. We trotted along after her, bravely hopping onto the first train that stopped—and eagerly watched from the windows as sprawling industrial and suburban areas passed by. We had no idea where we were going.

While sitting on the train, Anna told us about her life in Virginia, attending classes at George Mason University, her fiancé, her wedding plans, about the Kellys and how she came to join them on this trip to Okinawa.

Anna could decipher many of the Chinese-origin *kanji* symbols—which makes Japanese one of the most difficult written languages in the world. There is no rhyme or reason to the formation of the *kanji* symbols, and elementary school students usually have learned around 400 *kanji* symbols by the time they are ten years old. One must master at least 1545 *kanji* symbols just to be literate enough to read a newspaper. There are 40,000 *kanji* symbols in all and rote memorization is pretty much the only way to master *kanji*.

At one time, shortly after the American occupation ended in 1952, with General MacArthur's postwar reform campaign of Americanization, it was suggested that the Roman alphabet replace *kanji* characters in the written language. The plan never materialized and many foreigners who are still struggling to learn the Japanese language wish it had taken place!

I tried to prepare for this trip by picking up an English-to-Japanese dictionary and also by studying a foldout chart to help me with Japanese phrases for dire straits!

I mastered the phrase, "*watashi-wa,*" which translates into "okay with me" which could be quite useful in a variety of situations. I never quite figured out the context, though. Anna definitely had to become our "new best friend." No doubt about it.

We didn't want to travel too far away from the Kansai Airport, so when we discovered an interesting-looking area about three stations away, we jumped off the train. We walked a short distance and encountered a narrow street lined with shops. The first was a little shop full of old things, and Julia could hardly contain her excitement. Everything looked familiar from our past—wooden carvings, ceramic figures, and wall hangings! Julia found a porcelain fisherman with a long beard that she dearly loved but passed up because she figured we would find many similar items on Okinawa. Julia regretted not buying that little statue.

It turned out that we were in the village of Higashi-Kishiwada. A celebration clearly was under way. I learned later that it was the village's annual *Danjiri* Festival. An elaborately-carved, four-ton wooden wagon was being towed through the winding streets by men and young boys dressed in black and purple *haori* coats, tight-fitting cotton leggings called *momohiki*, and rubber-soled *tabi* foot coverings. The challenge was to maneuver that huge wagon through the winding streets with coiled towing ropes. A degree of skill was involved in this effort. Several men with cloth banners tied around their heads stood atop the wagon while it was swaying. We watched while the parade made its way through the narrow streets of the village. The fall festival had its origin three hundred years ago when the Lord of Kishiwada Castle wanted to ensure a good harvest.

We spent more than an hour wandering the streets and then decided we'd better get back to the station for a return train to the airport. Anna didn't seem worried, but Julia and I were "older and wiser" and nervous about missing the scheduled flight south to Okinawa. As we passed through the train station, I saw a rack of fliers advertising the ABBA musical *Mamma Mia* at the Osaka Shiki Theater and snatched a few—always on the lookout for more items for eBay!

We scurried past that bank of bright chartreuse pay phones once more, and hurried up the steps and were back just in time to claim our bags and meet up with the rest of the trekkers in the airport.

There may be a "no tipping" policy in Japan, but that's not the case with smoking. With smoking still socially accepted throughout Asia, the Osaka Kansai Airport had a designated smoking lounge that appeared to be pretty crowded. Julia and I wandered among the shops and saw coolers full of sushi-to-go and Japanese treats, including something cake-like, made from green tea. Everything was so wonderfully foreign.

The two-hour flight was uneventful with the high-heeled, gloved and hatted Japanese stewardesses ever-attentive and polite. They served ice cream. The Haagen-Daaz ice cream cups were so solidly frozen and impermeable, that the stewardesses brought us little cups of hot water to try to thaw the tiny containers. That kept me busy during the flight—chipping away at that silly little cup of ice cream.

Coming Home

As we neared Okinawa, flying south over the Sea of Japan, the two-hour flight gave us time to think about our return to the island after more than forty years' absence.

When our ANA flight approached the sixty-mile-long island, the clouds cleared (just like in the movies) and in bright sunshine we saw the familiar shape below. *Okinawa-Honto*, the largest island of all the tiny islands in the Ryukyuan Archipelago, could be seen clearly from this strategic vantage point. I'd never seen it from the air before. Okinawa is about three hundred and fifty miles south of Kyushu, the southern-most island of mainland Japan.

Since the end of World War II, Okinawa had been occupied by U.S. military forces. One of the Dragons pointed out that Okinawa is considered a "country cousin" to sophisticated mainland Japan. In other words—what we once referred to as the "boondocks" apparently now *is* considered just that by mainland Japanese. In my opinion though, Okinawa is the most "Western" of the prefectures. "*Gaijins*" (foreigners) can get around much better on Okinawa than anywhere else in Japan.

We all strained to see out of the right-hand side windows of the plane. At long last we really were coming home!

A sprawling metropolis appeared below as the plane descended for its final approach and landing. There was nothing rural-looking to Okinawa any more.

We debarked down a metal stairway that rolled up to our small plane.

Julia and I were back on "the Rock" at last!

Heat and humidity blasted our faces as we walked across the tarmac and approached the lower entrance into the terminal, and I remembered how tropical it was when we lived here. We followed one another into the lower level of the Naha Air Terminal where we collected our luggage, loaded it once more onto those handy little baggage carts like we used in Osaka, and proceeded out to the street where several hotel buses were waiting. We did not have to deal with customs officials because we simply passed from one Japanese prefecture into another. It's all one country now, since the reversion of Okinawa back to Japan in 1972.

Warm and humid, it was nothing like those tropical summers from long ago, where shimmering waves of heat and humid air left you perpetually clammy. Those steamy Okinawa summers were what drove my mother to her lifelong quest for air-conditioning. It was nothing out of the ordinary to walk into the living room and find Mom standing in front of the window air-conditioner unit, holding her blouse open to the cold air...clearly dreaming of being someplace else...in her Maidenform bra!

And I remembered carrying those little Wash-n-Dri moist towelettes in my purse to wipe down my face. They didn't last long before they turned into dried-out pieces of parchment. While at school, I folded wet paper towels in the restroom to carry off to class in an attempt to combat the sweltering heat. At least this trip was carefully planned for October—officially at the end of typhoon season—and when the extreme tropical heat of summer tapered off.

Fascinated with what zoomed past the bus windows—at sixty

kilometers an hour—nothing at all looked familiar! This clearly was not "our Okinawa" from the fifties or the sixties; and although we had been warned repeatedly that things had changed, we were stunned. We couldn't stop staring in amazement at the high-rise office and apartment buildings. The sleepy island was now a metropolis.

Known simply as Highway One back in the sixties, built by the Army Corps of Engineers, the sole paved road on the island ran north to south and was limited to a speed of twenty-five miles per hour. Now called Highway 58, this futuristic multi-lane highway even had overhead pedestrian walkways.

One of the trekkers sitting behind us, Clinton (Class of '64) Cummings, explained to his wife about the metal bars that covered many of the windows on the buildings. Designed to protect windows from typhoon winds and damaging debris, they did serve another purpose. Clint was telling her that they kept out the "stealie-boys."

Julia and I looked at each other. *Stealie-boys!* I hadn't thought about "stealie-boys" in a long, long time. And I hadn't uttered those words in many years. That expression was unique only to our shared past.

Did Julia remember what Mom surely must have told her back then? What happened to our neighbors off-post in Oyama? How loud voices outside my bedroom window awakened me in the middle of the night?

When it was hot, I slept with my windows open because there were iron "stealie-boy" bars across them to keep me safe. That night, I looked outside and saw Dad and the MPs talking with the American civilian couple who lived next door, Bud and Bobbi Hansen. They had been victims of "stealie-boys" who broke into their house. The "stealie-boys" had been so bold that one of them pulled the diamond ring from Bobbi's finger as she slept. She woke up, screamed, and they ran out of the house and were never caught. Bud and Bobbi moved out of that house soon afterwards.

Another family moved in. A Filipino family with about five or six kids, and the husband had just come back from a tour of duty in Vietnam. He gave me a Vietnamese doll, dressed in a purple *ao-dong*. I displayed it in my doll cabinet, along with all my other dolls. There was a story going around that the dolls had been booby-trapped by the Viet Cong. If you raised the doll's arm, it would explode. I worried about that story and Mom assured me that it wasn't true. I had nothing to worry about.

But I still wondered. I finally got up the courage to raise my doll's arm. Nothing happened.

But stealie-boys...hmmmm...that was something altogether different.

While riding from Naha airport to the hotel, we noticed tanks on the flat rooftops and someone explained that they collected rainwater. We remembered the water shortages that occurred back in the sixties. And I remember when we encountered signs above faucets that read "Non-Potable." Sometimes the water looked rusty. You could still wash your hands with it. You just couldn't drink it.

We used to have frequent power outages. An old navy ship called the SS Jacona, was anchored in the East China Sea. We could see it from our driveway. Dad always pointed it out to visitors. I don't know why, but it was a topic of conversation.

After the war, the Jacona was brought to the island as a floating power barge, to serve as a generator for electricity. The Jacona had quite a history and already had provided electricity to the destroyed city of Nagasaki after the bombing. During the Korean War, the Jacona was towed to various ports, and ended up supplying power to Okinawa until 1971.

The bus continued its slow climb through the hills and narrow streets along the Pacific Ocean side of the island toward an ultra-modern, high-rise hotel, and strained to make it up the steep driveway—coming to a halt in front of a covered portico with a two-story high wall of ceramic *shisa* dogs—each one with its own unique expression. A *shisa* resembles a combination between a lion and a dog. Many people put a pair of *shisa* on their rooftops or outside the gates to their homes. It's a Shinto animalistic spiritual belief that *shisa* protect from various evils. When found in pairs, the *shisa* on the left traditionally has a closed mouth, and the one on the right has an open mouth. The open mouth wards off evil, and the closed mouth keeps in good.

We were at the Tokyo Dai Ichi Hotel, which would be our base of operations for the next eleven nights. The bright, modern lobby featured a towering colonnade support with lighted fabric panels shaped like lotus blossom petals. A huge glass wall provided a view of the Pacific Ocean below. The lobby was decorated with orange and black Halloween die-cut decorations of black cats and jack-o'-lanterns. It was obvious that this hotel catered to Western holidays.

Our advance man, Larry Laurion, had everything well under control. He and Amy Nitahara had arrived the night before, allowing the rest of us to experience landing on our beloved island in bright sunlight. We were to meet up later in the banquet room for a welcome dinner.

The Dai-Ichi was a modern 300-room high-rise hotel that fit in with the new image of Okinawa as the "Hawaii of the Farther East." We checked in and got our keys. The two young Okinawan women behind the desk were pleasant and one covered her mouth shyly as she smiled. Yes. That charming, characteristic shyness was something we remembered…

And then the clerk answered the phone, not as I expected, with "*Moshi Moshi*," a hello from the past, but with the name of the hotel and a standard greeting. Too professional. Not what we expected to hear. Not what we remembered…

Our room was large enough to hold two beds with a built-in

nightstand/radio/alarm clock between them, a coffee table and chairs, a desk, television, dressing area and bathroom—but no *TOTO*—just a basic flusher. We had all we needed: a mini-fridge, a sink and a hot-pot to make tea or coffee. There was a built-in safe in the closet for our valuables. Julia plopped down on the floor and set to work, coming up with a combination so we could stash our airline tickets and travelers checks.

Down the hall, there was a little room with a Sanyo stackable washer and dryer. Three 100-*yen* coins were all it took to wash and dry a small load of clothing. Several vending machines offered canned coffee and beers, and exotic juice drinks—one was an Okinawan fruit drink called "*Shiikiwasha*."

From the balcony of our ninth floor room, Julia and I looked down upon several single-family houses and yards, stretching across the sloping hillside toward the ocean. Julia couldn't stop staring at the familiar skyline.

"It seems like this is the exact view I used to see when I looked out from our house in Awase," she said. "We were way high up on a hill and could look down at the Pacific Ocean. I spent a lot of time staring out at that ocean."

Bay Gillion had located an off-post rental for his family in the Awase area, while Dad found a rental house for us in the Oyama area. We lived on opposite sides of the island but visited frequently. Arrangements to visit on the weekends had to be made through Bay and Dad, through phone calls when they were at work.

Life was primitive back in 1963, and isolation made up much of the daily routine. We kids had school to take up our time, but our moms had a quiet day—every day.

Our little cement house in Oyama had no source of heat, except for a small portable kerosene heater on chilly nights during the rainy season. Okinawan households used a *kotatsu*—a charcoal or electric heater positioned in the recessed floor that let you warm your legs around it while seated at a table. For Okinawans, it was a relatively inexpensive way of providing space heating.

Okinawa had two seasons—wet and dry—with low temperatures during the wet winter months dropping down into the 40s. That was cold for the tropics. At least we never got snow like they did in the mountains of Japan.

Dad was into creating those "Rube Goldberg-inventor-style" contraptions and made a canopy out of aluminum foil and bent wire coat hangers to deflect the heat and keep it from rising straight up to the ceiling. We would wake up in the mornings with our nostrils black from soot from the kerosene fumes. Could we have died from carbon monoxide poisoning? I'm surprised we didn't.

It's interesting that Dad actually used a dangerous kerosene heater to warm our house—considering his "theory of spontaneous combustion" —Dad always warned us kids that something could suddenly erupt into flames or simply blow up—more of Dad's propaganda.

My husband often wondered why I would worry that something could "combust spontaneously" or "catch on fire." Like the refrigerator.

Now he understands why I say the things I say. It's the *Dad factor.*

There were three bedrooms in that cement house, a living room and a kitchen. We had a front door and a back door that led out to an area with a clothesline for hanging laundry. All of the windows to the house were covered with "typhoon/stealie-boy bars" and had wooden sliders that could be moved in place when a typhoon bore down on the island.

The kitchen had only a small refrigerator and a two-burner hot plate for cooking.

There were light bulbs burning in all of the closets of our house. They burned constantly to add warmth to the closet and combat the high humidity levels. If you didn't keep the bulbs burning in the closets, your clothes and shoes could mildew.

Dad always warned us kids to make sure there weren't any geckos or roaches inside our shoes, so we made sure to shake them before we put our feet inside. I never really knew if this was true or not. Dad came up with a lot of things on his own.

The bathroom was made of one-inch-square mosaic tiles and there was a drain in the center of the floor. The bathtub was made from the same tiles, with a back that sloped at a 45-degree angle. You could only lie back at that angle in the tub.

I'm positive I'm not imagining the huge cockroaches that came up out of floor drains in the utility room and the bathroom. They were real. Julia remembered them too.

"And don't forget those giant snails," said Julia. "They were always on the plants and flowers... "

I had almost forgotten them. At least the snails didn't get inside our house. The U.S. Army kept us supplied with handy olive-drab cans of DDT which we sprayed liberally throughout our quarters.

DDT, one of the best-known and most effective synthetic pesticides, wasn't banned until 1972. But before then, if we saw a bug, we grabbed a can—and sprayed it until it was lying dead in a puddle!

And each time a family would move out of quarters, they were cleaned to "white-glove" inspection standards—and then sprayed with apparently even more DDT before the next family moved in.

We used to joke that when someone moved, the roaches just scurried to the next-door-neighbors until the spraying team finished.

Many of us remember the pesticide spray trucks that would move slowly through the housing areas, spraying clouds behind them. No one thought to stay inside and close the doors and windows back then. Who knew what was being released upon us? I remember riding our bikes through the streets while the trucks were spraying.

Gecko lizards (*tokagemodoki*) crawled along the walls and ceiling, and Dad said we weren't supposed to harm them because they ate many of the other bugs crawling in the house. I remember the time we found a mama gecko with a parade of baby geckos trailing along behind her. We just left them alone and watched them.

Our furniture was issued by the quartermaster. Beds, dressers, tables and the most wonderful rattan sofas and chairs, with flowery tropical cushions. Everything was extremely durable.

We had mosquito netting that could be stretched from the ceiling over our beds—to keep the mosquitoes from biting. The mosquitoes bothered Danny in particular so Mom kept netting around his bed. Encephalitis was worrisome. Mosquitoes didn't really bother me or Ray.

We had no telephone. If we wanted to make a phone call to Dad at work, we walked to the little *mamasan/papasan* store at the corner and handed *mamasan* a dime. The little building was a combination store, with a living area in the back. When the pull-down metal shutters were up, an array of goods were displayed in front of the living area, where the floor was covered with *tatami* mats and where you could look right into the home. Shoes were lined up outside the door. Usually the homeowner was watching *sumo* wrestling on Japanese TV while waiting for customers to come by. We always came up with an excuse to go to the store. When Mom ran out of laundry detergent, we bought boxes of *Blue Wonder*, a Japanese brand, and with the spare change, bought *Fusen* bubble gum and *empitsus* (pencils).

We knew a few words of Japanese: *sukoshi* for little, *takusan* for lots, *kudasai* for please, *gomen nasai* for excuse me. And of course my brothers and the other kids on the bus would shout *bakatade ne* from the open windows at any passers-by on the street—pretty much calling that person a stupid fool.

In our little neighborhood there was a beauty shop, where Mom got her hair washed, set, teased and sprayed for a dollar or two. It was a bargain and she went often.

There was a little dressmaker shop nearby, where we could have clothes made to order. Mom and I would flip through the pages of a Sears or J.C. Penney catalog, clip a picture and take it off to the "sew-girls." We would stand barefoot, in the center of the *tatami* mats, while the "sew-girls" took our measurements. We would select a length of fabric from the bolts of cloth, and come back within a week for a fitting and then again a few days later for the finished item! Those women worked all day long at treadle sewing machines. Mom taught me to sew back then, but why? Those ladies made their own custom-fit patterns from newspaper and could turn out a garment for next-to-nothing. Mom and I had matching cotton shifts made, as well as skirts and blouses.

Peddlers knocked on our door…*mamasans* walked along the streets with huge bundles balanced upon their heads. We would invite them inside and they would unpack their wares upon the living room floor. I specifically remember clothing items…and even framed artwork. We bought a painting on black velvet of a *mamasan* whispering into the ear of an old *papasan*.

Living on Okinawa was rough on marriages. I can remember listening in on Mom's conversations with other military wives when we lived on-post, about wives whose husbands had been shipped off to Vietnam—who picked up GIs—and who were as Mom said, "playing around."

I remember a friend of Dad's—a guy named Grimes—whose wife arrived on Okinawa and just couldn't stand it there. It was a rough life if you weren't up to adventure. She came to our house in Oyama several times because I think Mom and Dad were trying to talk her into staying with Grimes. Dad always referred to people he worked with by their last names—that was army style. Each soldier's name was stitched on his uniform. I think a lot of guys probably didn't even know each other's first names.

One day, I walked Mrs. Grimes down to the corner store where she telephoned someone to come and pick her up. I can still remember her saying into the phone to someone, "This is all a big snow job and I've made up my mind. Get me out of here." She was a fashionable woman, with short platinum blonde hair, miniskirts, and hot pink lipstick. I thought she was so glamorous.

She left Grimes and returned to the States. She was not prepared for the life of an army wife. This was not what she signed up for. Grimes got involved with a local Okinawan woman, Yoko, who had a little girl of her own named Donna. He moved in with Yoko. She lived nearby in the Futenma area and we used to go to her second-floor apartment to visit. I remember going to a picnic with Grimes, his Okinawan girlfriend Yoko, and her little girl. We all got along well.

I suppose Yoko was classified as a "barracks rat," a woman who was "shacking up" with GIs. To us, she was a nice woman who was trying to make a life for herself and Donna. I guess she was a "whore" and probably an outcast with her family because of her mixed-blood child. When Grimes PCS'd back to the States, I suppose another GI moved in with her. It was a common thing back then. The women who lived with GIs were not respected and the resulting mixed-blood children never knew their fathers. Whoever Donna's father was probably didn't know she existed. It was like what was taking place in Vietnam with all those babies fathered by GIs.

I remember Mom talking to Dad about trying to adopt Donna. They approached Yoko about it, but she clearly didn't want to give up her daughter.

Mom had a hysterectomy while we were stationed on Okinawa. She clearly must have wanted more children and that hysterectomy must have affected her deeply.

Adopting an Asian child would have been totally acceptable in the army. Integration, blended families, mixed blood—all were commonplace. The girls I went to school with were stunning, with their straight shiny coal-black hair and exotic features. These were the AmerAsian girls, whose fathers were American and mothers were Asian. I thought they were beautiful, with their exotic, blended features.

Ainoku. That's what those girls were called.

I learned the term many years later. I heard it from one of those girls with blended features. She told me, "It literally meant 'love child'—and it was a very derogatory term. It was after the war, in the fifties, when there was strong anti-American sentiment in Japan. I went to Japanese school and it was very rough being half American in those times."

She went on to say that the situation has totally changed now and that racially-mixed women are referred to as *hafus* and are successful models in Japan.

She was known as an *ainoku* in the fifties. Little Donna was an *ainoku* as well, in the sixties.

Soon after we arrived on the island, an elderly bowlegged Okinawan woman knocked on our front door. She asked for work as a maid and told Mom, "*Okasan*, I very good maid. Lot of experience."

Obviously, we had never had a maid before, but on Okinawa almost all Americans employed local residents as maids and gardeners. Her name was Toshiko.

Mom and Toshiko communicated with one another through broken English and a lot of frantic pantomime gestures. I think Mom must have pointed to a day on the calendar and that was how they set up a schedule for Toshiko to work one day a week for our family.

On the agreed-upon morning, Toshiko arrived to clean our house. She set to work, washing dishes. Mom showed Toshiko where she kept the cleaning supplies and equipment and went outside with a basket of wet clothes to hang on the line.

When she came inside, Toshiko was busy vacuuming in the living room—but the vacuum was not plugged in—she was just pushing the nozzle around the floor. Mom told this story many times through the years—how she had to show Toshiko that the vacuum should be plugged in first!

It was a good thing that Mom was patient and saw the humor in the situation, because a short time later, she discovered Toshiko in the bathroom, with the toilet brush in her hand—scrubbing the floor.

You had to admire Toshiko for her determination. She was trying so hard, and clearly had no experience as a maid. It's not like Mom had anything else to do, so she worked with Toshiko and showed her how to clean, American-style.

Toshiko hustled around the house with her bowed legs—which I've learned can be blamed on the way that Japanese women carried their babies—tied onto their backs with their little legs straddling. The thing I remember most about that old lady was her constantly mumbling, "*hubba-hubba*" over and over while she worked.

When we moved into our quarters on post, we had to say goodbye to Toshiko. Maids who worked on post had to be approved and carried ID with them to get past the checkpoint gate. Toshiko didn't have the necessary clearance.

Our new maid was a shy young woman named Yoko who came to our house once or twice a week. Yoko knew how to clean American houses and spent the afternoons ironing. Back then, everything was made of cotton. And everything needed ironing. My task on the day before Yoko arrived, was to dip shirts, blouses and skirts into a bucket with starch. Then I'd roll them up and stack them in the ironing basket. For all that work, I'm pretty sure Yoko earned one dollar a day, the average pay for a maid. I can remember Mom raising her salary to $1.50 for the day and Yoko kept saying, "*domo, domo*" over and over. Mom treated Yoko very well and made sure she ate lunch at our house and even offered her the use of our shower before she went home. I wondered about her family life and where she lived, and how far she had to travel to work for us. We really knew nothing about Yoko. We never took a picture of our Yoko, but I can still see her youthful face. She was probably around seventeen or eighteen years old.

Julia and my mother worked around the house and cooked supper, waited for their children to come home from school and their husbands to come home from work. Julia was very isolated in her Awase location and told me about her frequent attempts to walk from her house "up high in the hills" to a village she could see below.

"There's only so much cleaning you can do," said Julia. "I tried to get out of the house, but each time I walked down that dirt road with Gary, who was only two and couldn't walk very far, we never made it. I ended up carrying him on my shoulders back up to our house. We were so far from anything. When Bay finally got home from work, we often drove somewhere after dinner just to get out. We'd come visit y'all."

Julia told me how she walked those dirt roads in her mind through the years of memories, and it was so wonderful to be back on this island. So often, it was Julia who seemed even more excited to be back on Okinawa than I was. She needed to come along with me.

We watched from the balcony of our hotel as a GI came home from work and let his dog out to run through the yard below. Tossing a ball for his dog, we watched and wondered if one of those houses below us could be the one that the Gillions had lived in.

69

"Our house was so similar to that house right down there—with the tiled roof. That style was called 'Manning Housing.' I really do have a feeling that this is where our house was. What if this hotel was built on it?"

We were so excited. We couldn't wait. We headed for the elevator. We needed to explore.

We had time before meeting the other trekkers for the welcome dinner, so Julia and I started walking...not far...down the steep driveway of our hotel...toward the spot where Julia thought her house might have been. There was no pattern to the narrow alleys and streets, so all we could do was wander around the area surrounding the hotel before it got dark. The brightly-lit Dai-Ichi would serve as a landmark high up on the hill. We couldn't get lost.

We walked past cement block houses with tiny courtyards, surrounded by fences with decorative ceramic *shisa*. Flowering red and yellow hibiscus trees, golden trumpets and purple turmeric surrounded us. Okinawa still was the botanical paradise we remembered. When we lived here, we had all of these flowering beauties and even poinsettia bushes in our yard.

We came across a row of family tombs—constructed in the gabled-roof style—situated just on the other side of a cement fence where two boys were tossing a ball to one another. We could reach right out and touch those tombs!

The tombs we remembered from the past were *kameko-baka*, turtleback-style, and were far off on the hillsides, away from houses—not like this—not right next to someone's back yard fence!

Okinawan spiritual belief involved ancestor worship, dating back to the fourteenth century, and the family tomb was the site for a system of rituals performed in honor of one's ancestors. The turtle shape symbolized long life. The Buddhist philosophy of "returning to the source" from where one originally came, was illustrated by the shape of these tombs—resembling a female womb—with the belief that we will all return to our source after our earthly passage.

Three years after death, the bones of the decomposed body are cleansed and placed in a decorated urn for thirty-three more years, until a final memorial service is conducted, signifying final passage into the spiritual world. Responsibility for this task falls upon the oldest female in a family. That person would be me, if this was our family custom!

The Buddhist festival of *Obon*, to honor the dead, is celebrated in mid-July, and involves music and folk dancing. Ancestral spirits were believed to return to the living world and on the final day of *Obon*, *Eisa* folk dancers parade from house to house, playing drums along the way.

I recalled an *Obon* festival celebration held at Kadena Air Base back in the sixties. We were all sitting on the sidelines as spectators, when the folk dancers encouraged us to join in. I found myself following along in a line, trying to copy the movements of the dancers. It was just for fun then, and I didn't really even understand what it was about. Now I know so much more.

Julia and I kept wandering. Land seemed at a premium now. Cement houses were built close to one another, and the driveways opened onto tiny sidewalks. But in almost every available spot, something was growing. Gardens were still an important part of Okinawan life.

A mixture of rich scents hit us as we wandered through the neighborhood—the pleasant scent of the flowering trees and the not-so-pleasant pungent odor of the *benjo* ditches that still abound on the island.

"Oh, oh, oh," exclaimed Julia. "It's the familiar smell of Okinawa."

I heard that little "oh, oh, oh" whenever Julia got excited, which was often. She drew in a deep breath, and I told her, "It's just the *benjo* ditches that you smell, Julia."

Julia's right. If you had to search for one familiar smell, I guess that would be the one that stood out. *Benjo* ditches—open cement sewers that ran along the sides of the roads—now had cement lids covering them, probably so no one could drive a car off the side of the road and get stuck.

"When I could keep the car, I would drop Bay off at Torii Station and then drive over to visit your mother. I remember how hard it was to drive down that little dirt road in front of your house. Those open *benjo* ditches ran along each side and I had to be careful not to get the tires stuck in them. One time, I met up with one of those three-wheeled trucks and he wouldn't back up, so I had to back up all the way down the road to let him get by."

Actually, *benjo* ditches were convenient for toddlers. Little Okinawan kids didn't wear diapers. They were potty-trained to squat over the *benjo* ditches. It was common to see bare-bottomed kids walking along the dirt road, clad only in t-shirts

Another common road hazard was the honey-bucket driver. That's what they called the wooden wagon, pulled by a water buffalo, with an old *papasan* in the driver's seat. All I remember was that the "honey-bucket" most definitely did *not* contain honey. Human waste or "night soil" was collected from the *benjo* ditches and deposited in the wagon. It was used to fertilize the crops. You definitely didn't want to bump into one of those wagons!

Okinawan farmers were known for using "night soil" to fertilize their crops, and we were strictly warned against consuming any fresh produce grown by farmers on the local economy. The produce we saw in the off-post market stalls was appealing, but we ended up back at home eating whatever Mom found at the commissary, which wasn't all that fresh after it traveled for weeks in the hold of a navy ship.

The sun was dropping behind the horizon as Julia and I walked past free-standing vending machines, isolated and brightly-lit, on street corners just waiting for a customer. The machines sold everything from *Orion* beer to *Pocari Sweat* soft drinks.

We turned a corner and came face to face with Tommy Lee Jones staring back at us from another vending machine. Jones endorsed *Suntory's* BOSS line of canned coffee drinks.

Nothing "lost in translation" here. Celebrity endorsements net big bucks for American actors, who appear in some pretty cheesy commercials. They don't expect American fans back home ever to see them—except now we have the power of YouTube! Nothing goes unnoticed. Some of those commercials can be embarrassing.

Mainland Japan has the greatest concentration of vending machines anywhere in the world—selling everything from drinks and cigarettes, to umbrellas, to kerosene for your space heater—to used underwear and pornography! I heard that there is even a Hello Kitty vending machine that pops popcorn!

Julia recalled how when upon their arrival, her husband, Bay, took them on a tour through the Koza shopping area, and while they walked along the street, side by side, with the children following behind, a young Okinawan woman walked right up to her husband and asked, "Long time? Short time?"

Bay just shook his head and kept walking. Julia wanted to know what that woman was talking about. Later she learned that the woman was offering her personal services—for a long time—or a short time.

Koza B.C. Street had a reputation for bars, hookers, pawn shops and rowdy GIs drinking and fighting. It was where GIs went after work to let off steam and party. I remember driving along with my family at night, sitting in the back seat of our car, staring out the window at the gaudy neon lights of the bars and strip clubs, *pachinko* parlors and pawn shops. Everything bad was located along that street. There were GIs walking along the sidewalks with Okinawan bar girls on their arms, while loud music blasted from the doorways. People were partying. Bands were playing rock and roll...and there was a lot of drinking and dancing going on. These were places that I saw only from the car window in passing, as I imagined what went on inside.

Dad liked his beer and was a drinker. I'm sure he hung out in those same bars with his buddies before we arrived. After we joined him on Okinawa, he pretty much did his beer drinking right after work at the NCO club and then at home in the evenings.

Drinking is expected among the Japanese *"salari-men"* office workers, and they routinely stop off for drinks with coworkers at the end of the work day. The ability to hold your liquor is expected. *"Salari-men"* eventually make it to the right subway and get home late, only to do it all over again the next day. In Japan, being able to out-drink your coworkers is something to be proud of.

Julia remembered fondly the little alleys full of shops in Koza where she and Cathy found wonderful treasures. She hoped we could find some of those alleys once more. We both expected to have plenty of time to wander.

Julia and I finally sat down to rest upon some stone steps near a playground. We said nothing. After a few minutes, we started the uphill climb back to the hotel to get ready for the banquet dinner.

In a private banquet room, our leader, Larry Laurion, made introductions and passed out a handwritten itinerary, bus passes, and Kubasaki t-shirts. We each introduced ourselves and explained our connection to Kubasaki. I proclaimed that I was apparently the youngest alumni at age fifty-five. The oldest person on this trip was eighty-six.

As the plates were served, some of the trekkers took photos.

Course after course of artistically-arranged Japanese cuisine was delivered to our tables. I was determined to eat and not think about or ask what was being served; but when a plate arrived, featuring a fish with its head still in place, I could see Julia trying not to look. I'm sure she was wishing for a lettuce leaf...so that she could cover up that poor fish's head. She finally leaned over and whispered, "It's staring at me."

We managed to eat most of what we were served. I reminded myself that this was an adventure.

Back when my family lived here, we tried nothing that wasn't one hundred percent all-American. I remember the time our neighbor lady in Oyama, Mrs. Higeru, came to our door with her little daughter, Hidome. They brought us a plate of rice cakes to celebrate the New Year,

They were called *mochi*, which I now have learned is considered a delicacy. The cakes were made from cooked sticky rice, rubbery in consistency, and I think rather tasteless, but I remember Mom throwing them away. I tasted them, but she was afraid to eat them. She had no sense of adventure and at the time, military families were constantly warned about eating local food.

Military personnel were not supposed to eat at any restaurant off-post unless it had a sign above the door, with a large "A" indicating that it had been inspected and approved for dining. As a result, we never explored the restaurants outside the gates. My parents were secure only in their on-post world of the commissary and the PX—and the only time I can remember dining out on the local economy was at a little pizza place that had the requisite framed "A" sign above the door, indicating that it had passed inspection and was "approved" for all military personnel.

One trekker was still MIA, despite numerous e-mail updates that he was on a business trip to Taiwan and would catch up with us today, tomorrow or the next day. Maybe Emerson Edwards would make it for the next meal, but for now we had one extra plate of everything to pass around our table. So when each course was served, we selected what we wanted and kept his plates moving! Julia certainly could have had *his* fish! Later we learned that we even ate a local delicacy—a pig's ear!

We sized up our fellow trekkers and decided that most were pretty congenial; a few seemed aloof. And three trekkers had actually walked the hallways of Kubasaki High School with me: sisters Marlene (Class of '67) Dulay and Jane (Class of '68) Dulay, and David (Class of '68) Knowles. Their names were familiar, but because I thought of myself as such an "invisible" student back then, I didn't really know them. What a waste of time—being the shy girl.

Clearly, the six trekkers who did the landmark trip back in 2001 had a lot to talk about, and they reminisced over old times. They shared so much in common, and they had been here before. They were the genuine Kubasaki Dragons from the early 1950s classes—some were more than middle-aged, with graying hair—all certainly "card-carrying AARP members." And our designated leader, Larry Laurion, was fond of wearing a t-shirt emblazoned with the motto: "Old Guys Rule."

Pioneers from the first classes of students who attended Kubasaki High School in the post-war days, they attended high school on an island that was the site of the bloodiest battle of the Pacific Theater of World War II.

We learned from the original trekkers just how rough it was to attend high school on post-war Okinawa. Larry (Class of '56) Kelly talked about how he was ordered to carry a weapon with him when he went out on a date back in the fifties.

"If a boy escorted a girl out at night, he was ordered to carry a gun," he said. "If you knew how to drive, you could drive a Jeep. Licenses weren't important."

Our First Day

Our first morning on Okinawa, and Jay (Class of '68) Wentworth picked up Julia and me at the hotel to drive us around. We met Jay the night before at the banquet. He had lived on Okinawa for the past fifty years, and after graduating from Kubasaki, attended college in the States and then came back to live and work where he'd been raised. Now a successful businessman, Jay had an enterprise related to the government under SOFA (Status of Forces Agreement between the United States and Japan) and lived here with his wife Merri and son Justin.

We couldn't believe our good fortune! Julia and I had talked about paying a taxi driver to chauffeur us around for a day, and figured we'd try to arrange something through a hotel clerk. This was much better.

We climbed into Jay's right-hand-drive SUV. He drove us through many winding streets, turned left through a busy intersection, and zoomed along a busy divided highway, right past the Futenma Housing Area and the gates that my family passed through long ago. The gates were still surrounded by fences, now with large signs that proclaimed the area an "ASBESTOS HAZARD AREA."

"That's definitely the gate that led to our old quarters!" I exclaimed. "We've come all this way and now we can't go any farther."

"Everything back there is being torn down to make way for new construction. They started the project a few weeks ago," explained Jay.

While waiting for the traffic light to change, I could see the road curving off to the right and remembered that our house was only a few streets inside the gates. I couldn't believe it. Under destruction! We'd come so far. I could cry.

Quarters 886 Futenma Housing Area was a typhoon-proof cement house with a flat roof, a screened-in porch at one end and another smaller screened porch at the back, with concrete laundry tubs. Tropical in design, there were louvered screened openings along the bottoms of the sliding glass windows so that ventilation was optimum. At one end of the house near the driveway was a wooden plaque, where SSGT KRIHA was stenciled. When you drove through a military housing area, you could read the names on the quarters to see who lived there.

Jay continued on, driving through an intersection I remembered, then down a hill that I definitely remembered, down toward the East China Sea, and then into nothing I remembered at all!

Jay told us that we were driving along what was once old Highway One, except it was a four-lane highway now called Highway 58. There were so many unfamiliar buildings around us that all I could do was guess where we should make a turn to the right. I was wrong.

We were in the old Oyama neighborhood, and I relied upon Julia's "driving" memory to help find the cement block rental house that looked out toward the East China Sea, beyond a sea wall and rice paddies. What we didn't expect was the change in terrain. The past twenty years had seen land reclamation on both sides of the island. The rice paddies were long gone and new land that was reclaimed from the sea had been developed into prime real estate. The shape of Okinawa was changing, despite opposition from local environmental groups.

The area where our house once stood along the coastline of the East China Sea was now a congested labyrinth of narrow paved roads with traffic coming from both directions that forced pedestrians off to the side to walk upon the covered *benjo* ditches.

"There was a large pink cement building called the Club Daimyo Steam House where I used to stand each morning for my school bus," I told Jay. He didn't remember it. But I remembered it so well. It was the landmark Dad used when he gave directions to people about how to find our house.

I can still hear Dad saying, "Take Highway One and turn down the dirt road by the pink steam house. Follow that road all the way down the hill until you can't go any farther and turn right at the bottom. Go past the rice paddies until you see the second American-style concrete block house on the right. That's us."

So Jay turned to the right, down a paved road—one which could have evolved from the dirt road that we used to bounce along in our Plymouth.

We drove along until I thought we should turn to the right, while Julia thought we should turn to the left. We ended up driving in both directions for a while but could not find my house. When I dreamed about returning to Okinawa, I kept picturing that cement house as I walked to it, down the winding dirt road, past the *mamasan/papasan* store, continuing down the dirt road with the *benjo* ditches, past the rice paddies, right up to our gravel driveway surrounded by the decorative cement block wall.

The cement house with a flat roof that Dad found for us to live in was in the Oyama neighborhood along the western side of the island about a mile away from Highway One, the only paved road on Okinawa. Beyond our driveway were rice paddies with a man-made sea wall at the edge of the East China Sea.

We walked that dirt road daily and observed women bent over in knee-high water—wearing peaked straw hats—many with babies tied onto their backs as they transplanted the little rice seedlings into the waterlogged paddy. Planting rice is a complicated procedure that involves controlling the amount of water that floods into and out of the paddy until harvest time. Eventually, after the feathery ears of rice are harvested, water buffalo are led into the paddies to feed on the remaining shafts of rice. All this activity took place right across the road from our house. I knew very little about the inner workings of a rice paddy back then, but now I fully understand it.

Something else took place not far from the corner store, at a local water source—a stone wall where water poured from spigots into a large stone-lined pool. Late in the afternoon, local women would gather there to wash their vegetables and laundry. My brothers were far more interested in watching the women washing vegetables and laundry, than planting rice in the paddies. All too often, the women removed their blouses and washed themselves after they finished with their vegetables and laundry.

Titties. That's what appealed to my little brothers.

Jay drove us along more narrow dirt roads, and past more cement block walls with decorative trim along the tops. There were flat-roofed cement houses all around with typhoon bars protecting the windows. But nothing was the same. Nothing.

Jay was patient as we tried to decide where to turn next. I was certain that all we had to do was head toward the East China Sea, except the sea as I remembered it, had moved.

At one point, when Jay turned down a street, Julia got excited over what she was certain was my house. We pulled over to take a closer look, and she was "Oh, oh, oh-ing." But it wasn't my house. Not at all. I was humoring Julia's certainty, but finally told her that we would have to continue the search on our own later. We were running out of time that day, and Jay was scheduled to pick up some more trekkers back at the hotel.

Next Jay drove us on post to Camp Foster. As he showed his ID at the checkpoint gate, he greeted the Okinawan guard with a "*Konnichi-wa.*" That just seemed all wrong!

What once was called Fort Buckner by the army is now called Camp Foster by the marines. With the reversion in 1972 and the Japanese renaming almost everything on the island, and then the marines taking over the facilities, it's all new. We came across the NCO Club where we used to go for dinner, the Topper Club—now renamed the Globe and Anchor. We drove down the long hill we remembered, toward Sukiran Pool, and Julia got emotional over a set of three little cement steps stuck in the middle of nowhere, leading to nothing, the very spot where she used to tell the kids to wait for her when she picked them up after swimming lessons!

Jay drove us past Sukiran Chapel, where we'd attended Sunday Mass, often wearing flowery cotton *mu'umu'us* and *zoris*. It was just as I remembered it.

Sukiran Chapel was special for Betty and Larry Kelly. At the welcome banquet the night before, Larry had shown us all an old black-and-white wedding photo taken on the steps of Sukiran Chapel. They had been married there in 1965.

We passed the old Sukiran Hobby Shop, where I remember learning to make leather wallets and purses. Then we found the building that we were pretty sure was the dental lab that Dad once had worked in. Still there. And then Julia announced that Dad had made her first pair of false teeth!

False teeth! What?

Julia explained that a severe calcium deficiency from pregnancy led to the demise of her teeth. Only in her early thirties, she had no choice but to be fitted for dentures. And Dad was the lab man who made them.

"Those were the best teeth I ever had!" proclaimed Julia. "Your dad made dentures that fit me so well. I never had another pair fit as well as that set."

We wondered about the dates we saw stenciled on the sides of the buildings. Jay explained that when the marines paint a building, they date it. He said, "The army and air force kept records when a building got painted, and had to look everything up. The marines keep it simple. Just read the building."

Julia recalled how marines were not allowed to bring their dependents with them overseas back in the sixties. Jay agreed, and told an oh-so-familiar anecdote about a general who proclaimed, "If the marines wanted you to have a wife, they would have issued you one!" That tired old story brought fresh laughter from Julia and me. Jay was full of amusing anecdotes and we were his captive audience.

Jay told us how he helped backstage at Stilwell Field House when he was in high school. A lot of USO shows performed on Okinawa. Stevie Wonder and Ricky Nelson entertained the troops, and there was some guy in the band who offered his autograph. Jay wasn't impressed with him and told us that he thought to himself, "I don't want *your* autograph. You're playing back-up. Can you believe, that guy turned out to be Glen Campbell!"

A lot of big-name talent passed through Okinawa on the way to Vietnam to entertain the troops. If extra tickets were available, dependents could join the audience. We saw Johnny Mathis and Roy Acuff and his Foggy Mountain Boys. But the biggest thrill for me was when extra tickets were available for dependents to see *Hello Dolly!* Mary Martin was playing the role of Dolly and was taking the show to Vietnam to entertain the troops in 1965.

Hello Dolly! introduced me to the world of Broadway musicals. I was captivated. I have an autographed program from the production because Gloria Moeller's mom volunteered to help with wardrobe and needed extra irons...our iron was called into service...so she brought me a program that had been signed by everyone in the cast, including Mary Martin!

Mom bought me the Broadway cast soundtrack album from the PX! I played that album over and over until I knew the entire score by heart. It remains my favorite.

Forty years later, Carol Channing, who originated the role, and recorded the soundtrack, came to Cleveland with the anniversary production of *Hello Dolly!* I finally saw the woman behind the voice that I had listened to for years.

Soon we were in an area that once was our center of activity. Jay pulled over, and Julia was out of the SUV and running toward an area right behind the PX and commissary. I chased behind her as she walked briskly toward the hillside that led up to the Chatan Housing area. Jay pointed out that Chatan also was being demolished—to be replaced with newer housing stock. Disappointment once again!

Julia stood behind the PX, staring up at the hill, lost in memories from the past. I gave her time alone and talked with Jay. We didn't expect this turn of events. I expected to walk right up to our old quarters and find the poinsettia bushes by the side of the house. I expected to knock on the door, maybe even be invited inside. The Okinawa we remembered was now forever gone.

The Fort Buckner Theater looked the same—except the marines had renamed it Foster Theater—and we laughed about how Cathy and I waited in line for hours with our brothers for the first Beatles movie, *A Hard Day's Night*, and when we finally made it inside, everyone was screaming like they were at a real Beatles concert.

Movies were our primary entertainment back then and the films changed every few days. Admission was 15 cents for kids and 25 cents for adults. Always on the cheap side, Dad would walk up to the ticket booth and mumble, "two adults, three kids" every time we went to the theater. I must have been fourteen going on fifteen at that point and Dad was still passing me off as a child. It was embarrassing.

We saw everything. We had no criteria. Any movie released during the early 1960s was deemed worth seeing—all the James Bonds, the Doris Days and every single one of those *"Beach Blanket Bingo/Party/Wild Bikini"* movies. We were a family with way too much free time.

The thing that drove me crazy was that Dad was one of those people who never paid attention to the starting times. Often, we would arrive midway through a feature, watch the second half first—and then have to wait to see the beginning of the film! I got used to it. I saw many movies "out of order." For some reason, Dad liked to sit way in the back of the theater—and as soon as the film ended, if we had managed to get there for the beginning, Dad jumped up and we all had to follow him out, as the credits were rolling. I wanted to read those credits.

At the start of every movie, before the newsreel or coming attractions, everyone stood at attention—while the National Anthem played against a background of an unfurled flag. Everyone stood. No exceptions.

When *Soldier in the Rain* arrived at Buckner Theater, we couldn't wait to see it. While we were stationed at Fort Ord, the film crew had been on post for location shots. They used the army barracks and "created" fake rain with huge shower heads atop poles for the wet-weather scenes with Steve McQueen and Jackie Gleason.

We were part of the crowd of onlookers watching the filming. I brought my little autograph book from Woolworths along with me in case I encountered any movie stars. I was looking for Steve McQueen, but someone pointed out a pretty young woman with long blonde hair, wearing a simple brown shift dress, and told me she was Tuesday Weld. I didn't know who she was at the time, but asked for her autograph anyway. (Who would name someone after a day of the week, I wondered?)

Julia and I hoped we could make our way back to Camp Foster to do some shopping at the PX because she had her retired military ID card, so that should get us inside. We piled back into the SUV and Jay dropped us back in front of our hotel. I don't know what we would have done without him. Thank you, thank you. *Domo arigato!*

Good to Go!

A USMC Tour Bus parked near the wall of *shisa* dogs at the entrance to the Dai Ichi, and as we climbed aboard, Larry Laurion took a headcount. Marines Corp Tour Guide Chris Majewski was greeted enthusiastically by the original trekkers—they all seemed to know him from the first trip in 2001—and were thrilled to discover that he would once again escort the group around the island.

Larry and Amy Nitahara took the front seats and chatted with Chris while he maintained his balance at the front of the bus. It was amusing to watch him riding backwards, never falling, keeping his footing, as he swapped old stories with the first group of trekkers.

Chris told us where he was taking us—and ended a lot of his comments with "Good to go!" It started to get on my nerves until I got used to it and realized that this was just the way he was. Julia and I chuckled as we heard it over and over again. It eventually became endearing...good to go! *Semper Fi!*

Part of the Marine Corps Community Services (MCCS), these tours were big business on Okinawa and heavily advertised in the local *Okinawa Marine* newspaper.

I discovered that Majewski was quite the expert on battle history.

He really knew his stuff. And it wasn't until I returned home and became even more obsessed with all things related to Okinawa, that I discovered his fame extended far beyond the island, to The History Channel, and an episode of *Cities of the Underworld* that focused on the network of caves on Okinawa. When I watched the episode, I expected Chris to be involved and was not disappointed. There he was, the "go-to" guy, the absolute expert on the battle of Okinawa, crawling though the caves...with the camera crew following close behind.

Majewski also was listed as a source in the credits for a PBS-TV production of *American Experience* about the battle of Okinawa.

The first place Chris took us was to the ruins of *Zakimi Gusuku*, located in the village of Yomitan, on a peninsula providing an excellent view of the East China Sea. We climbed ancient limestone steps up to a wide moss-covered stone wall and walked along the top. It was hard to imagine that these ancient walls once were a castle enclosure. Zakimi Castle dated back to the beginning of the fifteenth century. It was totally destroyed during the battle of Okinawa, like almost everything. Like so many *gusuku*, only ruins remain.

I scribbled notes in my steno book, and whenever we got back on the bus I wrote frantically. By the time I returned home, I had filled a steno book front to back—and back to front—with a combination of shorthand and English notes that only I could decipher. I felt compelled to write down everything I could, so I would remember this trip forever.

Marlene Dulay clearly was the best-outfitted trekker among us. She wore some serious footwear, sturdy hiking boots, with thick socks. She appeared to be one serious travelin' gal...and her boots were made for walking. I admired her practicality. Marlene continued to wear her sensible footwear throughout the trip—with skirts, shorts and slacks. You knew her feet weren't sore. She walked along in comfort with her husband, Ken, while Julia and I managed to keep up by alternating our assorted sandals and sneakers, and still ending up with tired feet.

Not until we returned home did I learn that Julia had been in quite a bit of foot pain. Her feet had been bothering her, but she didn't want to risk any type of surgery that could jeopardize the trip. So she said nothing, determined to soldier on in silence. I wish I'd known.

Himeyuri

The next stop on our bus tour brought us to the Himeyuri Peace Museum. There, more than two hundred students and teachers from the First Prefectural Girls High School and the Okinawa Women's Normal School were mobilized into action as "nurses." They were ordered to treat wounded Japanese soldiers at the Haebaru Army Field Hospital, in underground caves. Schoolgirls were forced to become battlefield nurses under horrendous conditions.

Chris told us how girls were pulled from their classes and quickly trained on the job, and then forced to treat wounded Japanese soldiers in dark caves under deplorable conditions. The girls expected the battle to be over in a few days, not months, and even brought their school books along with them, somehow expecting to find time to do schoolwork.

We walked up a tree-lined path toward a large opening in the ground that we learned was a mass grave, where the bodies of many of the schoolgirls were entombed with the bodies of the Japanese soldiers they were caring for. At one point, explosives had been tossed into the caves, along with white phosphorus gas and rounds of machine-gun fire.

Surrounding the mass grave were colorful streamers hanging from trees and as I drew closer, I discovered that they were not streamers at all, but hundreds, more like thousands, of paper origami cranes; tiny replica birds that were strung by thread into very long chains. These cranes were snugged tight against one another so that the cranes became tightly stacked into streamers. Those long colorful streamers appeared to draw the visitors closer to the memorial. I was amazed at how much work had gone into these creations. The emphasis clearly was focused upon peace at the memorials we visited.

The crane is a symbol of peace and often appears at shrines. Japanese folklore has it that for every thousand paper cranes folded, a wish will come true. In this case, the wishes are for peace.

A haunting melody continued to play over and over while we wandered through the memorial and paused to read the words of the students who survived that "typhoon of steel."

Youthful school portraits of the nursing students lined the walls of the memorial…and the girls who survived, recounted their stories as "testimony" to the horror of war. We read translations of handwritten accounts…about how they dealt with injured soldiers…insufficient medical supplies…with no water to treat wounded soldiers in dark caves under deplorable conditions.

"A patient with no legs was crawling in the mud,"
> –16-year-old Shizuko Oshiro

"Bloated corpses as large as gasoline drum cans,"
> –17-year-old Toshi Uehara

"I could hear maggots eating the rotting flesh,"
> –15-year-old Tsuneko Kinjo

"I just can't die in a place like this, I said to myself."
> –18-year-old Ruri Morishita

After three months of battle, the girls were told by the Japanese soldiers in command that they were "on their own." But they had nowhere to go.

General Mitsuru Ushijima had ordered his army to fight to the last man and never surrender. Then Ushijima and his deputy committed ritual suicide—*seppuku*—at Mabuni Hill, leaving the non-combatants totally on their own in the raging "typhoon of steel."

There were about ten thousand patients in the caves and orders were issued to leave the seriously-wounded behind. The end of the battle was near and those left behind were directed to dispose of themselves in a way befitting the members of the Imperial Army. Hand grenades and doses of poison were distributed.

Despite shouted calls from American soldiers—*"dete-koi–dete-koi"*—to come out of the caves and surrender, eighteen-year-old Sada Arakaki told how nine students had only two hand grenades and were unsure that the two grenades would be enough to kill all of them at once. The students argued over who would get to hold the grenades close to their bodies, when a soldier snatched them from their hands. He urged the girls to leave the cave and surrender to the Americans. That Japanese soldier wanted the grenades for himself.

Many girls believed the Japanese propaganda about how surrendering to the Americans meant certain rape and murder at the hands of the GIs, so they left the caves under cover of darkness and threw themselves off the cliffs at Mabuni. Eighty percent of the students and teachers perished in the area that eventually became known as "Suicide Cliffs." Only eighteen girls survived to tell their stories.

Julia and I remembered going to Suicide Cliffs. We have similar photos in our family albums—of our families standing atop those high windswept cliffs—where hundreds of steps led up to a tall monument. That was all that was there back in the sixties. And all

91

we knew then was that fear of the American soldiers led schoolgirls and their teachers to throw themselves from the cliffs. Now we know so much more. Now we know how much the Okinawan civilians suffered. Himeyuri remains with me as the most moving place we saw.

Larry Kelly sat down beside me on a bench while we waited for the others to complete the tour. We said nothing. Himeyuri was a solemn place and hardly anyone spoke above a whisper while inside.

While we wandered around the museum, several elderly Okinawan women stood quietly along the wall. It wasn't until we were back on the bus, that Chris mentioned that those old women were among the eighteen young girls who had survived. Now aging *obasans*, they volunteered at Himeyuri. I wondered how they could handle that.

The rest of the trekkers had been waiting for us across the street, at the "Okinawan donut shop." I missed out on the *sata andagi*, little round balls of deep-fried dough. I didn't care. Donuts were the last thing I was thinking about.

On the first day of April, Easter Sunday, 1945, April Fools' Day, the last battle of the Pacific Theater of World War II began. One of the bloodiest...the 82-day battle took place primarily in the southern part of the island, resulting in 70,000 deaths. June 27th marked the end of the Battle of Okinawa.

I felt so ignorant. All I could remember about the battle of Okinawa when I lived there came from the military history museum at Fort Buckner. We sat beside a huge three-dimensional relief map of the island that would light up during a recorded narration. All I learned back then was that it was a decisive battle and the last one before the atomic bomb was dropped on Japan.

I asked Chris about that museum, and he said that it had been shut down a while back and the contents, including that huge map, all had mysteriously disappeared.

Later that afternoon, we found ourselves stopping by the typical tour-bus stops, and it was obvious that we were being "dumped" into places where we were likely to spend some money.

The tour of a lacquer factory was educational and I lusted after some of those amazing items in the gift shop, but they seemed extremely expensive. I figured I could do better when we found some of the little alley shops that Julia and I hoped to find from the past.

True lacquered items are made from a wooden base, and then many coats of lacquer are applied by hand, thus increasing the value of the item because of the time involved.

Another stop at the glass factory known as the Ryukyu Glass Village brought back memories from the past. The Ryukyu glass industry had its origins during the postwar military occupation, when artists created many souvenir items to sell to American GIs. There was an endless supply of discarded glass bottles that the GIs tossed out. Those glass beer and soda bottles were recycled into works of art.

I remember going with my family to a local glass factory back in the sixties where we watched, as beer bottles were being smashed and melted down. Then the molten glass was recycled and mouth-blown into tall decorative vases and even artistic pieces of glass fruit.

Mom was so proud of her amber-colored Ryukyu glass punch bowl set that had been made in a "crackle glass" style with rough-cut pontils along the bottom where the glassblower had cut it off. That huge punch bowl rested upon a large, round tray and there were at least ten small uneven little cups surrounding it. No one in the States had seen anything like it before. It was always a topic of conversation.

Okinawa has evolved into such a modern resort island that the only place to experience the rural Okinawa from the fifties and sixties is to go to "Okinawa World" or "Ryukyu Mura" cultural theme parks where you can see traditional *Ryubyu*, classical Ryukyuan dances, and experience life like it was in the rural areas.

Despite Julia's protests, while at Ryukyu Mura, we did wander into Habu World, where we sat in front of a small stage where a divided display case housed a *habu* snake and a mongoose. Julia and I recalled *habu*/mongoose duels from back in the Kadena Karnival days. We knew now that we wouldn't be seeing anything bloody.

Political correctness had arrived for this "odd couple."

While on the bus, Chris explained that the traditional fights were now outlawed because of the cruelty issue, so we would see a film of a death match from the past. He told us about a major SNAFU that occurred when the mongoose was introduced onto the island back in the post-war days, to combat the prevalence of *habu* snakes.

"What started out as a good idea fell apart because someone forgot about the fact that the mongoose is a nocturnal creature—and the *habu* is only active during the daytime. The two never got together—except at show time!"

Julia and I sat surrounded by families and children who eagerly awaited the filmed fight. Julia tried to be brave and said she would close her eyes. An Okinawan man explained everything in Japanese to the audience—we didn't understand a word.

I whispered to her, "I read somewhere that you are never supposed to suck the poison out from a *habu* bite."

"I don't want to hear it. Don't tell me those things," she wailed. "Oh, oh, oh."

Finally a screen dropped down from the ceiling and the lights dimmed. A film showed an overview of the island and apparently explained the *habu*/mongoose history of martial arts. We were sitting off to one side at an angle and everything appeared a bit blurred.

There was a fight that lasted only a few minutes, and predictably, the mongoose won.

The lights came up. Everyone moved to the exit, and it was only then that we realized what we were still holding in our hands—the multi-colored 3-D glasses that we had been handed when we walked in! A box was placed by the exit to collect them! We looked at one another. We obviously didn't catch the command in Japanese, to "Put on your glasses!" No wonder those little kids behind us were laughing at the "*baka-no-gaijins*" sitting in front of them!

When we toured Okinawa World later, we sat through traditional folk dances with an old *mamasan* and *papasan*, bent over with age, surrounded with dancers and wild *shisa* dogs shaking their heads.

Chris told us that Okinawa World was the only place left where we would see a building with a thatched roof. Once commonplace, houses with thatched-roofs had dotted the island years ago. They surrounded us in our Oyama neighborhood. Now they were just another part of the past.

Construction of the traditional Okinawan home involved no nails! So for purposes of tourism, apparently some of those authentic houses were disassembled and reassembled here in the park!

When the folk dances ended, Julia and I met other trekkers for lunch at The Kingdom Village Restaurant. I ordered the traditional buckwheat *soba* noodles with pork and decided to sample the specialty beer brewed exclusively at the Village. *Soba* noodles are traditional Japanese cuisine and the technique for making these noodles dates back to the seventeenth century. The beer was okay, but since I'm not a beer connoisseur, I guess I didn't fully appreciate it.

After lunch, we wandered through the brewery and encountered a display of sake bottles with dead *habu* coiled inside. The *habu* snakes were coiled neatly into the bottles, and a young saleswoman encouraged one of our fellow trekkers to try a sample. She took a hearty swig—and began to gasp!

"Don't light a match!" she choked.

The sales assistant immediately offered her a glass of water. I took a close look at the *habu sake* bottles and decided that I probably wouldn't be able to get one through customs anyway. Something told me that a coiled, dead snake would raise questions. And it was in a liquid.

The story behind *habu sake* is that it is made from the poisonous venom of the *habu*. The venom loses its potency in the alcohol, which is not really *sake*, but *awamori*. So what's with calling it *habu sake*?

Traditional rice alcohol, known as *awamori*, was also available. *Awamori* is extremely potent, and is commonly diluted with water before drinking.

After lunch we walked through the little streets and observed Okinawan life created for tourists—as we observed it forty years earlier.

There, Julia encountered an old gentleman dressed in a *bingata* cloth *yukata* with a straw hat, and she immediately struck up a conversation with him. The old *papasan* told her that he used to be a manager at the Fort Buckner PX—but now he worked here at the Okinawa "village" portraying an old *papasan*!

He just shrugged his shoulders when Julia asked him what he thought about the changes on the island since the 1972 Reversion to Japanese control. It was apparent to us that his life had not changed for the better. He probably earned much more money when he was a manager at the PX.

Julia and I agreed later that the Reversion appears to have changed little on the island. The military installations remain and if the Americans left, it would severely affect the economy. It's been more than thirty years, and if things were going to change, it would have happened by now.

Battlefields Tour

Our next USMC tour with Chris Majewski took us to the sites of the last battle of World War II. Chris brought the Battle of Okinawa to life as we all walked along a grassy hilltop in bright sunshine. Standing here, on the actual battlefields, I looked around and tried to imagine these hills covered in blood and bodies—dead Okinawan, Japanese and American bodies. I was ashamed to be so ignorant of the details of this important event in history.

When we moved to Okinawa, I was just a girl of twelve, and not very interested in military history. It's never too late. I want to know more.

Chris Majewski's enthusiasm and knowledge of battle history was apparent as he pointed out the specific battle sites around Shuri Castle. This was where the majority of the fighting took place during the "typhoon of steel."

Standing in an attentive group atop Sugar Loaf Hill, encircling Chris, we learned how in the course of five days, from April 3rd to the 8th, American forces lost 1,510 men and the Japanese forces lost 4,489.

Pacing back and forth with his hands stuffed into the pockets of his cargo pants, Chris described the battle as the largest American amphibious assault in U.S. history. *"The largest,"* he emphasized.

Anticipating the obvious questions headed his way, he said, "Whoa, whoa, whoa! What about D-Day? D-Day put ashore 157,000 Americans. But Okinawa put ashore 180,000 Americans. Okinawa was bigger. We expected to hit the beach and fight our way off the whole way. But there was no resistance. The Japanese placed the first specially-established regiment, called the Okinawa Home Guard, all alone on that beachhead."

The Home Guard offered no resistance. The Japanese soldiers were hunkered down below ground, safe in a network of natural caves with connecting tunnels that they had forced the Okinawans to dig. I could now appreciate what the everyday people, the farmers, their families, and especially those schoolgirls at *Himeyuri* had gone through.

Walking through the Sugar Loaf Hill area, I asked Chris about the many books that have been written about the Battle of Okinawa and what he recommended.

"Feifer's book, *Tennozan* is really good," said Chris. "Find that one."

I tracked down Feifer's book soon after I returned home. Five hundred-plus pages of solid research and anecdotal detail from interviews with Okinawan, American and Japanese survivors told the real story. At times it was pretty gruesome, but I read all of it. *Tennozan* is the word that the Japanese used to describe what took place on Okinawa—a decisive struggle on which everything was staked.

It was the "first battle that took place on Japanese soil, and the last battle before the start of the atomic age," said George Feifer in his introduction. He pointed out that half a million Americans were involved in the Pacific Theater of battle, but no more than a handful of them had any real knowledge about Japan.

The Japanese belief in invincibility was rooted in the image of themselves as a unique people whose ideals and values were unattainable by others.

The Battle of Okinawa lasted eighty-two days. More than 12,000 Americans were killed or missing in action. More than 70,000 Japanese soldiers and Okinawans were killed, and it is estimated that up to 150,000 Okinawan men, women and children lost their lives.

Right off, Feifer told how the *Yamato*, the largest Japanese battleship in its fleet, was sunk two hundred miles north of Okinawa by the U.S. Navy.

He also described how Japanese survivors were amazed at the rescue efforts by American forces—and how often several lives were risked to save only one person! They didn't understand it, with their *kamikaze* mindset.

Feifer pointed out how the Japanese were puzzled that, during the attack on the battleship *Yamato*, not one American plane took a direct nose dive at the battleship. That's all it would have taken—a simple *kamikaze* suicide dive. Instead, the Americans kept hammering away at the target with artillery until it sunk.

Feifer explained that "when American strategists began preparing for the campaign, their problem was ignorance: intelligence discovered that the Ryukyus were among the world's least explored inhabited areas. Japan had kept foreigners away from the islands for over sixty years."

A young sailor on a battleship preparing to join the initial naval bombardment—which alone would ravage the land with over 60,000 shells—gazed at the target and compared it to looking at a beautiful painting.

He said, "I was struck with the utter incongruity of it all. There, the Okinawans had tilled their soil with ancient and crude farming methods, but the war had come, bringing with it the latest and most refined technology for killing. It seemed so insane."

The highest ranking American killed in World War II was killed on Okinawa.

Chris told us that General Simon Bolivar Buckner's bravado led to his demise. He died on June 18th after he ignored warnings to postpone a visit so close to the action. Buckner wanted to observe the 2nd Marine Division in action. "He insisted on standing out front at an observation point along Maesato Ridge…and with his obvious rank prominently displayed, Buckner was a target of sniper fire from a Japanese artilleryman."

"As of April 1st 1945 at 0430 hours, there was nothing but American warships out there in the water…they began pounding… and every ship in that fleet hammered Okinawa for three hours. At 0730 hours, the bombardment lifts, we fly in…strafe-and-rocket the landing beach, and push farther inland. At 0820 hours, the landing begins. Every book you read, except for one or two, says 0830 hours. But the 6th Marine Division jumped the gun by ten minutes. They put the first Marine on deck at 0820, north of Yomitan, up by Torii Station."

"Ten minutes," I thought to myself. "So what's the big deal? What's so important about ten minutes? Just ask any marine. Obviously, they were of extreme importance."

When the 6th Marine Division took control of Yomitan Airfield, one Japanese pilot wasn't aware that the Americans were there.

Still pacing back and forth, Chris said, "Our fleet's in blackout… in comes a Japanese Zero…the Japanese army and navy didn't talk to each other…so the Japanese army didn't have a clue that there was no Japanese navy left…nobody let the pilot know that the Americans had landed."

"So he flies over our fleet, lands at Yomitan Airfield, rolls his canopy back, pulls up to a hangar, hops out, lights up a smoke and starts diddy-bopping over to his ground crew, which just happened to be armed U.S. Marines. That pilot came to his senses, realized who he was looking at, and went for his six-shooters! Those marines turned that pilot, that plane and the damn building behind him into Swiss cheese!

"One marine sergeant walked up, looked at that dead pilot, rifled him for souvenirs, and said, 'See that? There's always one poor bastard who's the last to get the word.' "

Julia and I now can fully appreciate that master sergeant's cryptic comment from the deck of the USNS Barrett back in 1963 when we docked in Naha Port. What he saw back then truly had been all blown to hell.

While we wandered through the battlefields, Julia began to pick up a few rocks to bring home as souvenirs. I urged her to stop before gathering rocks got out of control.

"Julia, didn't you ever see that Lucy movie, *The Long Long Trailer?*"

I encouraged Julia to at least trade in some of her larger rocks for smaller ones. I wasn't sure she'd even be able to identify where they were from after she got them back home.

Back on the bus, Chris talked about his family—his Okinawan wife, Saya, and his two little girls, and told us about how he met his wife. His folks came over from Michigan for their wedding ceremony. Clearly, Chris is one of those men who appreciates the allure of Asian beauty. I just hope that he ends up with a son some day, or that one of his daughters develops some "tomboy" traits. Somebody needs to crawl through those unexplored caves with him.

"Go-time" once again, and we were back on the bus to our next destination, Camp Kinser and the Battle of Okinawa Historical

Display consisting of several huge rooms of military artifacts on the second floor of a building at Camp Kinser. Founded in 1992 by Chris and his buddy, Dave Davenport, its mission was "to keep the spirit of the 6th Marines Division alive."

Chris explained how he and his buddies went trolling for treasure at construction sites whenever they heard about an area of the island that was being excavated. Like excited boys, they raced off to the excavation site and used metal detectors to locate weapons, ordnance and equipment that had been buried for the past sixty years.

He and his buddies formed a group called the "Tunnel Rats" and unearthed battle artifacts as they dug inside the natural and man-made caves throughout the island for artifacts from the many soldiers and civilians who died in those caves. They even recovered an old toothbrush with a soldier's name scratched onto the handle.

Chris talked about how he had tracked down many items for the museum through eBay auctions. "I always seem to be in debt for the things I find on eBay," Chris added.

He told us how a veteran who came to Okinawa during the fiftieth anniversary of the battle could recall the exact spot where he buried a World War II Japanese weapon—so Chris took him to that area. They searched and searched, but never found that gun.

Later that day, while the old soldier walked around the museum, Dave Davenport overheard the story—and produced the weapon in question—he had just unearthed it a few days earlier. The old soldier and his weapon were reunited. Sounds too good to be true; but that's why it is.

We paused in front of an aquarium filled with salt water, and Chris explained that it held a flamethrower that had been recovered deep off the coast of Yomitan, submerged since the battle. At this point, it was best to leave the weapon underwater, than to try to restore it.

"It's at least a two-year process to clean it and it requires almost constant monitoring, so I just put it right back in salt water...and will leave it there."

In another room, I found myself most impressed with a full-size *jinrikisha*—a real *rickshaw*—leaning upright in a corner, with sandbags under the wheels to keep it from rolling away. That's what I am drawn to—the *rickshaw*. Forget the guns and ammo!

Yamada-san's Buddha

We wrapped up our stop in "touristy" Okinawa World and were back on the bus, "good to go," heading off to the Peace Memorial Park, where Julia and I knew that the carved Buddha we remembered from the past was located. Chris Majewski told us that this stop was unscheduled, so we had only a limited amount of time in the park. One hour. We would return for another tour later in the week.

That was okay with us. Julia and I were here for only one thing. We'd been waiting for this stop. Our goal was to locate the Buddha.

The rest of the trekkers wandered off in the direction of the Cornerstone of Peace, a long wall of engraved names of more than 200,000 Japanese and American military personnel, and many Okinawan civilians who lost their lives during the battle.

We hurried along the gravel pathways in a different direction, pausing a few times to ask directions from uniformed school girls, and then from some Japanese tourists—"Where can we find the large Buddha?"

Everyone directed us to the top of the hill, and pointed to a huge white concrete tower that resembled a nuclear reactor cooling tower. Who designed this?

Apparently that's where the Buddha must be.

We started climbing. Halfway up the steep flights of steps, Julia paused to catch her breath beneath a shelter covered with flowering red hibiscus. Sitting there on a bench, she started to laugh when she spotted me shooting video. I was equally out of breath, from carrying around a few extra pounds and my camera equipment. We had to get a move-on. We had to accomplish our mission and get all the way back down to the parking lot and back on the bus.

We finally finished our climb to the entrance of the tower at the top of hundreds of steps. Once inside, we scanned historic black-and-white photographs of the man who carved the Buddha back in the sixties—Shinzan Yamada. A line of framed photos along the wall depicted his progress through the years.

We entered a spacious chamber, where the centerpiece was the Buddha. When we finally saw the huge Buddha in its splendor in that enormous hall, we looked at one other in amazement because we found something that we could both identify with from our past—a tangible piece of *our* presence on this island.

Julia and I walked up to the massive Buddha, measuring about thirty-five feet high, now reflecting a glossy red lacquer coating. Hundreds of chairs surrounded the raised circular stage and paintings lined the curved walls. The theme of the artwork was "war and peace."

We recalled how back in the sixties, we observed Mr. Yamada at work on the statue. Down one of the many narrow alleys in Futenma, we stumbled across a large wooden building in which an old *papasan* patiently worked every day carving the huge white stone figure. Outside the barn-like building was a traditional Japanese garden, with a *koi* pond and a small bridge. It was wonderful. It was serene. It was peaceful. We had no idea back then what the future held for the Buddha statue.

When we wandered outside Gate Two, into little shops down

the alleyways, to buy *Shiseido* makeup, *bunka* embroidery kits, and bootleg LPs and forty-fives in colored vinyl from Taiwan, we often stopped by to check on the old *papasan's* progress. We left a small donation in a basket by the doorway. Yamada-san was so focused on his work that he never paid attention to the people who wandered in and out of his building. He continued to carve.

Through the years I occasionally wondered what became of the old man and his statue and it was not until the G-8 Summit took place on Okinawa in 2000, did I discover that "our Buddha" had become the centerpiece of the Peace Memorial Park, located in the vicinity of the battlefields around Mabuni Hill. It was dedicated to all those who died during the Battle of Okinawa.

Covered now with three-and-a-half tons of lacquer through a unique lacquer application technique known as *tsuikin*, Yamada-san's Buddha figure differs from the traditional Buddha. This non-religious Buddha design represents human harmony and world peace, and is decorated with a flower whose six petals represent the six world continents.

Back in the sixties, Julia and I both remembered standing there observing the old man hard at work and not quite knowing the background behind his project and what would become of the huge statue. Julia and her husband, along with their three children, would also stop by to see how *papasan* was progressing.

"He fell off the scaffolding several times while he was working," said Julia. "Did you know that?"

That I didn't.

Yamada-san was relatively old at seventy-two, when he began to carve the massive Buddha. He was over ninety years old when he completed his life's work. (A well-known artist back then, his designs appeared on many Ryukyu Islands postage stamps.)

The statue symbolized Yamada's hope for peace and was a tribute to his two sons, forced into service and lost during the Battle of Okinawa.

I continued to videotape while Julia sat quietly in the huge hall, lost in her memories. All alone with a rare item from our past, we had the hall to ourselves. There was no one around, except for a little Okinawan lady who was busy using a vacuum in the outer reception area. I kept waiting for her to shut it off so I could complete my videotaping. I captured some additional footage when a local tour guide, attired in a business-like suit, hat and gloves, led a small group of Japanese tourists inside and told the story behind the Buddha in Japanese. Perfect! It could only have been better if a group of schoolchildren in uniforms and caps had wandered through.

Resting serenely upon a carpeted circular platform with artwork done by schoolchildren displayed around the base, were thousands more folded origami paper cranes, threaded onto long chains. We found several tables with guest books at the back of the auditorium and sat down to sign our names and add comments about how we had lived on Okinawa in 1964 and observed Mr. Yamada at work, carving the Buddha.

Squares of blue and white origami paper were stacked on the tables so that visitors could fold origami paper cranes and deposit them into large Lucite containers. And because I still had not re-mastered the art of folding the origami cranes, I snatched a few folded paper cranes as souvenirs.

After walking around our Buddha one last time, Julia and I realized that we'd better get back to the bus. We stepped outside into the bright sunlight and looked at each other, eyes filled with tears. We still had to get down all those steps!

This proved to be the most emotional moment of our trip. Julia and I had finally found something from our past. I tried to lighten things up and cautioned Julia that we really had to get a grip on ourselves so we could see clearly through our tears—or we both were going to tumble down all those steps! Soon we were laughing and not crying!

We regained our composure by the time we got back to the bus and found the rest of our trekkers on board and ready to go. No one else had intruded on this visit to "our" Buddha.

We had it all to ourselves. Despite what we were warned about by previous trekkers, Julia and I *did* expect to find our past. We didn't want to believe what others had told us. What we remembered from the past couldn't all be gone. Surely we would find more. We were running out of days, but we still wanted to find my family's old cement block house off-post in Oyama. We needed a little more time. We needed to keep looking for the past.

Once more Julia exclaimed, "Your mother should be here. She would be amazed at what we're seeing."

I reminded her that this trip wouldn't have been possible for Mom. Just getting her on and off the bus would have been an ordeal. Mom did not have any of the fond memories that Julia had of life on Okinawa. Mom had a vastly different outlook on life.

"And they definitely would have voted her off the island!" I proclaimed.

Later that night, Julia and I lay awake in our beds, discussing the amazing odyssey we were on and what I should do about my writing project. I told her that it could very well turn into more than just a travel story. It could become a book if I included details about my family and growing up as a military brat.

"But with the publishing industry today, there has to be some explicit sex," I complained. "Books don't sell unless there's something to titillate readers. And there's nothing I can add into my memoir that would make it sexy—nothing took place among my little circle of friends when I lived here on Okinawa. At least nothing I knew of."

"Well somebody's got to be having wild sex somewhere," said Julia. "Maybe even some of our trekkers. Write something about that. We've got to stay up late one of these nights and get into that hospitality suite. It sounds like they all gather up there and drink and party. Let's check it out before we leave. There's got to be something going on up there."

We agreed to do that. Soon we fell asleep; Julia as usual, snoring lightly, escalating into louder crescendos and then tapering off when I rolled her over and aimed her toward the window. I lay reading in the next bed, until my eyes finally closed. The hospitality suite was the last thing on my mind. We'd try to get there the next night. Until then, all the explicit sex in my book would simply remain "off the page!"

Kokusai Dori

Around five thousand people had returned to Okinawa to celebrate this four-day event. The festival was an opportunity to reconnect those of Okinawan heritage around the world with their homeland. The first *Uchinanchu* Festival took place in 1990. I don't know how it came about, or who was responsible, but it was such a success that it led to plans for another festival five years later...and then another... and another.

The slogan for this Fourth Worldwide *Uchinanchu* Festival was "Reaching out with an earnest spirit are beautiful hearts joined as one." The term "*Uchinanchu*" translates to "Okinawan."

The hotel bus let us out along a street where the only monorail on the island passed overhead—yes, a monorail! We never rode that monorail—one more thing that we ran out of time to do.

We gathered in a dusty schoolyard with many other groups for the kick-off of the opening parade for this fourth festival.

Larry unfurled a ten-foot-long banner that identified us as Kubasaki alumnae and we tried to figure out who would handle it while we walked down *Kokusai Dori*—Okinawa's "Miracle Mile," where stores and restaurants lined both sides of the street. This was the street in downtown Naha where demonstrators once gathered to denounce the U.S. military presence.

Our banner sagged in the center, with only two poles to support it, so Larry Kelly tried to find something else to use to prop up the center. After scrounging around the schoolyard, he came up with a crooked stick and tied it to the center. Julia and I looked at each other: "Tiny Tim's crutch!" Somehow it worked, and only we could see it from the back while we took turns holding up the banner during the parade.

We waited in the dusty schoolyard playground, ready to fall in with the parade, surrounded by crowds of people representing transplanted Okinawans who were now living in Argentina, Brazil, Bolivia, the Philippines, France, Germany and of course Hawaii, where the concentration of Okinawans is highest. Each group carried banners proclaiming the origin of their "*kenjin-kai*" (organized groups scattered all around the world), and many were dressed in native costumes from those countries.

"Those GIs really got around," someone in our group proclaimed.

Crowds lined the sidewalks as we walked down the street, waving and reaching out to shake hands with us. It was like a triumphant victory parade. "Miss Julia" was absolutely glowing as she walked along, doing her best "Queen Elizabeth wave" and pausing to shake hands with Okinawans lining the sidewalks. She was having a grand time!

I kept hoping that Julia just might encounter her long-lost maid Yoshiko. I kept hoping that somehow, along *Kokusai Dori*, a little old *mamasan* would suddenly step out from the curb and shout to Julia, and then the two women would soon be hugging and crying. Anything was possible. After all, we never thought we'd see this island again—but we walked the entire 1.6 kilometers and my hoped-for reunion didn't happen.

While we walked, we spotted interesting-looking shops that we wanted to get back to after the end of the parade—and tried to remember where they were. We had another few hours before we had to meet back at the bus, so Julia, Anna and I decided to stick together.

The very first place I wandered into was a bookstore, a two-story Japanese bookstore. My goal was to collect all of the Harry Potter books in Japanese, and I was on my way. My first purchase ended up being a heavy one, and I dragged it around for the rest of the evening. In Japanese, many of the Harry Potter books are two-volumes. Japanese books are read from back to front and the *kanji* symbols are read vertically. Line drawings were interspersed among the *kanji* symbols. The cover art is unique to all foreign editions, and I was thrilled to have found *Harry Potter and the Order of the Phoenix.* I can't read it of course—but I just had to have it for my collection of many Harry's in many languages!

One item was crossed off my list.

We were on a "shopping high" as we wandered in and out of the little storefronts. The stores were small and in many of them, you carefully had to climb up a step or two to enter the shop. In one shop, we encountered two friendly *mamasans* who greeted us with cups of tea and little cakes in an effort to keep us inside. Their plan worked. We bought many gifts from them.

Just as in the past, the items we purchased were wrapped in colorful paper. We recalled how everything we bought was carefully wrapped by the shopkeepers. No bags. Small cloths, called *furoshiki,* were often used.

Back then, our items would have been totaled on an abacus. I can remember flying fingers, and the clicking sounds of the wooden beads as the shopkeeper arrived at a total. The ladies here used a modern calculator to arrive at a total. They kept laughing and offered us *"presentos"* with our purchases—little bonus scarves and handkerchiefs or seashells. They were trying to hold onto us, but we finally left the shop and moved on.

One store had large turtle shells encased in Lucite display boxes, but I couldn't imagine how I could ever get one of those home. There could be an embargo on bringing them into the States. I saw several *sanshins*—in faux snakeskin, as well as colorful *bingata* cloth. The *sanshin*, a three-stringed instrument similar to a banjo, has a neck made of lacquered wood and a body covered in snakeskin. The *shamishen* played in mainland Japan is a derivative of the Okinawan *sanshin*. The original Japanese *shamishens* were covered in white cat skin. I don't want to think about that. I'll take the fake snake!

It would look great on a wall back home. We found many shops with Ryukyu glass as well as *bingata* cloth purses. We were doing some serious "deadline shopping!"

Another street called *Heiwa Dori*, once known as "Black Market Alley," ran off of *Kokusai Dori*. Just one kilometer long, it's where the Mitsukoshi Department Store was located. We put that on our list for later.

Finally, we decided we must eat something but didn't want to waste time in a crowded sit-down restaurant. We ended up at a McDonald's and had no trouble ordering from the universal "McMenu." If you don't speak the language, you simply point to the menu on the counter in front of you, where the items are grouped in photos. This far from home and here I am, eating a Filet-O-Fish and fries! I simply pointed to the picture.

We moved on. We ran into some of our trekkers who were gathering for the bus ride back to the hotel. A discussion was under way about making the most of our festival bus passes while we were on Okinawa. Larry Kelly was determined to show us how to read the Okinawan bus schedules, which were posted on cement bus poles scattered around the island. He led us down the street to the nearest bus pole—and we trotted obediently behind him.

I hung back with Anna while Larry explained everything in great detail to Julia. She appeared to be nodding in comprehension. I whispered to Anna that Julia probably wasn't getting a word of it—because she couldn't see much of anything in low light with her growing cataracts—and I didn't know how good her hearing was either. I simply didn't feel like paying attention anymore, so I left Julia to deal with "Larry Number Two."

We followed Larry back to the pickup point for our hotel bus and he was certain that we now understood how to read the posted schedules and would be able to get around the island and make the most of our four-day passes.

Actually, Larry would have been horrified to know how many times we thought about taking the bus—but after a short wait at a bus stop, tossed in the towel and hailed a taxi!

One day, Julia and I did take the bus around town—only to hop off when things looked interesting. We didn't really plan where we were going on that ride and just looked out the window until something caught our attention. Sometimes it's good not to have a plan.

The *Uchinanchu* Festival officially opened on October 14th for four days, so we went to the Convention Center where each group or "*kenjin-kai*" was assigned to a section of the event hall. Above the entrance to the hall was a huge "WELCOME HOME" sign. There was excitement in the air. It seemed like we were attending the opening ceremony for the Olympics! The two Larrys led us up into the balcony of the Convention Center to our assigned seating area.

It was awe-inspiring and magical. A sophisticated opening ceremony marked by the most haunting song, "*The Wind to Nirai*," was performed by some extremely talented vocalists, Natsuki

Higashihama and Yutaka. And when the tempo picked up and the massive *taiko* drums kicked in, getting louder and louder, so that we could feel the reverberations, I got goose bumps.

The *taiko* drums, part of Japanese history, date back centuries. They are indeed primal.

Two words: "King Kong."

Okinawan dignitaries made speeches and the governor of Hawaii spoke. VIPs from Okinawa and the delegations were expressing gratitude, but we really wanted to see what was taking place outside on the grounds of the Convention Center in Ginowan Seaside Park. Anna, Julia and I slipped away as the ceremonies and speeches continued. Larry Kelly frowned as we crept out, but we just couldn't lose any more time listening to politicians and welcoming speeches.

Across the field outside the auditorium, booths set up by *kenjin-kai* from all around the world displayed items and foods from their homes.

That was where we encountered the first "squat-style" trench toilets as we searched for a restroom and decided that we could hold it forever if we had to. Some giggling schoolgirls noted our *gaijin* distress and pointed us to a Western-style toilet located nearby in another building with a long line of ladies eager to use it.

We walked out to the main highway and consulted one of those bus schedules posted on a cement bus pole. When we figured out that we would have to wait forty minutes for the next northbound bus, we flagged down another taxi. Larry would have been absolutely horrified if he knew how we were wasting our bus passes. A taxi driver braked to a stop, and the doors swung open remotely at the touch of a button. We jumped in, and we were off!

The driver was friendly and practiced his English with us, but when he discovered that Anna was fluent in Japanese, he directed all his comments to her.

He asked us where we were from and what we liked to eat, so we ended up talking about food! He told us what he liked to eat and what his mother cooked for him. She cooked *goya*, the bitter melon that was so popular on the island. And he still lived with his ninety-eight-year-old mother—moms are alike all around the world!

At one point, the driver questioned us about a helicopter crash that had occurred on Okinawa—something that I vaguely recalled from CNN. Like I said, whenever I heard "Okinawa" mentioned in the news, I paid close attention. (I "Googled" when I returned home, and discovered that the crash took place in 2004 when a Marine chopper grazed one of the buildings on the campus of the University of the Ryukyus before crashing to the ground and catching on fire. There were no civilian casualties, and the injured marines were treated at a local military hospital. But that incident reinforced the strong resentment of the locals toward the military presence on the island. They still wanted us gone!)

Our driver dropped us off along the street where I once walked with Mom more than forty years ago. The little wooden *Shinto* shrine was there off to the side, up from the street. I remembered when women shuffled along the street wearing colorful *kimonos* and wooden *geta*. Back then it was a quiet, peaceful area along a somewhat busy two-lane street, but now it was situated right in the middle of a very busy intersection.

The Futenma Shrine was one of eight shrines built about five centuries ago under the order of *King Sho Kinpuku*. Known locally as *Futenma Gongen*, the shrine was definitely from our past. Many people came here to pray, evidenced by the racks of prayer tablets, hanging from ribbons outside the shrine.

Behind the shrine was a large cave filled with calcium deposits that formed over hundreds of years. At the cave entrance there was a pair of stones symbolizing fertility. The stones are one reason why so many young couples visit the shrine.

It was believed that the water from the shrine would purify your body and spirit, so when you visited the shrine, you were supposed to rinse your hands and drink the water at the entrance.

When we left, I selected a rock of my own, my piece of Okinawa, one wonderful striated rock that looked like it had a lot of history.

"Julia, this is the only *one* I'm hauling home," I announced.

We climbed the steps leading to an "over-the-highway" crosswalk and descended down the other side. At each intersection now there were traffic signals and crosswalks with state-of-the-art "chirping" signals.

"Remember how we used to cross the street?" asked Julia. "There were those little buckets with crossing flags in them along each side of the street, and you would pick up one of those flags and hold it in your hand as you walked out into traffic. After you crossed the street, you dropped it into the bucket on the other side."

Where we walked, there once was a Japanese movie theater. Long ago, when Mom and I walked past it, I remembered staring at the poster for *Love Is a Many Splendored Thing* with William Holden and Jennifer Jones locked in an embrace, surrounded by *kanji*. I didn't know if the sound would be dubbed in Japanese or if there would be subtitles. I wondered what the theatre was like but never got inside.

There was a little shop down one of these alleys where we bought our *bunka* punch embroidery kits—the craft that we learned while on Okinawa. From our cement block house we could look over the concrete fence right into the Okinawan family home right next door. I tried not to be obvious, but peeking inside their house was fascinating. The sliding doors were open throughout the day and Mrs. Higeru knelt upon the *tatami* mats and punched on those *bunka* embroidery pictures. One day, Mom and I discovered the kits in a shop. I bought one and took it next door to show Mrs. Higeru. Somehow, through my pantomime, she realized that I wanted to learn how to make the picture. She showed me how to use the tin punch needle and the crinkly rayon thread. We didn't speak but I learned because she simply showed me how to hold the stitches in place with my finger. I completed that first "rather lumpy" *bunka* embroidery picture for Grandma back in Klamath Falls. I was so proud of it that we had it framed before sending it off to Oregon. She had no choice but to hang it on her wall. Fortunately, as time passed, my work improved.

The only thing that appeared to be open for business was the "Futenma Antiques Mall" and upon entering, Anna exclaimed, "It's like being back in my grandmother's basement!"

Loaded with garage-sale collectibles and plenty of clutter, the building appeared to contain everything that the GIs didn't drag back home. We found abandoned Corning Ware, Pyrex, and kitchen utensils lying upon Formica tables. There was an old Maytag wringer washing machine beside an old gas stove. Toys and games, stuffed animals, and Barbie dolls surrounded us.

The prices were all in *yen* and some quick conversions told me that they were simply outrageous! Did anyone ever really buy any of this stuff? I shot some video of the interior and we soon wandered outside, and down the alleyway. Somewhere nearby would have been the old wooden building where Mr. Yamada worked on the Buddha.

We hailed another taxi and ended up at the Plaza House Shopping Center. Once a few simple storefronts, it had now evolved into a multi-level shopping center with an escalator and specialty stores—where I found several Ventures CDs with Japanese paper obi-strips to bring home for Don.

Still standing was a Tuttle's Bookstore—once the only place where English language books could be purchased. Charles E. Tuttle founded his company in 1948 in Tokyo and was dedicated to publishing "books to span the East and West." Tuttle published many books on Japanese arts and culture, as well as translations of Japanese works into the English language. The company's main focus still was on Asian and Pacific themes.

I bought more books. I had to. I would never see this store again.

Shujiro Castle

Reduced to piles of rubble after the Battle of Okinawa ended, that rubble was all that we remembered from the sixties. There wasn't much to see back then at what we called the Shuri Castle ruins. But now! It had become a total tourist extravaganza.

Six years of serious renovation restored it to its original fifteenth century splendor in 1992. But could this really be the way it looked back then? Overwhelming opulence? Chinoiserie and gilt dragons? Like a modern-day Chinese restaurant?

Shujiro Castle dated back to the fifteenth century and was attributed to King Satto of Urasoe, the first Ryukyuan king to start trading goods with China.

Larry Laurion led us to Shuri on a hotel bus, and we climbed the steps and gathered in the wide courtyard of Shujiro Castle. Wearing his "Old Guys Rule" shirt, Larry passed out tickets for the tour of the castle and we proceeded to the entry point called *Seiden*, the State Hall, where we removed our shoes and carried them along with us in plastic bags.

Julia and Colonel French remained behind at the bottom of the steps and decided to take a rest. The Colonel had gotten a taste of some bad ice cream earlier in the day and decided to sit out the tour.

Julia didn't have any ice cream, but the "sitting it out" part definitely appealed to her.

The tour was rapid and something that I would like to do again, but at a much slower pace. There were way too many people and not enough time. We were led through room after room and eventually came to the banquet hall where the 2000 G8 Summit dinner took place.

I recalled the CNN updates about the Summit that was hosted by Japan and held July 19-24 on Okinawa—when world leaders from the "Group of Eight" —Canada, France, Germany, Italy, Japan, Russia, the U.K. and the U.S., with Tony Blair and Bill Clinton as representatives, went to the Far East for their annual gathering.

I remember watching footage when they gathered at the Peace Park, as well as in Shuri Castle. And now, I had been to both places as well!

Large photographs of the dinner hosted by Prime Minister Yoshiro Mori were on display, as well as the full table setting with the dinnerware that was used for the banquet. The menu for that dinner consisted of pigeon meat wrapped in soybean milk skin and pig's ears. At least they were able to wash it down with fine vintage Chablis and chase it with chilled sake.

July was definitely the hottest time of the year to be on Okinawa. It must have been a sweltering Summit! At least no one became sick at the dinner, like former President George Bush did eight years earlier in Tokyo in 1992, when he actually became so ill that he vomited into the lap of Prime Minister Kiichi Miyazawa. Reports were that Bush was suffering from an intestinal flu at the time, but it made for a memorable Summit with plenty of media attention.

When the guided tour wrapped up, we put on our shoes and were directed to "exit through the gift shop," which was absolutely exquisite. I could do some serious damage here! Too bad Julia was down at the bottom of the hill with the Colonel. I bought Shuri

Castle guidebooks for both of us. I found so many lovely items in the gift shop, but I was trying to be selective because I didn't know how much I could squeeze into my luggage.

The most amazing red and gold "lotus" flower hat was on display—a *yotsudake*—encased in a Lucite display box. I couldn't possibly get that home! I was trying to be reasonable. At least thirty-six inches across in diameter, I could only admire the stunning *yotsudake*, which is the traditional headpiece for the *yotsudake-odori*, the Ryukyu folk dance performed with bamboo castanets.

On the way out of the castle, I lingered until everyone had gone ahead of me down to the bus. I wanted to try to find a small stone, a tangible piece of Shuri Castle. Something I could bring home. But I couldn't find anything lying loose and it's not like I had any tools with me to pry off a piece of antiquity. I hung back and slowly walked along the outer wall of the castle. There, I saw several small stones and waited until there was no one around. I climbed up onto the wall and snatched them. I hurried to catch up with the rest of the group. Julia was already on the bus and was wondering where I was. I was never the last one on the bus!

Cape Hedo

We climbed aboard the USMC tour bus, only to discover that Chris was off on another assignment, so we had a young woman named Robin as our guide. She introduced herself as a "marine wife" who was working as a tour guide while her husband was stationed here.

She provided historical information, but she didn't have the high level of enthusiasm and the stories that Chris did. He truly loved his job, and it showed. Chris Majewski lives and breathes Okinawan history.

Julia and I whispered to each other, "I miss Chris."

The bus ride to Hedo took us along the western coastline, past fishing villages and beaches surrounded by cliffs. The waters of the East China Sea were a deep blue that seemed unnatural. The farther north we went, the rockier the terrain got. This was a mountainous area I'd never seen before. We were headed to the northernmost tip of the island—Cape Hedo—once unreachable because of a lack of roads.

We climbed down from the bus and the wind was so strong that I could hardly stand upright. I was determined to shoot some video and fought the fierce winds. I soon lost track of Julia. She wandered with the others while I captured some great footage of the waves breaking and crashing down upon the rocky beach below. As I stared down, I couldn't help but wonder how many people might have made a suicidal leap from this scary point at the top. I didn't want to get too close to the edge. I turned away to find the others.

Colonel French and Patti were gathered beside the memorial tower for photos. The Colonel lost his hat in the high winds, and Patti ran to catch it. He put it back on and they repeated the procedure one more time. She didn't give it back to him.

The Memorial Tower for the Reversion of Okinawa had an inscription in *kanji* on the front, which translates, "Present People of Japan and the World" celebrating the reversion of Okinawa. It explained the previous dissatisfaction of the Okinawan people, being separated from Japan, although some might disagree. The Okinawan people are a unique people, and the ancient Ryukyu Island kingdom dates to before the fifteenth century, with ties to both China and Japan. They have their own history. It deserves to be recognized.

When you look across the water to the north, you can see Yoron Island, situated at the 27th parallel, the designated line that separates the Ryukyu Islands from Japan. Each April 28th, Okinawans gather at Cape Hedo to look north to the 27th parallel. Now many Okinawans have their wish—and Okinawa is another prefecture of mainland Japan.

Under U.S. military administration since 1945, Okinawa was the site of numerous anti-American demonstrations, especially during the escalation of the war in Vietnam. The drone of warplanes constantly landing and taking off from Okinawa was a constant reminder of the changes taking place and the buildup of troops on Okinawa. Angry protesters took to the streets.

I remember seeing crowds gathered outside the gates to our housing area, as well as the gates to Kadena Air Base. When I asked

Dad what was going on, his response was, "They're just a bunch of crazy Commies...don't look at them."

Julia said she remembered listening for advisories on AFRTS (Armed Forces Radio & Television Service) radio about where local demonstrations were taking place. Most of it happened down in Naha. Those were the areas to stay away from.

"One time, Cathy and I were wandering in the Koza alleys, when a group of Okinawans spit on us. They looked so angry. And we looked so American. All I could think was to get out of there... fast."

Again, I was so happy that Julia was along for this trip. Julia's memory replaced my mother's lost memory and was invaluable. I needed to hear what she recalled. At age 73, Julia's memories were pretty sharp and she filled in many of the practical details of life on Okinawa in the past that were so important to my writing project. She could recall specifics that I didn't because I was only a girl riding around the island in the back seat of our family car. Julia was driving their family car. Our perspectives were different.

The Gillions were much more adventurous than my family. Probably because Julia was so desperate to get out of that house she'd been cooped up in all day! Bay would come home from work to find her ready to go, with a gas can in one hand and little Gary in the other...and Cathy and Jim holding Blackie on his leash!

She talked about the time they loaded up the car and drove on unknown narrow dirt roads into the northern part of the island, to find some waterfall that Bay had heard about from the guys he worked with at Torii Station.

"I don't know what we were thinking back then. Can you imagine what would have happened if the car broke down...in the middle of nowhere? We didn't speak Japanese and if we found a phone, who would we have called for help?"

Not my parents, that's for sure. Mom was always talking about how crazy the Gillions were to do something that dangerous.

I remember wishing that I'd been able to go along with them.

Julia was still talking about the waterfall. "I can't remember the name, because we didn't know it even had a name back then."

We overheard several other trekkers at the front of the bus asking Robin about taking a trip to *Hiji Ohtaki*, known as the Hiji Waterfall, located somewhere along the west coast. Thirty meters high, there was a wooden walkway to approach the falls. It took about forty-five minutes walking one way just to reach the waterfall—or you could hike through the river at the start of the trail. Robin explained that it definitely was a real hike and would have had to be a day-long excursion.

Could that have been Julia's waterfall?

Now Julia was asking me if my mom thought they were nuts back then to go off exploring remote places on their own.

"Oh no," I lied. "Mom and Dad didn't think you were doing anything crazy or dangerous. Not at all. They probably wished they would have gone along."

Our next stop was at the Okuma Beach Resort in time for lunch at the Officers' Club. Several long tables were set up outside on a deck overlooking the ocean, along the back of the club. We all ordered sandwiches and some people recalled how they spent time here at Okuma. Since our families were enlisted personnel and not officers, Julia and I had no memories of Okuma. What we remembered was Ishikawa Beach and Yaka Beach, the resort for enlisted personnel, which had small cabins for getaways.

Back in the sixties, a rare vacation was arranged, with the Gillions and us.

The sandy beaches along the shoreline were inviting, but I

remembered how we went wading in the water, wearing Keds. Your feet had to be covered and protected from dangers in the water that included stinging jellyfish and dangerous shellfish. Dad warned us about cone-shaped shells that harbored a creature inside with a harpoon stinger. If you picked it up, the creature living inside would inject its deadly venom! We touched nothing. The only souvenir shells we have from Okinawa are those that we bought from roadside souvenir stands where local villagers sold "kitschy" artistic creations from chunks of coral and seashells.

Another warning involved what appeared to be simple stones in the shallow water. If you stepped on them or picked them up, you could get stung. Those "stones" really were fish and were really called "stonefish!" Simple enough—who could blame those poor fish for stinging the person who stepped on them?

And of course, we were warned about the *habu* that populated the island. Like any snake seeking concealment, *habu* hung out in what else? *Habu* grass! As a result, we were also warned against playing in high grassy areas. No wonder we went to so many movies. There was nothing else safe for us to do.

Julia recalled how their old *papasan* gardener cut back the tall "*habu* grass" in the back of their yard when they lived off-post. One day *papasan* knocked eagerly at the door.

"*Okasan*, come look. I find a nest of baby *habu*."

"All I could do was look at him in horror, shake my head and say 'No, no, no.' *Papasan* just laughed at me," said Julia.

That weekend at Yaka Beach was a fun getaway for our families and it turned out that we took pretty much the same photos. Those in our family album are nearly identical to the ones in Julia's family album. There were black-and-white snapshots of us in the swimming pool, along the beach, and climbing a gnarled old tree.

Back then, Cathy and I looked like almost every other girl from the early sixties, with our stretchy elastic headbands, teased bouffant hair, glasses and skinny flat bodies. There's a classic black-and-white snapshot of all six of us kids in the gnarled old *banyan* tree, known on the island as a *gajumaru*.

That snapshot is like a page in black-and-white from a *Where's Waldo* book. You really *do* have to look closely to find each of us hidden in the tree.

After lunch, our final stop was at the Nago Pineapple Factory for a tour. Pineapple is one of the main exports from Okinawa, pineapple in all forms. Land is far too valuable now for fields of sugar cane and rice paddies. As we wandered through, we sampled pineapple wine, pineapple cake, more pineapple wine, pineapple cookies, another splash of wine, and finally, pineapple ice cream!

We exited through the gift shop of course, where "all things pineapple" could be purchased. I picked up an artistic Ryukyu glass decanter that was shaped like a life-sized pineapple, and full of pineapple wine. Yum.

Behold: The Power of eBay

I entered the search-word "Okinawa" into eBay one night and soon found myself in a long-forgotten world of Okinawa-related memorabilia. I could buy things I remembered from my past, from people all around the world, and in particular, a woman in the Air Force, stationed on Okinawa, at Kadena Air Base, whose eBay handle was *"Maneki-Neko-Nook,"* and whose name was Kathleen (KC) Watson.

I had put the world of Okinawa out of my mind years ago; it was lost in the past.

But I surrounded myself with reminders from my past. I decorated my first apartment with Asian décor and when Hello Kitty came ashore in America, I was drawn to all those comforting little trinkets that American girls became so fond of. Hello Kitty reminded me of the past—it was a Japanese creation similar to the early anime designs that were commonplace on Okinawa back in the 1960s. Hello Kitty gave me a good feeling.

KC had just what I wanted! She offered antique *kimonos* and *obis*, Okinawan pottery ashtrays and *shisa* dogs, and many more things I remembered from the sixties.

Through eBay, I located reference material about the 1972 Reversion of Okinawa back to Japan, and an account of what life had been like at the turn-of-the-century by a missionary woman based on Okinawa.

I bought "home-movie-style" videotapes from a guy in Montana who had been stationed on Okinawa in the late 1980s. His ever-patient wife handled the steering wheel while he panned his video camera through the window to capture endless footage of Okinawa. I desperately kept my voyeuristic eyes peeled for some street or neighborhood that might look remotely familiar!

Sometimes the radio was playing and the kids were talking, but Mick McClary kept on taping and narrating the sights for his relatives back in the States. I enjoyed spying on his family.

I even came across a doll made in the sixties by an army wife who was a member of the Shuri Women's Club. Many military wives signed up for classes back then. Mom took a Japanese doll-making class and made one of those fierce-looking *kabukis* as well as a *geisha* doll.

When I had some details about my trip, I e-mailed KC to see how she felt about meeting in person. Some eBayers are quite friendly during a transaction, but don't ever expect to meet their buyers face-to-face. KC was not shy; she was enthusiastic and responded that she would be happy to meet me and my friends, and even offered to take us to a local flea market! What an incredible opportunity! This was right up my flea market alley! Julia was equally excited. She didn't have a clue about eBay, but was up for any adventure I could provide.

I e-mailed KC with the name of the hotel where we would be staying. Soon after Julia and I walked into our room on Friday evening, the phone was ringing.

"Some man is asking for you," Julia whispered, as she handed the phone to me.

It was KC. And she did sound like a man over the phone. She had a raspy voice, and said she would be at the hotel early the next morning at 0700 hours to take us to that Okinawan flea market she mentioned.

When I hung up, Julia and I just looked at each another. We already had discovered one thing we had in common—we definitely weren't "morning people." We called Anna in her room to alert her to the early morning rendezvous.

I hit the shower, and Julia busied herself setting the alarm on the nightstand clock radio—for what we both agreed was "way too early."

We were up at a punishing 0530 hours, and were first to arrive in the dining room. The waiters were setting up the same fare that we faced each morning, a repetitious buffet of scrambled eggs, fried potatoes, cereal, toast and assorted fruit. As always, we passed on the pale-pink-looking *buta* sausages. We needed to fortify ourselves, so we "chowed down." We had no idea what was the day would bring, but we were "ready to roll" and "good to go," with full stomachs, water bottles, and plenty of *yen* in our pockets.

Sure enough, at 0700 hours, a woman casually attired in shorts and sandals, with a confident air, strode through the door to our hotel, right on military time. After introductions, we climbed into a right-hand-drive 1996 Toyota Corolla sedan that had over 120,000 miles on it—still going strong and ready to roll over to the next hundred thousand miles. KC explained that she bought the car "sight unseen" when she got orders for Okinawa.

"GIs can't bring their cars over from the States any more. You have to find something to drive while you're here, and that's why these used cars keep changing hands. When I leave, it will move on to someone else."

Julia and I remembered how our American cars came along with us when we docked in Naha Port in December of 1963. The Gillions brought their 1958 Ford Galaxie, and we brought our "trendy two-tone, red-and-cream-colored 1957 Plymouth Belvedere." Cars were stowed in the hold of the ship. Once out of the hold, husbands and fathers loaded up their dependents and baggage and drove away.

We wondered what was involved in buying a new Japanese car and transporting it home. KC explained that the modifications necessary when a Japanese car goes to California are far too costly because of emissions standards and upgrades that must be put in place. And the biggest thing you can't change is obviously the right-hand steering wheel!

KC wasn't exactly flying jets for the Air Force, but she had a pretty significant job—one that involved investigating fraud for AAFES (the Army and Air Force Exchange Service network of PXs). She covered installations throughout Asia and spent a lot of time traveling to Korea, Japan and Hawaii.

A "short-timer," KC would be leaving the island in less than a year and told us she would retire to her ranch in Colorado, where her husband, Rick, kept things under control until her return.

She told us that when the roads were changed to driving on the other side—the speed limit on the island was dropped to ten miles per hour until things settled down. There must have been some scary moments. Drivers were encouraged to place a little sign in their cars—STAY LEFT—as a reminder whenever a driver got behind the wheel. Everyone obviously got the hang of it, but I was still having trouble every time a taxi driver made a right turn from the left lane. It just seemed all wrong—and frightening. I should have closed my eyes.

With KC behind the wheel, we set off for an undisclosed location somewhere across from Kadena Air Force Base Gate 3, stopping along the way at a local convenience store for coffee—a Lawsons store! Lawsons was our neighborhood place back home in Ohio, for milk, bread and lunchmeat! The chain disappeared in the States, but apparently made it big in the Far East.

A considerate smoker, KC held her cigarette close by the car window while driving along. We drove for what seemed like only a short distance and turned to the right, down a bumpy little dirt road, past a smelly cow farm, and then onto a narrow paved road with ten-foot high chain-link fences along each side. KC explained that the fences were erected in an effort to keep the Saturday morning flea market from taking place, but determined—and rather stubborn—Okinawans continued to show up and park along the narrow road to sell their things as long as there were customers looking for bargains. The attempted closing had something to do with an old grenade… that exploded…accidentally of course…it could have happened anywhere…but the military didn't like it.

An Okinawan man waved to KC and moved some bamboo poles aside so that she could park the Corolla right behind his van.

"Reserved parking," explained KC as she greeted the man with a gift of assorted baked goods and cigarettes.

KC unpacked a folding shopping cart from the trunk of the Toyota and passed around plastic shopping bags. Soon we were walking along one side of the road, looking at assorted items spread out on blue plastic tarps—great junk from our past, everything from cassette tapes and magazines to ceramic *shisa* dogs and pots and pans. We started out organized, but kept wandering back and forth as those "kitschy" items from the sixties beckoned. Soon we had enough lucky finds in our arms that we had to return to the car to unload. Then we wandered back for more.

One of the regular vendors greeted KC with a big hug. The woman was selling elaborate kimonos displayed on hangers positioned along the chain-link fence, and Anna was enchanted with an embroidered white brocade wedding kimono. Julia and I put our heads together for a quick conference, and agreed to split the cost of the kimono—eight thousand *yen*—about eighty dollars, as a wedding gift for Anna. Anna was thrilled. The same woman was also selling *hakata* dolls in glass cases. I ended up with two, a *samurai* and a *daruma*. I bought them only because KC assured me that she could ship them back to the States through the post office at Kadena. (Thank you, thank you, thank you! *Domo arigato!*) So I ended up with both of them—for an amazing bargain price of six thousand *yen*—around sixty dollars!

Without KC's help, it would have been pointless to even consider them.

Hakata dolls were made from clay found near Fukuoka City, Japan, and each was carefully crafted by a single artisan from firing to final painting. They were highly prized, and their origin dated back to the early seventeenth century when Fukuoka Castle was built and a worker making roof tiles for the castle began to create pottery dolls and presented one to the lord of the castle.

Anna and I came across some unfamiliar items, which KC explained were *battledores*—"*hagoita battledores*"—to celebrate the New Year. They were decorated wooden paddles used to play a game with shuttlecocks, similar to badminton.

KC knew all the regular vendors and they pulled her aside to show her special items they brought for her approval. They all seemed to know what she liked. One old man on crutches—missing a leg, beckoned from the back of his van. He showed KC a large carved wooden bear, an *Ainu* bear. *Ainu* are the native people who populate Hokkaido, the northernmost island of Japan, and are sometimes compared to our Alaskan Eskimos.

Vintage carved *Ainu* bears can bring big bucks on eBay, so KC shrewdly negotiated a good price in what worked for her—a combination of English and some Japanese, mixed with many gestures.

I couldn't believe how little Japanese KC spoke. It didn't seem to matter.

Another old man pulled KC aside to show her some Japanese fishing magazines. KC had a regular customer on eBay for them. We found ceramic ashtrays, oil paintings, framed *bunka* embroidery pictures, a lacquer tray with a dragon figure in relief, and even a souvenir baseball bat with a signature in *kanji*. The man told me that it was signed by a "Yankee-san," so I added it to my pile for a young Yankees fan back home. It turned out that it was signed by Hideki Matsui, who played for the Yomiuri Giants in Tokyo. They nicknamed him "Godzilla." Now he was a Yankee-san, and I somehow doubted New Yorkers were calling him Godzilla.

"Beso-ball" is very, very big in Japan.

We arranged all of our treasures carefully in the trunk of the Toyota and piled back into the car. I was in the left front seat, balancing a large wooden *Ainu* bear on my lap, and Anna was behind me with a large glass doll case on her lap. Finally, Julia was in the back with another glass doll case on her lap. And between the two of them, they balanced the third glass doll case—the one containing my *daruma*! KC drove us to her off-base rental house to unload our treasures.

With all that glassware in the back seat, we slowed to a stop in front of KC's off-base rental, a rather modern pastel-colored row house. KC gave us a tour of her two-story, three-bedroom home, which was complete with indoor and outdoor cats. It was clear to me that KC loved animals.

"I feed hungry neighborhood cats and keep cat food inside the outdoor grill. When I am out of town, which is often, a friend feeds them for me," explained KC. She had a postage-stamp-sized front yard with a few flowers and the requisite clay *shisa* dog statues. "One day, I came home from work to find one of my *shisa* in pieces. And a few days later, I came home to find that someone had taken the time to glue it all back together! Imagine that. My neighbors are so thoughtful. I never did find out what really happened."

Her house was cluttered like mine—something I totally understood—with treasures she found at the flea market, with packing material, with items to be photographed, items to be packed and packed items waiting to be shipped—it's how we eBayers do business!

KC had an amazing collection of *tsuboya* pottery—huge earthenware pots that she planned to send home to Colorado in her allotted 18,000 pounds of household goods. What I wouldn't give to have one. Too heavy. Couldn't even think about it. Impossible to ship.

KC suggested lunch at the hottest new restaurant on Kadena Air Base—Romano's Macaroni Grill—which was a surprise. It had just recently opened.

"This restaurant already makes the most money in the entire chain," said KC.

As we drove around Kadena, Julia and I were amazed to see Burger King, Popeye's Chicken, Subway and even a Cinn-A-Bon. Off-base, McDonalds and A&W drive-ins were abundant.

When we lived here, we ate hamburgers and hot dogs at the NCO Clubs and at the American Legion Club. Military clubs were bar/restaurants with live entertainment, usually consisting of Filipino cover bands singing American pop songs.

Eating out was a treat back then because families ate home-cooked meals. Moms cooked. There was no carry-out. Mom made her special spaghetti sauce and Dad made his special chili—every week. There was not a lot of variety in our menu.

Julia and I recalled a snack bar near the PX where we would eat hamburgers and hot dogs.

"That's where we found each other after we all got off the ship," said Julia. "Remember? We bumped into each other in the snack bar! We pushed some tables together and figured out that we were living on opposite sides of the island. After that, we went back and forth almost every weekend to each other's houses."

Okinawans could very well be doomed! America's fast-food culture is rapidly taking over. The gravest threat to Okinawan longevity is the Western diet influencing their traditional simple diet of complex carbohydrates, vegetables and fruit, combined with plenty of activity well into old age. KC pointed out that so many locals eat in restaurants now that they are starting to get fat.

Published in 2001, *The Okinawa Program: How the World's Longest-Lived People Achieve Everlasting Health—And How You Can Too,* called attention to the large number of centenarians thriving on Okinawa—hard-working old folks like the ninety-three-year-old flower lady and the octogenarian fisherman—as profiled on ABC-TV's 20/20, who were still active and thriving on the traditional lean cuisine. Staying active was key to stayin' alive.

Okinawa still has the highest percentage of centenarians anywhere in the world.

But the current generation doesn't stand a chance of emulating its ancestors, and are likely to follow Americans into obesity and health problems.

"Are you guys up for another road trip?" KC asked.

We pushed back our chairs.

Like we would say no!

KC told us about an Okinawan woman she knew who sold *kimonos* and *obis* from her home in Nago, the northern part of the island—and she was willing to drive up there. KC explained that each year Sachi made several buying trips to mainland Japan to purchase items for her antiques shop. Sachi was well-known among womens' clubs on base and apparently had an exclusive clientele. And best of all, Sachi just came back from one of her mainland buying trips.

"Take us to Sachi!"

We hit the road on another adventure—as KC was fond of saying, "just a few more 'clicks' in the Corolla."

We found ourselves speeding along the Okinawa Expressway, a "super-highway" that can take you from Naha to Nago in about forty minutes! While on the expressway, cruising along at around eighty kilometers an hour, in the warmth of the afternoon sun, we all dozed off—except for our driver...

Julia started to snore softly in the back seat, Anna also zoned out, but remained "snore-free," and I got one of my refreshing "power naps." Ten minutes later, my head bobbed up, and I once again was conscious, but embarrassed. KC was grinning. I was apologizing... and I can only hope no one was drooling...

Sachi lived in the Motobu area and when things started to look familiar, we realized that we were once again up at the northern end of the island, the same area we were in two days before on our bus trip to Cape Hedo.

KC suddenly maneuvered the Corolla into a sharp right turn up a steep gravel driveway toward the top of a hill. She parked in a clearing, and we found ourselves surrounded by assorted cement yard decorations—most of them creatures that KC explained were *tanuki*, which resembled a cross between a raccoon and a dog. *Tanuki* typically are found outside of restaurants and bars, where they beckon guests to enter. More widely-recognized is the beckoning cat figure— the *maneki neko*—with its raised right paw, which is found outside of retail establishments.

As we approached Sachi's traditionally-designed Japanese home, we encountered little dogs and puppies scattered in pens around the yard and tied to trees. Anna stopped to pet one puppy and he immediately clenched his baby teeth into her pants leg. We worked to set her free.

We removed our shoes at the doorway to "Sachi's Antiques & Tea Room." There were several levels to the spacious Japanese house, with many sliding doorways. Clearly, Sachi also lived in this house. I would have loved to explore and see what the rest of her home was like.

Sachi was busy with customers as KC greeted her and led us over to a small alcove containing racks of assorted *kimonos*. A nearby table was covered with folded *obi* sashes that wrap many times around the waist. Most of them were elaborately embroidered in brocade and gold. They would make wonderful table runners. Waves of greed washed over me.

Everywhere I went, I figured I'd never, *ever* be back. So when I found something lovely, it was hard to be sensible or practical. And when KC offered us her post office connection, what more could I ask for?

Sachi had what seemed to be very fair prices on almost everything we found, including furniture, *shoji* screens and *tansu* chests.

I selected several lovely brocade *obis*. I also found a simple *kimono*, in a *bingata* cloth fabric that seemed Ryukyuan in design. And then I found a black *kimono* embroidered with gold thread. I had to have that too.

KC led us to another building where we found racks of *haori* jackets. *Haori* are lightweight coats designed to be worn over *kimonos*. I held up several to see if they'd fit me. Maybe. Too warm to try them on, I found a few that were possibilities for myself and another to bring back for my mother.

While I tried to locate a few more treasures, Julia sat down and leaned back upon a bench outside the building, fanning herself, in search of an elusive breeze. It had been a long day. Clearly, she was pooped.

I continued to search through the racks; and came across a *koinobori*, measuring over six feet in length. It was one of those huge cotton carp flags, flown to celebrate Boys' Day, *Tango no Sekku*, but it was so old and sun-bleached that I put it back. It had clearly been flying outside too long. When we lived here, my brothers each had a large cotton carp flag. Ray's was black and Danny's was orange, and we would fly them outside on Boys' Day, on the fifth day of the fifth month of each year. Chinese legend has it that carp swim upstream and turn into dragons around that time.

Girls' Day, celebrated in early March, featured a doll festival, called *hina matsuri*. Families displayed dolls in their homes, upon shelves that could be from five to seven tiers high.

Anna found several things and I finally narrowed it down to just two *obi*s and two *kimonos*. Because of our connection to KC, Sachi generously lowered the prices on our purchases. I can't remember now how much *yen* I handed over, but it didn't seem like much.

I was already planning to toss some of my clothes to make room for these treasures in my suitcase.

Late that afternoon, as we drove south toward our hotel, we saw the signs for the Nago Pineapple Factory. Definitely time for a snack! KC told us that she had passed it often on her way back from Sachi's, but never stopped. We led the way and sampled ourselves through tables loaded with trays of pineapple chunks, cakes and wines, topping it all off with a single-scoop of pineapple ice cream.

As we passed the display of Ryukyu glass pineapple wine bottles, KC said, "I found one of these empty bottles at the flea market, and sold one for seventy-five dollars…so of course, I picked up one more bottle for eBay. Julia and I had to remember to drink this stuff before we left. I didn't want to pack full bottles in my suitcase.

As we approached the central part of the island, traffic was backing up along the highway and we slowed to a standstill.

"It gets like this often on Saturday nights," explained KC.

Still a small island experiencing rapid growth, traffic was incredibly backed up and afforded us a "slo-mo" view of Okinawa's one and only Ferris wheel, brightly-lit in neon against the dusky sky. A landmark in the Chatan area, the "American Village" features plenty of American-style shopping and a seven-screen movie theater, known as the Mihama 7-Plex, showing Western and Japanese movies.

Julia and I remarked that the Ferris wheel was so sophisticated, compared to the makeshift "rides" that were created for the annual Kadena Karnival.

"Remember the military version of a merry-go-round? It was a large construction crane, rotating in circles, with a closed cage-box at the end. Kids were thrilled to sit inside and just go around in circles," said Julia.

"Did Cathy ever jump from the parachute tower?" I asked.

"No, but Jim and Gary did," said Julia.

I didn't think she did, and I know I sure didn't. It was a "boy-thing." My brothers must have been jumping from that tower as well.

There were official parachute training jump towers, with Air Force guys standing up on top, fastening kids into harnesses that were hooked to a zip line. You jumped, slid all the way down to the ground, where another airman unfastened you. And then you got in line again.

We finally made our way past that Ferris wheel (apparently every island should have one), the congestion cleared, and we made our way through the winding streets of Awase, back to the hotel.

An event was scheduled to take place after the cultural dinner— something that Larry Kelly described as a musical celebrating the re-introduction of pigs to the island of Okinawa. It was hard for Julia and me to get excited about it, but that didn't stop Larry from telling us that as a young boy living on Okinawa, he was an eyewitness to the return of swine to the island of Okinawa after those that had existed on the farms had been killed by the soldiers.

Pigs From The Sea (*Umi Kara Buta ga Yatte Kita*), the musical based upon the totally true adventures of a group of Hawaiians with ties to Okinawa, who managed to purchase 550 pigs from Oregon and transport them to Okinawa after the war, was to be presented in Japanese with opera-style English subtitles or translations. The Hawaiian Uchinanchu accompanied the swine on a 28-day voyage to Okinawa on the deck of a military transport ship—the USS John Owen. Those pigs apparently mated like bunnies and managed to serve as a continuous source of food for the Okinawan people.

I wasn't taking this production too seriously and referred to it as the original "*Spamalot*," because back in the States, a big hit on Broadway at the time was Monty Python's musical spoof, "*Spamalot*."

And coincidentally, *buta*—pork—was really big on Okinawa. Canned SPAM was sold in stores everywhere. America's "miracle meat" had found its niche in the Far East—harkening back to the days of the GIs.

Hormel Foods must be happy.

After spending the entire day with KC, who had now become an old and dear friend, it was time to say goodbye and never see her again. Another one of those military farewells.

The next morning, over the usual breakfast buffet, we told our fellow trekkers about our adventures—the flea market, Sachi's house, Macaroni's for lunch—and clearly, some of them wished they had teamed up with us. Julia and I agreed that the day with KC was one of the best days of our trip.

"Some of those other trekkers appeared 'pea-green with envy,'" she laughed.

School Days

Two flags now fly together side-by-side over Kubasaki High School—
the Stars and Stripes right beside the Japanese *Hinomaru*. Since the
1972 Reversion, both flags have flown together to signify the joint
presence of the United States with Japan.

The white background of the *Hinomaru* represents honesty and
purity, with the red circle symbolizing sincerity and passion. This flag
was adopted by Japan in 1870.

The bolder design of the "Rising Sun" flag was meant for battle
and used by the Japanese navy during World War II.

"Coup d'etat." I remember the day that Miss Zirkle boldly scrawled
those two words across the blackboard—and then spent the rest
of history class talking about what it meant and the effects of the
coup—the coup that took place in Vietnam, when Ngo Dinh Diem,
the president of South Vietnam, had been assassinated on November
1, 1963. Another significant assassination that took place halfway
around the world.

Our teachers had plenty of current events to work into classroom
discussions. News headlines were reality, and for Kubasaki students,

the war in Vietnam was all too close. You could graduate, get drafted and go to 'Nam.

When things heated up in Vietnam, I remember talk about evacuating all of the dependents off of the island. It had me worried, because I didn't know if Dad might have to go to Vietnam. And I didn't know where we would go if we returned to the States on our own. Fortunately, it never happened. But Okinawa continued to be a staging area for troops deploying to Vietnam.

There was a constant roar of fighter jets streaking through the skies overhead, and if it wasn't the planes making noise, it was the protesters gathering outside the gates of the military installations. They objected to our presence on the island.

The bus pulled up in front of the high school I was so proud to attend back in 1967—Kubasaki. The buildings were the same ones I remembered, and the only addition appeared to be an ROTC building.

It was exciting to attend a real high school back then. No longer were there makeshift classrooms in Quonset huts or in military barracks. Kubasaki finally had a permanent home in permanent buildings with a library, cafeteria, gym and lockers.

Kubasaki was the first dependent school in the Pacific region of the DoDDS and opened on September 15, 1946 with thirty students in a large Quonset hut. It was known as the Okinawa University School then. The site changed through the years. At one point in its history, students used a barracks building during the day, and when classes ended, military personnel took it back for the night.

In 1950, the school became known as the Okinawa-American Dependent High School and moved to an area known as Camp Kubasaki, with classes in more Quonset huts. The high school relocated once more to the Naha Port Wheel Area and finally to this campus in 1964, where it remains, instantly recognizable by its "crinkle-cut" roofline that everyone I knew called the "french-fry" roof.

The ornamental cement wall remained as I remembered it, along with the large *shisa* standing upon a pedestal in the center of the courtyard. I still have photos from my last day at Kubasaki. I brought my little Kodak camera with me to school that day and shot a roll of black-and-white film, taking pictures of my friends, Laurel Armstrong, Yumi McGarvey, Valerie Emme and Debra Lee.

I was happy to be there. But before the school year ended, my family was already on the move to another place. Dad was ordered to make another PCS stateside, to Fort Campbell, Kentucky.

As we walked through the hallways of the two-story building, things did look familiar and I was quite certain that the lockers along the walls were the same blue color when I was there. The indestructible poured cement construction style of the island had preserved these structures. Weathering countless typhoons in the past forty years, the buildings were connected with covered walkways—great in good weather, but not offering much protection against windswept rains during monsoon season. While some kids in the States got days off from school for "snow days," our only days off were for typhoons.

The girl behind the glasses...the girl beneath the white elastic headband...the shy quiet girl...that was me.

I remember sitting outside reading, if I wasn't inside reading. English was my best subject, and geography came easy. Geography was a snap for military brats. Knowing where you'd been and where you were going was simply something practical. I was totally capable of mapping my way around the world.

Mom had been trying to talk me into a career in nursing and told me that I needed a background in Latin. Mrs. Peabody taught freshman-year Latin. When I began to conjugate all those verbs and then realized that the nouns came in declensions, I decided to drop Latin and take Spanish.

Mrs. Wilbourn taught algebra, and I was determined to master algebra. Math had always been a weakness for me. But once more, we moved in the middle of the school year. Mrs. Wilbourn gave me assignments and I seriously tried to do them on my own while we traveled back to the States by ship. By the time I ended up at Fort Campbell High School in Kentucky, I had missed too many school days and was placed in a general math class. When Dad retired in 1968 and I was in my senior year of high school in Ohio, all that a counselor could suggest was that I wrap it up with some "general math" and call it a day.

I didn't have to deal with math again until I found myself in college, near tears, with my future husband tutoring me through a college-level basic algebra course.

"What do you mean, you never learned this stuff?" Don sputtered. "How is that even possible?"

Don wasn't the most patient tutor.

Somehow Don helped me master combinations and permutations and I managed to pull a "B" out of what I referred to as "Baby Math 101." I had successfully fulfilled my liberal arts math requirement! I would graduate! With a better background, I probably could have been solving quadratic equations.

We congregated in Kubasaki's library to begin the tour. I spent much of my time in libraries, and the school library at Kubasaki was one of those places. I wandered around among the stacks, looking at the books, the posters depicting poisonous snakes indigenous to the island, the Asian artwork, the *kabuto* helmet, the Japanese *ningyos* in glass cases, and finally took a seat at one of the tables.

Principal Steve Sanchez welcomed us all to Kubasaki. And guidance counselor, Harvey Getz, introduced himself and explained how he came here in 1962, returned to the States for a while, came back to Okinawa in 1992 and had been here since then. Getz proclaimed himself Kubasaki's unofficial "school historian."

"Kubasaki is very much a part of my personal history," said Getz.

"It moved to this site in 1964 from the Naha Port Wheel area. Now there are 625 students in grades 9 through 12, and we have a Marines Junior ROTC Building."

As a result, many students—boys and girls—roam the hallways wearing fatigues and combat boots, an ordinary sight here.

Getz proceeded with his "power-point presentation" of historical slides that showed the very first group of teachers coming across the Pacific aboard the USNS Sultan. They were a group of teachers who were tossed together on the ocean, much like the families aboard our ship—a group of teachers who forged friendships that lasted a lifetime.

Our teachers told us about some of the trips they took during school breaks. Teachers in the DoDDS system were fortunate enough to hitch rides on a "space-available" basis to nearby countries during the spring and summer breaks.

We actually planned one of those "space available" trips with the Gillions during one of our school vacations, by ship to Korea and Taiwan, and had it well-planned—until Danny came down with either the mumps or measles. I don't remember. We cancelled.

The adventurous Gillions took the trip and forty years later, I finally saw the photos when I visited Julia at her home in South Carolina!

I remember some of my teachers and classmates vividly. One geography teacher in particular told us about her adventure on safari in Ethopia, and how when they broke camp, everything was scavenged, even the shards of eggshells. Geography was something you certainly acquired first-hand while traveling around the world. I thought that becoming a teacher in the dependent schools system would be a good thing to consider.

One girl had learned Polynesian dancing while living in Tahiti, and tried to teach us how to dance while in gym class. It's much harder than it looks. Other students were highly skilled in the martial arts, before it became commonplace in America. They learned it where they lived.

Some of my friends seemed to know exactly what they were going to do after graduation. Like Dawn Nevling, who proclaimed that she was going to join the Peace Corps. I'd read a book by Peace Corps volunteers, a husband and wife who served in the *barrios* down in Ecuador. That would be a life of adventure. Maybe I would do that.

But I really thought that becoming a writer would be the best thing ever. I just didn't know how to go about it. Gloria Moeller lived across the street from us in Futenma when we moved on-post. Gloria wrote stories and kept a diary. She was so certain about her future. She couldn't imagine not writing.

Walking the halls of Kubasaki with Jane and Marlene and David, I realized that we once walked these halls together forty years earlier—passing one another in the same building at the same time back in the early sixties. I knew the Dulay girls' names, but not David's. My close school friends back then were Laurel Armstrong and Valerie Emme. Constant farewells were a fact of military life. I remembered many promises made to write and stay in touch. We wrote letters, but soon lost touch. People disappeared from your life as quickly as they appeared.

One friend, Nancy Miyahira, ended up in Honolulu and we did keep in touch with Christmas cards for a few years, until she married and moved. I lost track of her. Another friend, Sherry Ahl, was more determined and we have remained in touch all through high school, college, marriage (now Pearson) and children. We've exchanged Christmas letters for over forty years now.

Principal Sanchez led us on a tour of the school. Local media followed us around. *This Week on Okinawa* dispatched a reporter to cover our triumphant return, and a Marine Corps videographer from AFN-TV (Armed Forces Network) was tailing us, hoisting a camera and tripod on his shoulders, to get footage for the five-minute local news breaks.

He captured some footage with me in the background. Julia was shouting from the room while I was in the shower later that night… but I missed it.

We all gathered for a group photo, while crouching precariously on the side of Kubasaki's "Senior Hill," more appropriately-named now.

In the faculty conference room, adjacent to the library, we enjoyed a buffet lunch prepared for us by the staff. The principal brought in a collection of *TORII* yearbooks from the past years for us to look through, and I came to the conclusion that I was still the "unknown student" because there was absolutely no 1967 *TORII*—the one yearbook in which my picture should have appeared.

While everyone was passing around those yearbooks, pointing out their friends, laughing and reminiscing, I could only keep eating all that great food that the faculty had provided. There was nothing for me to look through. I wasn't there!

Maybe there really *was* something to my feeling of invisibility…I moved on…to the cookies and brownies.

Larry signaled. It was time to wrap up our adventure and get back on the bus. This visit was over. Always on the lookout, I snatched several Kubasaki felt wall pennants and a few Kubasaki water bottles—just a few more items for eBay.

1950 – Basic training. My mother actually *did* wear combat boots!

1953 – Camp Crowder, Missouri. Back from The Korean War, Dad stands beside his 1948 Dodge.

1958 – Tacoma, Washington. Showing off my first pair of glasses. Mom was cutting my hair and I had no teeth!

1961 – Fort Ord, California. A typical "nuclear" family: Mom, Raymond, Danny, Dad and me.

1963 – Okinawa, Joe and Grace Kriha standing in front of the little cement block house that I've been searching for—1498 Oyama.

1963 – Chris wearing her Christmas kimono and Danny and Raymond, wearing their yukatas.

1963 – Mom with her treasured carved camphor wood Hotei.

1963 – Raymond and Danny exploring a
bunker from the Battle of Okinawa.

1964 – Danny pointing out the sign on our quarters in Futenma.

1964 – Julia and Bay Gillion outside their quarters in Chatan.

1964 – Julia with her maid Yoshiko—the long-lost photograph!

1964 – Look closely! There are six kids in the *gajumaru* (banyan) tree at Yaka Beach. From left: Chris, Cathy Gillion, Jim Gillion, Raymond, Danny and Gary Gillion.

Whisky Tango Foxtrot!

Back at the hotel, I stayed up late each night, checking e-mail and watching TV. Julia didn't mind the TV being on and drifted off despite the noise.

She snored. At times, she *really* snored. Although she warned me, it did get pretty loud. I liked to read myself to sleep, so I used my "itty-bitty" book light while Julia snored. Several times though, I had to get out of bed, shake her by the shoulder, and tell her to roll over and face the ocean! As long as she directed her snores toward the Pacific Ocean, things worked out and I could eventually drift off.

The main English-speaking TV station still was the Armed Forces Network, but the selection was far different from what we remembered. Television programming now began with Sesame Street in the morning for the kids, a few select soap operas in the afternoon, and seemed to be as current as in the States. Prime-time in the evenings brought some of the shows that were popular back home.

Mom's favorite daytime soap opera was *As the World Turns* and she watched it as often as she could, before she left for work. I remember the spinning globe at the opening of the show. The characters were in black-and-white when we left them in 1963. Soon after we returned in 1967, those characters came to life in living color, and Mom liked to tell people, "I missed my soap opera for four years, but when I came back to the States, I could figure out what Lisa Grimaldi had been up to. There are only so many things those people can go through."

And if we were stationed here now, she might not have had to miss that soap opera.

The world of CNN indeed followed us around the world, with on-the-hour headline news updates. I paid attention to the latest bulletins about the nuclear tension with North Korea—a nuclear weapon had been detonated on October 9th, and the situation was worrisome. There's nothing like being too close to the action when there could be a nuclear standoff! I was *over here* and not *back there*!

The North Koreans gave China twenty minutes' advance notice that the test would occur. And then it happened. And now there were ongoing rumors that another test would occur on the 11th. That news was in the back of my mind the entire time we were there on Okinawa.

The Armed Forces Public Service Announcements (PSAs) were interesting. One PSA dealt with security and leaving your ID card out for someone to snatch, like that old "Loose Lips Sink Ships" warning from World War II. Each of us kids had ID cards back then. We needed an ID card to get into the PX, the commissary and probably even the theater. It was an essential gate pass for access to anything related to the military. As kids, we kept our ID cards safely in our wallets. I don't recall ever losing my ID card. We recognized its importance.

Today's PSAs also focused on family matters and the availability of counseling services, including hotlines for stressful family situations.

A girl who lived right next door to us on Okinawa was being

physically abused by her father. I remember hearing him screaming and yelling and swearing at her at night. I didn't know what domestic violence was. I thought her father was just mad about something. But it happened too often. It was not an isolated incident.

Her room was on the side of the house that was closest to my bedroom. When the windows were open, I could hear them clearly. I don't remember her name because I didn't really know her. She was a few years older than I was. I thought about her a lot.

This was back in a time when you just stood by silently and did nothing because things that happened behind closed doors remained behind closed doors. I heard that girl crying while her dad yelled and hit her. I remember asking Mom about it. She said we couldn't do anything. It was private. It was a private family matter.

No one considered getting involved. It happened often enough though, that it upset me quite a bit.

Family problems were weaknesses. Things were kept private. People didn't ask for help. You kept secrets. I'm sure quite a few secrets still are being kept.

Late one night, while sending an e-mail to my friend, Debbie Scotese, back in Cleveland, there was a highly-emotional baseball game taking place on Japanese TV, with the Yomiuri Giants weeping as they ran onto the field. I described the scene to her. I didn't get it. Baseball is very serious to the Japanese.

When we lived here in the sixties, the AFRTS station signed on at 3:45 p.m. with about fifteen minutes of warm-up with a black-and-white "test pattern." At 6 p.m. there was a local newscast, with a uniformed news anchorman. I'm almost positive that my classmate Cheryl's dad, Sergeant Major Eckhart, read the news. He literally sat at a desk and read the news from sheets of paper. That news was followed by *Sea Hunt*, *Gunsmoke* and the most popular show at the time, *Voyage to the Bottom of the Sea*.

Additional filler programming included odd Encyclopedia Brittanica educational films, like *Communism—Myth vs. Reality.*

We did see the "Fab Four" make their debut appearance on *The Ed Sullivan Show,* but not on February 9, 1964 like the rest of America. There was a week's delay while the film was flown across the Pacific. With the same historical significance as the Kennedy Assassination, we three kids sprawled out across the floor of the living room when Ed Sullivan introduced those four young lads.

Being marooned on an island in the Pacific Ocean left us out of the loop with the rest of our generation. We couldn't get our hands on any of the Beatles memorabilia that was readily available in the States. If we hadn't left California, maybe I could have made it to the Cow Palace or Candlestick Park for one of their concerts.

The Beatles toured Japan in 1966, but getting to Tokyo wasn't like driving up the California coast with a group of friends.

The British Invasion was under way, and it was a magical time. I was part of the generation that discovered the Beatles. The greatest bands were emerging, and we didn't even realize it then. The Rolling Stones, Herman's Hermits, The Dave Clark Five, The Beach Boys… they were all having fun making music and didn't envision the impact they would make on music. Those bands now are revered "old guys" enshrined in the Rock and Roll Hall of Fame!

AFRTS signed off around midnight and then there was nothing but the radio. When I babysat for the Florio family next door, I would read and wait for them to return, counting my earnings. I earned twenty-five cents an hour and charged double after midnight!

After midnight I was pretty much stuck watching the local Japanese TV channels. A lot of it involved sumo wrestling, which was incomprehensible to us at the time. We just stared at the massive buttocks on the massive wrestlers. They wore what appeared to be a diaper around them and there was a great deal of ceremony involved, including tossing sand into the center of the ring.

Some popular American TV shows aired on Japanese TV with dubbed Japanese dialogue. Local radio station KSBK would simulcast the English audio for shows like *Lost in Space* and *The Fugitive*. All we had to do was tune our radio to KSBK and the TV to Japanese Channel 12 and turn down the volume. Sound came from the radio and video came from the TV. It worked.

Emperor Hirohito opened the Summer Olympic Games on October 10, 1964. When we got home from school each day, we watched live coverage of the swimming, gymnastics and track competition on the Japanese channels on our little black-and-white Sanyo portable TV. Translation wasn't necessary. You didn't need English. The Olympics were universal.

We were fascinated with the swimming events and watched as Don Schollander won four gold medals. Judo was first introduced into the Olympic Games that year and we watched gymnastics—parallel bars, rings and pommel horse events. These were the first Olympic Games that we were old enough to really pay attention to. We tuned to endless hours of coverage as it happened, live on Japanese TV.

I stayed in touch with my husband, best friend Debbie Scotese, sister-in-law Paula, as well as Julia's three kids back home in South Carolina. The responses piled up each day and I relayed information from Cathy and her brothers to Julia.

Late one night, I found an e-mail from Don—just some frantic husband stuff—dealing with our son Paul who decided that he "just couldn't breathe" and needed immediate medical attention. A little planning and the kid would have had a fresh inhaler on hand. What could I do from over here? I learned that poor planning involved an expensive trip to the ER for a simple breathing treatment.

There's something to be said for a "need-to-know" basis when it comes to instant communication. And then a few e-mails arrived from my sister-in-law Paula, about my parents.

Julia was unaware of the turmoil taking place at home. I found myself trying to explain what was going on between my parents. And then one thing led to another, and then another. I had to come clean about the situation taking place on the home front. Paula's e-mails left me with no choice.

Mom and Dad had been bickering for the past several years and Mom once again decided that Dad had "threatened" her. Paula said that Mom phoned the police for a pickup. As they had done once before, responding officers took Dad off to the geriatric psychiatric unit of a nearby hospital for evaluation.

This time, though, when the officers arrived, Dad was waiting for them, sitting in his recliner in the living room, with his "U.S. Army Retired" baseball cap upon his head.

Clearly, Dad was "good to go." I think he was simply trying to get away from Mom's nagging and out of the house for a while, and even a stay at the so-called "psych ward" was fine with him.

Mom and Dad should have tried a separation and taken a break from one another. I'm sure they really still loved each other, but a short separation might have helped them to appreciate one another again.

Mom had no outside interests and when she retired from the hospital, all she did was watch her soap operas and talk on the telephone. And when Dad stopped working and they were both at home together, my parents clearly got on each other's nerves. Some time apart might have helped. Once, when I suggested this to Mom, she became furious.

I remember the day Dad came up with one of his brainstorms. There were many.

He walked in from the garage, and proclaimed, "We need to sell this house, buy a Winnebago, pack up the dogs and hit the road!"

He was serious. Dad was always serious. We usually just let him rant and get it out of his system.

Dad thought it would be great to drive around the country and stop whenever they wanted to. He'd seen RVs parked in the lot at Wal-Mart, with seemingly happy campers loaded down with bicycles and sports gear, sometimes even towing a small car on the back of the RV.

"We wouldn't have an address," he boasted. "There's no way they could track us down to pay taxes!"

Yup. That's what they would do.

Except Mom wasn't buying into that plan.

For every comment Dad made, Mom responded with a negative one. I tried not to get drawn into their discussion. Dad never realized his "ultimate road warrior" dream. I could just see him, driving cross-country, and cross-country, and then cross-country again. Dad was the guy who once zoomed right past the Grand Canyon without even looking!

Each night, when we got back to the hotel room, I logged on. Julia stood behind me and urged me not to check my e-mail. But I couldn't resist. It was like a bad soap opera. I just had to keep tuning in.

So there I sat in the hotel room, with my little IBM ThinkPad glowing before me, six thousand miles from home, linked to the battles taking place on the home front. It was more than I could handle. Don ended all of his updates with "Serenity Now!"

I felt better after I confided in Julia about what was taking place back at home.

And Julia said that she never knew that Dad had a history of drinking!

"That was because Mom loved to visit with you folks. You didn't offer beer," I told her.

Julia and I talked about how things are so very different now. Communication is 24/7. E-mails zap around the world. Calls back home are no big deal. Some of the trekkers on our trip told us how they had rented a cell phone as soon as they arrived on Okinawa and were simply using prepaid calling cards!

"The wives who are out there e-mailing their husbands stationed over in Iraq and sending pictures over the Internet don't know how lucky they are to have such a direct connection with their husbands," said Julia.

I agreed.

I could remember how much planning went into the one-and-only phone call that Mom made back to the States. For some reason, Mom wanted to call Grandma in Klamath Falls.

Scheduled in advance, it took place through amateur radio communication through the Air Force's MARS (Military Affiliate Radio System). The call was "patched" from Kadena Air Base's amateur radio position (KR6AF) over to one ham radio operator stateside in Arizona and then to another, until it finally got through to Oregon.

I remember how awkward Mom said it was to try to speak to Grandma by relaying a message in short sentences that ended with "over" so that the radio operator could transmit to wherever Grandma was waiting at the other end. The conversation went back and forth and was slow and cumbersome. She kept forgetting to say "over."

Most of the communication was by letter. So many letters were written over the years. I wish I had them now. No one thought to save them. Mom wrote to Grandma every week and Grandma wrote back to us.

Sam's By The Sea

Kubasaki alum Mark (Class of '69) Payne's family owned a chain of restaurants throughout the Far East and hosted a dinner for the trekkers at the site of the Okinawa Yacht Club, which is one of the locations in his family's chain of restaurants—Sam's By The Sea.

Jay Wentworth's wife, Merri, pulled up in front of the hotel to shuttle Julia and me, along with David Knowles, over to the restaurant. As we chatted along the way, Merri mentioned that she had relatives in Ohio—in Bay Village—and would be returning in a few months to help move her mother from the family home. I couldn't help but marvel at how small our globe has become. (Corny, but so true.) Merri said she got back to the States several times a year for visits with her family.

I heard a familiar squawking as we walked across the gravel parking lot and approached the dining area. An outdoor aviary held several hyacinth blue macaws. The birds side-stepped along their perch to one side of their cage to peer at me with curiosity. One of the birds tilted its head and said, "*Konnichiwa?*"

"*Konnichiwa?*" Well, of course. Should I expect to hear "Hello?" from Japanese birds?

I instinctively wanted to reach out and touch them, but was

worried that they just might chomp my finger off, so I left them alone. They probably spend the entire year outside in this tropical setting. They're *real* birds! Not spoiled little house-birds like my cockatiels back home.

A massive, carved Tiki towered in front of the restaurant. Inside the dining room, a large canoe was suspended from the ceiling, with fisherman's netting and glass floats. Drinks were served in souvenir mugs, shaped like fierce-looking *shisa*.

Julia and I shared a table with Betty and Larry Kelly, Anna, and Patti and Colonel French. The rest of the trekkers soon arrived at the restaurant, as well as many Kubasaki alumni living on the island.

The setting was wonderfully tropical, a balmy breeze blowing off what was once called Buckner Bay, now Nakagusuku Bay, with illumination from the full moon.

Flaming torches surrounded the dining area, making it seem like we were on a lanai in Hawaii. We stared at the twinkling lights from across the inlet and in the dark shadows, a few stray cats roamed nearby, waiting for us to go home so they could clean up our scraps. The Colonel grabbed his new digital camera and wandered off in the darkness to "shoot the moon."

American-born *shamisen/sanshin* virtuoso Byron (Class of '87) Jones arrived and greeted Betty Kelly with a warm hug. He was a fellow member of the Washington D.C. *kenjin-kai*. Byron was here to perform in the Uchinanchu Festival. Dressed in a *yukata*, Byron wore his black African-American hair tightly pulled up into a Samurai-style topknot. The topknot went well with his trendy goatee. Held in high esteem by fellow musicians for his skill with the *shamisen/sanshin*, Byron discovered the instrument while a Kubasaki high school student on Okinawa in the 1980s and now has a reputation for being "more Japanese than the Japanese." He released a CD in 2001 with another artist, entitled *"Miyagi-Jones nu aji goi,"* which translates into "A Taste of Miyagi and Jones."

Betty and I discussed our respective pet birds back at home, while Larry hit the dance floor with Amy Nitahara to make the most of the pure sixties music provided by a Filipino cover band.

I still don't dance. These songs may have been the soundtrack to my life, but dancing isn't something I ever felt confident about.

The food was plentiful and served buffet-style. Gifts of sake sets emblazoned with the logo of "Sam's By the Sea" were unwrapped, provided by our host, Mark Payne. The trekkers lingered long after dinner.

Someone asked, "Do you remember when Gemini 8 aborted its mission and had to make an emergency landing?"

Some trekkers remembered more than I did. There was a lot of excitement and our teachers discussed it in school.

You see, years before Neil Armstrong walked on the moon, he walked on Okinawa.

It was March 18, 1966, and the Gemini space capsule started to spin out of control, splashing down about 500 miles east of Okinawa. Astronauts Neil Armstrong and David Scott were picked up by a navy destroyer, the USS Leonard F. Mason and "choppered" to Kadena Air Base, where they immediately boarded a jet back to the States. A black-and-white photo made page one of *The Morning Star* newspaper—our English-language daily—and was the only photo to show the two astronauts on Okinawa.

Someone else said, "Remember the Alaska earthquake? And the tidal wave that was on the way over?"

Several of us nodded in agreement.

"It was really scary and the tsunami was coming across the Pacific, straight at us."

"We were supposed to move to higher ground."

"Yeah, I remember."

And then we all burst out laughing.

It was Good Friday at 5:36 p.m. when it hit. But for us, it was already Saturday.

The "Great Alaska Earthquake of 1964" as it became known, lasted nearly five minutes and struck the coastline of Alaska on March 27, 1964, causing devastating damage.

We first learned about the earthquake from official bulletins on AFRTS, but it was the local civilian AM-radio station with the call letters KSBK that had me petrified. The deejay kept frantically reporting that the huge (officially registering at 9.2) earthquake had churned up a great tsunami wave that was rolling across the Pacific Ocean and heading straight toward us!

Since we were living on a small Pacific island that was sixty miles long by two miles wide at the narrowest point, there wasn't much high ground. That narrow point was also the highest point on the island—the only place where you could stand and see the Pacific Ocean on one side, and on the other side, the East China Sea.

Radio was all we had back then. There was no 24/7 coverage of anything. Besides six hours of AFRTS TV and the radio station, there was a popular English language AM station that broadcast all the Top-40 pop hits. Maybe there weren't even forty top hits back then, but that's what I listened to in my room. And in my room, the deejay was getting more frantic as the night wore on. This was probably the biggest story he'd ever reported.

I was thirteen years old and lying awake in my bed. I don't think I ever fell asleep that night. I was so scared. I expected a huge wave to wash over the island at any moment and wipe us out. If I'd had a life jacket, I would have been wearing it. There was no safe place to go. There was nowhere to go. You can't go inland when you're on an island!

Finally, Dad came into my bedroom and simply switched off the radio. No more bulletins. No more news. "Just shut up now and go to sleep," he barked.

Mom and Dad said the tsunami wouldn't ever hit us. But how could they know that? It didn't reassure me one bit. I was the oldest and didn't believe them.

By dawn, nothing had happened. We were still alive, and I was still waiting. I'm sure I didn't fall asleep, but of course I can't prove it. We finally got official word on the radio that the tsunami did reach the Hawaiian Islands just five hours after the quake struck the Alaskan mainland. And the tsunami was officially measured at just three meters high. I guess I could have gone to sleep because Mom and Dad were right after all. Just a lucky guess on their parts. But then again, maybe they were up all night long. Maybe they were just as worried.

The hotel shuttle arrived to take some trekkers back to the Dai-Ichi, but we remained—until it finally dawned on us that the bus would not be returning. Patti and her dad were ready to go back, as well as Julia and me. Others were clearly going to make a late night out of this party. We phoned for a taxi, and waited outside, when Jay Wentworth's son, Justin, appeared and offered to take us back to the hotel.

We all squeezed into Justin's little car and zoomed off in the dark.

He told us about going to college Stateside, and how he came back to Okinawa after graduation.

"Because it's my home."

To so many of us.

So These Are My Siblings?

When little brother Danny started to walk, he moved fast. He was always on the run. And apparently he didn't come back when called, because Mom bought a leather harness for him. It worked. She was able to take him out in public and keep him within six feet of her.

Maybe toddler harnesses were *de rigueur* in Munich, but when we returned to the States, Grandma was absolutely appalled. "Grace, you can't keep your little boy on a leash! People will think that's cruel."

Mom dumped the leash. And Danny kept running away.

We were stationed at Fort Lewis, Washington then and living off-post in a house in Tacoma. Park Avenue Elementary School was within walking distance and I went there for second and third grades. I walked to school back then, apparently all by myself.

Danny was still running away. Mom finally discovered him missing in action and began to search. She found his tricycle parked at the end of the sidewalk, and our collie, Nosey, sitting beside it. Nosey knew her boundaries. She wasn't going to disobey Mom and leave the sidewalk.

No one thought about "stranger-danger" back then. No one

considered the possibility of kidnapping. There were no pictures of missing children on milk cartons.

Mom simply walked around the neighborhood, calling his name. Eventually she went back home to see if Danny had returned, and while she was there, someone from the school office phoned. Mom picked up. No one had answering machines.

I was out on the playground when Danny came running up to me. I took him to Mrs. Stevens. She let him sit in class with me until Mom arrived and walked him back home. Danny wanted to be in school. That's all. He wanted to go to school so badly back then, but all that changed through the years. Danny dropped out of high school two months before he would have graduated.

Little brother Danny could never become president. At least that's what Raymond and I kept telling him when he was a kid. A clear case of kid one and kid two, picking on kid three!

We knew exactly how to push Danny's buttons. And then he would start to cry and run to Mom. She would tell us to "knock it off" and threaten us with her wooden spoon.

You see, Danny wasn't born in the United States and wasn't a natural-born-citizen. When we came home from Munich, I remember all of us piling into the family Rambler, and driving off to government offices to process papers to "naturalize" Danny.

Another thing Raymond and I would tell Danny: that he was a German. That upset him, and again he would start to cry, run to Mom and whine, "They're calling me a germ."

But now "Dan, the Man" has more than his country of origin to worry about. I'm pretty sure now that a felony record could be the bigger obstacle.

We got to talking about health insurance one afternoon, and Dan told me how he doesn't worry about health coverage because he can always go to the Veterans' Hospital for treatment. Being a navy vet, Dan is entitled to lifetime health coverage. It was then that I asked about his one-year stint in the navy back in 1977 and about the hand injury that led to his discharge.

"What are you talking about?" asked Dan.

"Well that was what Mom told me back then," I responded.

I had just graduated from college and moved into an apartment. I wasn't living at home.

"I didn't know anything except that you got hurt and were discharged," I said.

Dan finally came clean. Boasting with an air of barroom bravado about his nearly one-year stint in the U.S. Navy, he told me how he had done ninety days in the brig after receiving a general court martial "for communicating a threat to injure and do bodily harm" to an undercover narcotics agent.

"I was made a blue-roper (which he explained was a company commander's assistant) right after basic training and lived in an apartment at Great Lakes (Naval Training Center) with another guy," said Dan. "I came back to the apartment and found that the door was kicked in. My roommate was gone. He was court-martialed for drugs and I never saw him again. When I found the guy who busted him, I hit him."

Well then. That would explain the hand injury that Mom was talking about. Of course, all I've got to go on now is Dan's side of the story, and he's actually quite proud of it. My brother just doesn't know when to stop talking.

Oh, and did I mention that Dan claimed there were also a few "short" AWOLs in his tour of duty? The long and "short" of it: AWOL is AWOL.

Dan didn't elaborate about where he was when he was designated as AWOL, but Aunt Mary told me that the Shore Patrol was cruising the streets of Oshkosh, trying to track him down.

Dan said that Dad drove up to Great Lakes to visit him while he was doing his time in the brig. Dad must have been so disappointed. And I had no idea that any of this was happening…just one more of the many things Mom kept from me…if Dan had made the navy his career, the navy might have made a man out of Dan.

Who *are* these people? Maybe my husband is right. Maybe I really *was* switched at birth. Anyway, Dan claims that he spent one year in the navy and ended up with a "general discharge under honorable conditions." Hmmmm. Okay, so clearly, the navy is not my father's army! As usual, there's always more to the story than my brother's telling!

Middle brother Raymond is another study in contradiction. Ray showed early signs of artistic talent when he was a little kid. He would sprawl across the living room floor with blank sheets of paper and using Mom's prayer book, copy the paintings reproduced on the pages. When people noticed what he was drawing, favorable comments were made. But no one paid much attention to the little kid who was making those drawings. Mom and Dad weren't into art and it wasn't until Ray took an art class in junior high school that a teacher acknowledged his ability!

While in high school, Ray took Saturday classes at Cooper School of Art in downtown Cleveland. When many of his friends from high school went off to pursue art in college, Mom and Dad urged Ray not to consider college, but instead to get a real job.

I was working at my first job out of high school as a secretary at General Electric and brought an application home for Ray to fill out. When I picked it up to take it to the personnel department, I couldn't believe that when Ray came to the part of the application where the applicant is asked why he wants to work for the company, Ray simply had written, "for the money."

Ray could easily have become an art major in college, but instead, he got a job. He worked as a light bulb inspector in the Pitney Glass Works Division of G.E. on second shift for several years. Ray worked second-shift and so did Mom. She dropped him off at the factory and then went to Euclid General Hospital. When she clocked out, she drove down to East 152nd Street and picked up Ray.

Both my mother and brother would wind down after their shift and that involved eating and watching late-night TV. Mom told me that the last thing she did before turning off the lights and going to bed was to climb upstairs and remove the plate from Ray's hand, push him down onto his pillow and turn off his TV. My brother had this uncanny ability to fall asleep while sitting upright in bed, holding a plate of food in his hand! And there were usually one or two dachshunds patiently watching that plate in his hand…waiting for it to tilt toward them…rewarding their patience.

Mom and Dad were pleased. In their world, all was well. Two of their three children were employed. But baby brother Danny was out there…somewhere…wandering the country…and wiring home for money whenever he got into trouble.

I think all children need to be encouraged when they show signs of talent. The only people encouraging me were my teachers. They were my inspiration. Mom and Dad did not understand creativity or the need for higher education. The only reality they knew was to tell us kids to go find jobs. I was the only one to graduate from college.

Needless to say, both of my brothers are pretty much out of the loop with technology. Dan's still trying to find the on-ramp to the information superhighway.

How did I ever wade into this gene pool? I should have climbed out long ago.

I updated Julia recently about Dan's latest exploits, and she just laughed and said, "Honey, he looked like trouble. I could see something in that little boy's eyes. He knew he could get away with stuff because he was the baby."

Maybe Julia's right. And she never even knew about Danny's leather harness.

Until now.

Frank Lloyd Wrong

"He's going to do *what*?" I shouted to Mom. "I'm coming right over. Don't let him touch anything."

I had to get to my parents' house right away—to stop "Frank Lloyd Wrong." He was fired-up and ready to go.

I could just picture Dad shaking and rattling in one hand his can of gold spray paint, while spreading out newspapers for his next project with the other hand. This time he was going to improve upon a vintage Art Deco mirror that Grandma and Grandpa had received as an anniversary gift back in the 1930s.

He had to be stopped. I had to save the mirror. Only I appreciated it as it was.

Dad always considered himself a "master craftsman" when it came to modifying furniture—but behind his back I referred to him as "Frank Lloyd Wrong."

In the fall of 1968, we weren't moving any more. When Mom and Dad bought a little bungalow in Willowick, Ohio, Dad began to remodel. By that time, he had perfected some of his techniques.

Dad's decorating and remodeling usually included sheets of dark wood paneling from K-Mart and self-stick mirror squares. For once, we didn't have to think about quarters inspections and rules about holes in the walls. We could hang things without worrying about patching the holes afterwards.

My brothers were free to tape glow-in-the-dark rock posters to their walls. And I finally got my choice of color on the walls of my bedroom.

Mom got carried away when she discovered DuPont Flair-Squares at K-Mart. She bought the Squares in a luminous green quilt pattern and stuck them on both walls all the way up the steps to the second floor. It produced a hallucinogenic effect in that hallway.

We were on a roll!

Extremely proud of his trademark method of creating knotty-pine paneling, Dad would explain the process to anyone who'd listen. "First, you nail sheets of plywood against the walls. Then you fire up a blowtorch."

Like a deranged performance artist, Dad randomly fired away at the wall, singeing black spots into the plywood, which served as his blank canvas. Once he was satisfied with the placement of these accents, he applied several coats of high-gloss varnish to the plywood—and *voila*! Knotty-pine! I remember distinctly two houses in which Dad used that blow-torch.

Another favorite decorating technique was Dad's use of Sears texture-paint. He always said, "If you texture-paint the walls and ceilings with a sponge, you don't have to worry about cracks or low spots. Texture-paint fills in any mistakes. Everything's covered over."

Except that the walls end up covered with tiny sharp projectiles and it hurts when you lean back against them! It's like the walls were one giant scratching post.

When we were stationed at Fort Lewis, Washington my parents somehow came across a second-hand, five-piece bedroom set—pure

1930s Art Deco. Soon it was in pieces when Dad decided he could make more functional items of furniture from the bedroom set.

He disassembled the set. The wooden frame that supported the massive round vanity mirror was transformed into a coffee table and accented with tiny mosaic tiles from Woolworth's that he inserted into the recessed portion of the frame. Four wooden legs were screwed into the "new" table and it was covered with multiple coats of high-gloss varnish.

The round mirror, out of its frame, simply hung on the wall. Actually, it looked pretty good all by itself on the wall. Dad couldn't think of anything to do to it.

The low vanity table dresser with drawers on each side soon became a much more practical desk—with the curved waterfall-edge headboard from the bed fastened to the top of it and four more screw-on legs beneath. Several coats of high-gloss varnish made it shine like the other piece. And now, everything had been re-stained into a reddish shade of mahogany.

The unique coffee table and desk traveled around the country with us. People remarked about them many times. And Dad told his story just as many times.

Ohio Bell workers showed up one morning to replace a telephone pole along Foxboro Drive in front of our house in Willowick. Dad convinced them to let him have the pole and not to haul it away. Dad couldn't pass up a full-sized telephone pole! He had another creative brainstorm and set to work measuring and cutting down that massive pole.

Dad took the cut sections and lashed them together with thick rope, sinking them into the ground at the end of our driveway. He was so proud. We were the only house along Foxboro Drive with what resembled a place to tie up your boat. It made it easy to find our driveway.

Lake Erie was about a mile away, but we were ready. We used to joke that Dad was anticipating the effects of shoreline erosion and that one day, our property would be "beach-front."

Dad's signature creation to this day, remains his pair of GI combat boots. Standing upright in the corner of the living room and filled with cement, he spray-painted them gold. I always warned my husband that we three kids would one day be fighting over who would inherit them.

Dad was most definitely "master of the house." When we were little kids, we looked up to him. As we got older, we more or less humored him, and figured things out for ourselves.

Dad was pretty good at fixing things—if those things happened to be old cars and household appliances. He wore his pin-striped Sears coveralls throughout the weekends and could almost always be found underneath an old Ford or Chevy in the driveway, carport or garage of whichever house we were living in.

Mom always said, "He's probably going to go, wearing his coveralls while lying on his mechanic's creeper. I'll just slide him out and call the undertaker."

It was another old story, but it always brought a laugh.

Dad was in charge of our motor pool and maintained our fleet of vehicles. We relied on him for advice. He picked out my first car when I began to drive—a used 1965 Rambler American, the color of dirt, with manual steering and no radio. "You can't drive and listen to the radio," Dad warned. "No distractions. Eyes on the road."

Well, Dad was obviously worried about distractions, but somehow managed to teach me to drive illegally! That would be two-footed. That's how Dad drove, and I thought everyone drove that way. I've been driving "two-footed" since then and not giving it a thought. It's only when someone points it out to me that I become flustered and get confused. So fair warning—if you're my passenger, I don't want to hear about it.

I've been driving this way for over thirty years now and use my left foot for the brake and my right foot for the gas. I'm an excellent driver. But I know that I can never let my license lapse, or I'll have to re-take the driving test.

Because Dad maintained each of our cars, he felt that he had a proprietary interest in them. We all got lectures from him about car maintenance whenever we stopped by the house. Especially me. I stopped by several times a week. Ray didn't stop by very often and when he did, it was only when his car was barely running.

Dan was off wandering somewhere and was pretty much out of the picture. After dropping out of high school, Dan was well on his way to "finding himself."

That left me to deal most often with the "parental units." After work, I would pull up in the driveway with whatever vehicle I was driving. Dad would pop the hood and tinker—all the while mumbling, "Oh shit" or "Jesus Christ." I stayed inside the house and played with the dogs.

Soon Dad came in to deliver one of his lectures on vehicle maintenance. I nodded and listened.

When I bought my very first brand-new car, a sporty two-door 1973 fire-engine red AMC Hornet with a black vinyl top and an AM/FM radio, Dad went along to the dealership with me to negotiate a good price. Dad was one of those guys who could always be counted on to outsmart the car salesman.

That's how I ended up with the innovative "Buyer Protection Plan" that American Motors promoted. Apparently there had been nothing like it before, and this "Buyer Protection Plan" would cover my car and protect me from expensive repairs. Dad was determined to make the most of that warranty. He became a frequent complainer.

As a result, I spent a lot of time riding the bus to work while Dad took my car off to the dealership.

My red Hornet was equipped with self-adjusting brakes. Dad insisted that the only way to keep those self-adjusting brakes in adjustment, was to "pump" them hard whenever I moved the car in reverse. Well, apparently I never did that to Dad's satisfaction because he would snatch the keys from my hand as soon as I walked into the kitchen.

Mom and I watched from the living room window as Dad drove in reverse down the street, with my little red Hornet furiously jerking to a stop every twenty feet—over and over again. I wondered what our neighbors thought.

But the neighbors were used to Dad. He was the guy on the street who kept an eye on things around the neighborhood, and in the winter he would fire up his huge eight-horsepower snow blower (that was four horsepower more than he needed) to clear the driveway. And because Dad was "suited up and ready to roll," and even had a plastic-covered windshield across the snow blower, he would do just that—roll on down the street, blowing the snow next door and then on to the house next to that—and the house next to that one. He kept clearing snow until he was done with the street. He would have been happy clearing runways at the airport.

Dad was strongly prejudiced against foreign cars—and when my husband and I bought a pair of matching Datsun hatchbacks in the early 1980s, I turned over the keys for the old Hornet to Dad. After all of his hard work through the years, I felt he should just take it for a spare.

Not happy with our crossover to Japanese imports, Dad never got another chance to work on my car again—mostly because it just kept on going. After the Datsuns, we moved on to Toyotas and then to Hondas. We switched teams and Dad never forgave us.

But Wait, There's More!

They were the pots that started the argument that put Dad in the doghouse.

The pots and pans, an eighteen-piece set of cookware that Dad stubbornly refused to take back to the guy in the NCO club on Okinawa who talked him into buying them...the set that endured as our family cookware for over forty years. And now they're all mine!

Somebody made a successful sales pitch to Dad, and he bought a complete set of stainless steel cookware, made by a company called Saladmaster. Mom was furious about how much money he spent. I don't remember how much, but I do remember how mad Mom was.

I was the one who washed those pots.

I was the one who read the words, "*Saladmaster, Stainless Steel, Dallas, Texas...*"over and over as I washed the pots, dried them, and stacked them back in the cupboard.

And wouldn't you know? It was just Dad's "dumb luck" to buy into something that has apparently cultivated a following? There are postings on the Internet and testimonials from savvy cooks who get excited about the "vapo-valve technology" behind what Saladmaster referred to as "waterless cookware."

So that's what all that clattering was about.

When Dad's chili or Mom's spaghetti sauce really got cooking, the little "top-hat" vent built into the lid went crazy with its rattling sound. That sound apparently was a signal. I doubt Mom or Dad even realized it.

Exclusive to Saladmaster, the "vapo-valve," was designed to take the guesswork out of cooking, and alert you when it was time to reduce the heat. It eliminated dreaded "pot-watching."

Testimonials abound on the Internet from aficionados of Saladmaster, which I still think is a strange name for a line of pots and pans. The name must have originated from the gadget that resembled a meat slicer that could be secured to the countertop with suction cups and had attachments to slice and dice carrots and potatoes into decorative curls and swirls. That piece never got used. It was always shoved way back in the cupboard, hidden beneath a plastic cover. It definitely disappeared during one of Mom's "moving purges."

One woman claimed that she bought her set in the early sixties and couldn't decide if she had done the right thing, adding that she had spent the equivalent of "half a new car" back then—around six hundred and fifty dollars.

I'm not sure Mom cooked as well as she could with those pots. The large one was used for chili and boiling spaghetti noodles; the medium one was for the spaghetti sauce, and the small one was for heating cans of peas or corn. There was a science behind this cookware. But Mom and Dad weren't people who read directions. They didn't do anything except cook with those high-tech pots and pans.

It was when Mom and Dad were hastily vacating their little apartment that didn't work out…after I returned from the big Okinawa trip… when I stood there, surrounded by piles of clutter that had to be out of there within the next few days. I don't know what made me toss those Saladmaster pots into my car. It must have been my dishwashing connection.

Now that I've done my research, I find that they are indeed still in production—and HOT, HOT, HOT! People are paying a lot of money for these pieces on eBay, up to $1000 for a complete set of used cookware.

My husband keeps urging me to put the pots and pans on eBay and make some money. But I can't do it. Dan has my mother's Buddha. I have the pots—a more valuable heritage, and I'm not letting go of them.

Mom shouldn't have been so mad at Dad. As the years passed, she was the one who fell hardest for anything "as seen on TV." That was all she needed to make a purchasing decision. And if something said, "Not Available in Stores," that was the clincher. Dad was fond of gadgets and gizmos—most of them "as seen on TV" items. If my parents saw something advertised on TV, they fell for it. They clapped their lights on and off, and at breakfast, they used the Inside-the-Shell Egg Scrambler for perfect scrambled eggs.

And every time another amazing piece of exercise equipment was introduced with a "free 30-day, no obligation in-home trial," Mom punched in the toll-free number. She usually kept whatever was delivered and when she tired of sitting and twisting, or bending and twisting, she tried to pawn it off on me. I remember one day, she had me try out a twisting machine with a floppy foam arm rest that offered absolutely no support or resistance.

Always looking for a miracle, Mom was positive that if she followed Richard Simmons' exercise videotape, *Sweatin' to the Oldies*, she would succeed in shaping up.

However, the tape could not be located anywhere but at the public library, so once we got our hands on it, we dubbed an illegal copy for her workout activities. I'm sure she watched the video. But I'm not sure she worked out. Richard was a good guy, and Mom totally believed in him.

Each Christmas, when commercials began to air for the "Chia-Pet," Mom would try just one more time to successfully sprout a Chia. And there were so many to choose from! She smeared Chia goop onto the Chia-Ram, the Chia-Bull, the Chia-Puppy and finally the Chia-Guy, waiting patiently, hoping for the best. She never had any luck with those things, but she was a constant customer.

But wait. There *is* more! Mom and Dad had trouble programming their VCR, especially when they paused so long entering the starting time, the ending time, the tape speed and the channel number, that they lost everything and had to start over before they could push the PROGRAM button to lock in their data selection.

Mom returned one Panasonic VCR to the store because of the problems she encountered with the programming procedure.

Don began a search for a VCR that would not "time-out" and located a Toshiba model that had unlimited programming time... he and the salesman stood silently together, in front of a Toshiba model, while the screen was frozen...guaranteeing no "time-out" on the programming function.

You could have dozed off while entering the data...perfect for Mom and Dad!

But still they still struggled...and soon they were ready to toss their VCR out the window.

Then something called the VCRplus+ came along; it promised to set everything up for you once you entered the "magic" digits that were assigned to listings in the TV Guide. Don and I located the highly-sought-after unit during the Christmas-shopping frenzy and wrapped it in Santa paper. Finally all would be well.

Unfortunately, the VCRplus+ couldn't determine when *60 Minutes* was running late because of a football game...

"Well, why not? Why doesn't it know that?" Mom kept asking.

Toss it, Mom. Just toss it.

And when they got their first cell-phones? You can just imagine.

Colorblind

Grandma bought me a brown vinyl Gerber baby doll in the late 1970s—because she said it reminded her of me! She wrapped it up for my birthday present, and then told me the story about how when I was a little girl, I insisted on selecting the chocolate brown baby doll at Higbee's, a downtown Cleveland department store. No one could change my mind.

I guess I was stubborn and because I probably was on the verge of one of those attention-getting "down-on-the-floor" tantrums that Grandma says I was known for, I went home with that little brown doll.

I don't really remember anything about this, but apparently I carried that doll everywhere. It must have provoked quite a few comments back in the early 1950s in Cleveland.

"You called that little doll your 'cugga-baby' because you couldn't say 'colored!'" exclaimed Grandma, while Mom stood in the background, nodding in agreement, and laughing. I added the Gerber doll to my collection.

One of the last books I checked out of the school library in California before we shipped overseas was John Steinbeck's *Travels with Charley*.

New on the shelf in 1962, the cover depicted a drawing of a poodle with a camper-truck in the background.

I read the book for a second time recently, but this time around I read a book that I own—a vintage first-edition hardcover from my Steinbeck collection. No more libraries. I hoard books.

Steinbeck set out in 1960 from New York City "in search of America." He traveled west with his black poodle Charley in a custom camper-truck with the name *"Rocinante"* hand-painted on the side. (A friend suggested that the camper be named after Don Quixote's faithful steed.)

Traveling through forty states, Steinbeck drove west toward his hometown of Salinas, California before turning back and crossing the Mojave, heading across the huge state of Texas and into the racially-torn segregated South. Stopping in New Orleans, Steinbeck wanted to see for himself the source of considerable uproar. Making headlines at the time was a group of protesting women who became known as "the cheerleaders." They appeared each morning right on schedule, to shout at a little Negro girl being escorted by four U.S. Marshals, as she walked into school.

Rereading that book from my youth, I can appreciate Steinbeck's comparison of the event to the opening of a show, with the sounds of sirens and motorcycle cops. He described how a "jangle of jeering shrieks went up from behind the barricades." And he further described how the little girl appeared "even more of a mite because the men were so big." And how the little girl half-skipped along, but then took measured reluctant steps between the tall guards as she entered the school.

Steinbeck must have known that he was observing a milestone in history. It was a news event. Steinbeck made his feelings clear; his feelings as a self-proclaimed "racist failure" were obvious. His book made a strong impression on me then. It still does.

We were colorblind in school. I know I was. My classrooms were filled with a mix of boys and girls—certainly colored kids—in shades of browns and yellows and white. I knew my classmates by name first, and maybe later I figured out their ethnic heritage. We were all first and foremost military brats. That was our shared heritage.

Military brats were children who traveled with their fathers as "dependents" and who had gained a global perspective on life, one that civilian kids don't understand. (I liked to think that my blood was tinged with army green.)

Classmates cycled in and out of my life. There was a boy named "Bodo" in kindergarten in Munich. I haven't a clue about him, just that he was actually named Bodo. And later on, there were other kids named Hirome Fujio, Bok-Nam-Lee, Yumi McGarvey, Dai Ling Yao, Khamla Bhatti, Chieko Starr, Irene Tanabe…my very own personal United Nations.

One girl named Gretchen had the best name of all. I'd never known another Gretchen, other than our little dachshund! Gretchen told everyone that her mother was a teacher and wanted to select a unique name that would not be duplicated, so that's how she ended up with her name.

President Truman issued an Executive Order back in 1948, calling for equal opportunity in all branches of the armed services. It still allowed for segregation, but called for "equality of treatment and opportunity." Truman's order did not actually integrate the army—it used segregated units during the Korean War—but it opened the way for integration in the early 1950s. True segregation in the military was between officers and enlisted men. That was reflected in the location of your housing area, how nice the housing was and who saluted whom.

Racial prejudice was left outside the gate. In the dependent school system, we were black, we were white, we were Asian and very often

AmerAsian! My friends were Caucasian, Colored, Latino, Asian and mixtures of all of those races. It must have been shocking to some civilians to see those bi-racial and multi-racial combinations.

I was enrolled in a civilian school, Seaside Elementary School, in California, for fifth grade just a few months before we got quarters at Fort Ord. There, my classmates were Jorge, Jesus and Juanita. I remember walking home one afternoon with a classmate named Donna who lived nearby. I thought we could play together at my house after school—and we stopped by her house to ask, but her mother just looked at me and said "no." That was the end of it. Donna went inside and I went home. We could not be friends. Donna was a colored girl.

Our friendship was discouraged and I didn't understand why. It was the early sixties. The civilian world was different.

When I look at my class picture from Seaside Elementary, most of my classmates were Latino and colored. When we moved on post, I attended the rest of fifth grade at Stilwell Elementary School, where a lot of my classmates were still Latino and colored. But there, we were army brats. Mary Wertsch asserts in her book that the military community is normally a stronger bond than the differences of race. Military brats grow up in communities that actively condemn racist comments. This results in brats who "aren't just non-racist, but anti-racist."

When the local Girl Scout troop geared up for the big "cookie sale" on post, I went to my friend Seglinda's house after school so that we could load up our boxes of cookies.

I remember my surprise when the door opened—and Seglinda's dad was a colored man! And then I discovered that her mother had a strong German accent!

There we were, a couple of fifth-grade girls, in our uniforms, trying to earn a cookie badge, walking around, knocking on strangers' doors, selling Thin-Mints for thirty-five cents a box until we ran out of cookies and went home. Our little world was safe. We were happy.

We kids didn't seem prejudiced, but obviously some of our parents were. It was how they had been raised. Dad was definitely prejudiced. But like any soldier who was prejudiced, he kept his derogatory comments confined to quarters—inside our home.

And when I was in high school on Okinawa, if I hadn't been way too shy to even speak to a boy, I might have actually gone out on a date! There were some cute guys in my classes. Clearly some were mixed-race. I thought of "cute" first, before ethnicity. But now I wonder what Dad would have said if I had come home with someone who was an AmerAsian guy? Or a Filipino guy? I wasted so many years being shy.

Out in public, Dad seemed like a really great guy, always smiling and wise-cracking, someone you wanted to spend time with. When he hung out with his buddies at the American Legion Club or the Castle Terrace Club, you'd hear Dad's exclamations of "No shit!" or "You shittin' me?" and then lots of laughter and shoulder-slapping. Everyone seemed to be having a really great time. And when we were at a cookout somewhere, there were lots of laughs, but I finally caught on that there was usually lots of beer too. At times like this, Dad was a fun-loving stranger. That guy was not the person we knew at home.

Behind closed doors, Dad was a moody man. He sat around and chewed his fingernails while he watched TV. He drank beer and barked orders and he kept track of us while Mom worked second shift as a nurse, wherever she could get work.

Mom kept the home front running smoothly as most army wives did. She ran interference for us when Dad was really grumpy and didn't want to deal with us. If we kids really misbehaved or did something seriously wrong, we got spanked. It's what parents did back then.

Army Nurse

Mom found part-time work wherever she could, at any hospital, civilian or military, depending where we were stationed. I can remember when we returned from Germany, we drove to the state capitol in Olympia, Washington so that she could renew her nursing license. Then she worked at Pierce County Hospital and at the Bellevue Sanitarium in Tacoma.

Once we made another PCS to Fort Ord, California, Mom worked at the army hospital near our housing area. It was right up the hill from our quarters.

Mom was a total "germ-freak" and she positively hated it when someone, usually a doctor, would grab her stethoscope...and put it into his ears...she'd have to wipe it down with alcohol wipes...she would even wipe off the phone!

When Mom arrived home from work, she would head straight to the shower, strip off everything and toss it right into the washing machine. She even wiped down the bottoms of her shoes! She never wanted to bring any hospital germs home with her.

Mom wound down after work by watching late-night movies and if I stayed up with her, she talked about her patients and what had happened that night. Many times, I heard her talk about how the nurses knew more about a patient than the doctors did. Mom loved nursing. It was what she was good at.

She especially liked working in the maternity ward at Fort Ord, California. I remember walking to the hospital after school and going up to the "baby window" to look through the glass at the newborns lined up in their tiny bassinettes.

Mom liked to tell the story about how she was on duty when Helen Beardsley was admitted to give birth to baby number nineteen—a little boy—in July of 1962. The Beardsleys were the couple who gained fame after they met, married and combined their large families—Helen North, a widow, had eight biological children, and Navy Warrant Officer Frank Beardsley, a widower, had ten children. They met and married, blending their many children into one enormous family.

Anyway, Mom was a nurse on duty in the OB ward when Helen Beardsley delivered that baby boy. Mom kept track of the Beardsley brood throughout the years, and when Mrs. Beardsley wrote a book called *Who Gets the Drumstick?*, she couldn't wait to read it. And when the book became the movie *Yours, Mine and Ours*, starring Lucille Ball and Henry Fonda, we eagerly awaited its arrival at Buckner Theater on Okinawa.

Mom couldn't find work at the army hospital on Okinawa, but she resumed her nursing career when we made our last PCS to Fort Campbell, Kentucky. Mom worked at the local army hospital, not too far away from our housing area. It was a one-story sprawling layout back then, where it seemed you just walked and walked through endless corridors to get anywhere.

Still hoping that I would consider a career in nursing, Mom gave me information about the "candy striper" volunteer program and during one of my summer vacations, I went through the training. My assignment as a candy striper? As soon as someone discovered that I could actually hit the keys, I ended up in a small office, typing up information on three-by-five index cards. I was alone with a typewriter. And I liked it.

That was the end of anything related to nursing and the start of all things secretarial.

Everything I've done so far has been linked to a typewriter. I didn't want contact with any sick people! Mom finally gave up, and stopped trying to make me into a nurse.

Mom sent us off to school each morning, took care of the house, went to the PX and commissary, and then left to work second shift. I can still picture Mom in her starched white uniform with the little "wing" style sleeves, white Supp-Hose stockings and leather Clinic-brand nursing shoes. I polished those shoes every few days with dab-on shoe polish, especially made for baby shoes and nurse's shoes. Mom always carried her starched nurse's cap with her, with a few bobbie-pins so that she could fasten it into her hair. It was like a little miniature "Flying Nun" hat and had the blue and white emblem of Jane Addams Nursing School at the edge.

The last thing Mom did before she went out the door was to grab a bottle of spray cologne or perfume—whatever was handy—usually Jungle Gardenia, and spray it down the front of her uniform.

"Patients tell me that I smell nice," said Mom. "There are so many foul odors. This is the only way I can fight them off."

When we retired in Ohio, Mom settled down at Euclid General Hospital and worked there on a part-time basis for twenty years. She worked in the Intensive Care Unit and was floated to Coronary Care and the Emergency Room. That was an exciting time for Mom. She worked with a close-knit group of nurses, who shared their lives, their families, their problems, their meals. They got along well and were always looking for an excuse to celebrate.

Someone could be counted on to say, "Tomorrow's Wednesday. We'll all bring in something to eat and celebrate."

They were a close group of nurses and nurse's aides. Like a family. I heard about Terry, Phyllis, Julie, Nikki, Margaret, among others, and got to know them like they were my friends too.

Mom loved pizza and for her birthday, someone who was into cake decorating, baked a birthday cake for her that looked just like a pizza! To me, it was not a pretty cake, but Mom thought it was the best-ever.

When you worked in those critical-care units, there was plenty of action, and as a team, they worked well together. I heard about life-saving procedures, stories about prisoners from the Euclid City Jail who were being guarded by police, aortic aneurysms, intubation, respirators, Foley catheters, Posey restraints, and Ambu-bags—I heard it all and became familiar with a lot of medical terminology.

When CPR instruction went mainstream in the 1970s, Mom was excited by its success and told me all about it. I enrolled in a CPR Class at the American Red Cross—hoping I'd never have to ever actually use it! My goal was definitely to maintain a "hands-off" approach to medicine. The closest I would ever consider getting into the medical profession was working as a medical transcriptionist. I could spell well. That wouldn't involve hands-on care.

Not every patient found a miracle. Death was part of the hospital and some people died because it was their time to go. And I specifically remember what Mom said one night when she came home from work. It was profound, and I never forgot it.

"Not everyone can be saved. You just walk a bit slower when you know the end is near."

Mom talked about how nurses knew who was the best doctor, and which anesthesiologist was suspected of a drinking habit. They had the inside scoop.

Mom took her job seriously and was often upset when something went terribly wrong on her shift. She would scan the death notices over the next few days to see if a patient made it or not.

Some nights she dropped off her close friend, Terry Parr, and that made her a bit later than usual arriving home. The dogs would wait anxiously by the front window, pushing their noses through the living room curtains, watching for her car to come down the street. But when Mom dropped off Terry, she came from the other direction. That totally confused them. Their heads were turned to the left, watching for Mom, when suddenly she pulled into the driveway from the right!

Mom would walk in with a sigh and say, "It's so hard to get out of there with Terry. She just can't leave anything unfinished! If she's got a patient caked in shit, she won't leave until every crack is cleaned. She's so thorough, it drives me crazy!"

We would have a good laugh over this. Mom always said that if she was ever a patient in the hospital, she definitely wanted Terry taking care of her.

And when AIDS started to gain notoriety, Mom became quite alarmed about how contagious and dangerous it truly was. She said that they kept AIDS patients in total quarantine and isolation, but things were going to get much worse. She and others close to it, knew that this was something that was going to change the world.

I know Mom worried about picking up some serious infection from the hospital. And despite her caution, she did.

I was in my own apartment at the time. It was 1978. Mom went to the doctor because she thought she had a bad case of flu. The doctor sent her home, but things weren't getting any better. I still remember vividly the afternoon that she called me at work and said that I needed to take her to another appointment. Dad was working and she didn't think she could drive herself. Mom always got everywhere on her own. This was serious.

I drove her to Euclid Clinic. When we got to the entrance, I couldn't get her out of the car. Mom was so weak that I had to get a wheelchair. She couldn't walk. I got her into the doctor's office and someone decided that she needed to be admitted to the hospital. No one seemed to know exactly what was going on.

I can remember Mom telling me to get Terry on the phone. Mom trusted Terry. Terry would know who to call for advice. I held the phone up to Mom's ear and somehow, she and Terry together decided who should treat her. (It takes a couple of good nurses to find a good doctor.)

They had faith in a new internist named Peter DeOreo and decided that he was the only one they trusted. He was young, inquisitive, and would pursue this. And they were right. He was the only doctor who came up with a definitive diagnosis of bacterial meningitis—not the flu and not something others were thinking might be Rocky Mountain spotted fever! Mom's suburban lifestyle had certainly not put her in the vicinity of a tick!

Mom was in bad shape. She clearly had contracted bacterial meningitis from one of the patients she was caring for. We all had to take sulfa drugs because of our close contact with her. Mom was in a private room by herself. I was worried.

I went back to work, and late that night in my apartment, the phone rang. It was Mom. And it was past midnight.

"Chris, get up here now. I can't go to sleep. I'm so afraid my IV will infiltrate. It did once and I just can't sleep because it could happen again."

It was scary to experience Mom like this, and I thought she was getting paranoid about her IV. But if it infiltrated, she would have to have it restarted again. When the IV needle dislodged from the vein, the fluid poured subcutaneously beneath the skin.

I drove down the street to Euclid General Hospital. I parked by the Emergency Room entrance and simply walked in through the back doorway like I knew where I was headed. No one paid any attention as I entered the service elevator. Mom was in a room by herself up on the ninth floor. Things were different back then. More casual and less secure. I simply walked down the hallway to Mom's room. She was so relieved to see me. I couldn't do anything but sit in semi-darkness in the chair beside her bed and reassure her. I promised to keep an eye on her IV bag and she got some sleep. I didn't get any, but Mom calmed down and felt reassured.

I remember sitting up all night long. I remember a nurse coming in to take vital signs and stopping in surprise when she saw me sitting in the shadows beside the bed. I whispered that Mom was upset and couldn't sleep, so that's why I was there. The nurse said that I could stay. And by morning, Mom was much better and calmer, so I went home to my apartment to get ready for work at my job as a legal secretary.

Mom was off work for quite a while, recuperating from the meningitis. Eventually she returned to work, but was more "germ-conscious" than ever before.

There came a time when licensed practical nurses were restricted in the procedures they could perform and Mom felt "demoted." She took a course in math and struggled through it to pass the test required for nursing pharmacology. It helped for a while, but a requirement that only registered nurses were permitted to pass meds and perform certain procedures left Mom out of much of what she once did routinely.

Now Mom felt like a nurse's aide. She could still care for patients, but had lost most of her responsibilities. She finally decided to retire and end her nursing career after more than twenty years at Euclid General Hospital.

For Mom, watching *"ER"* on Thursday nights was as close as she would come to the environment in which she once thrived.

Instead of being the nurse, Mom became the patient! So deeply entrenched in the medical profession, Mom gradually developed a lot of illnesses, some real and others imagined. As a result, her final years were spent in doctor's offices and undergoing procedures. Sadly, Mom evolved into one of those "frequent flyers" that she used to talk about from her active duty days as a nurse. Mom had some definite medical problems as she aged. She picked up a staph infection in the hospital that led to weeks of home IV therapy with visiting nurses, and she ended up having a toe amputated because of diabetes. Things were getting complicated.

About this time, my brother Dan offered to take Mom and Dad to live with him in his house because he and his wife Paula had split up. Everyone seemed to agree that it was a wonderful plan. So what could possibly go wrong?

Everything. Absolutely everything. Mom summoned the three of us kids and our "significant others" to the house for the big move. Dan borrowed a truck from the factory where he worked, and we were all in action once again—moving Mom and Dad out of their "slab-o-ranch" over into his "slab-o-ranch."

I started wrapping Mom's finest treasure: the platinum-edged Made in Japan, Seyei Fine China, Majesty Pattern, service for twelve dinnerware.

Mom bought that set while we were stationed on Okinawa. Those dishes had seen use probably only ten times since retirement, but they looked impressive in Great-Aunt Margaret's mahogany Duncan Phyfe corner china cabinet.

Things were packed and stacked, and the house was listed for sale. Dan moved some items of furniture and Mom's toilet. (Years earlier, Mom decided to replace her existing toilet with a taller toilet, one designed for handicapped people. It was great for Mom and Dad, but not quite the thing for a little boy. When Paul visited his grandparents, he had to suddenly aim a little higher than he did at our house.)

So the back bedroom was transformed into a sitting room with a bedroom set, TV and Mom's motorized lift chair. It actually was quite nice and had an adjacent handicapped bathroom now, thanks to some handrails that were installed in the shower. Mom settled in for her first night at my brother's house, and Dan went off to play bass with "The Burnt River Band." When Dan arrived home around three a.m., Mom was watching TV, and waiting up for him. Not good. He was fifty years old and forgot about his mother being at home to meet him at the door. And Dan was drunk.

The encounter with his mother did not go well for my little brother. The big move was unraveling rapidly in only the first few hours and turned into the big "un-move" the next day.

At seven a.m. I got a phone call with the breaking news that Mom was so angry with Dan that she called his estranged wife, Paula, in the middle of the night to take her back to her house. Once Dan sobered up, he brought back the furniture. The FOR SALE sign was pulled out of the front yard and stashed in the garage. The toilet stayed where it was.

Some things never even got unpacked. With Mom as the mastermind behind the move, things were deteriorating further.

Mom still had it in mind to move from her house.

It wasn't long before she dragged the FOR SALE sign out of the garage and planted it back into the same two holes in the front yard. The listing was activated once again, because this time, Mom found herself an apartment. I tried to convince her that the only apartment she should consider should be in a senior-citizen building.

Talking to her on the phone one night, Mom sounded wistful and said, "It was great when we lived in that apartment building in Perlacher Forst, in Munich. Everyone looked out for each other and we all spent time together. We were all young army wives with kids and were in the same boat. It was so friendly back then, living in those apartments."

"But that was a long time ago, Mom. And you all were young and had so much in common. You can't go back to that time again," I said. But clearly, Mom wasn't listening to me. She wasn't listening to anyone. Mom had made up her mind once again. No one could dissuade her.

She signed a lease for an apartment on the ground floor of a garden-style complex, with a patio, so that the dogs could be tied outside. (She actually found a place that would take small pets.) However, the laundry room was up on the second floor, and Mom still hadn't solved that problem. Whenever I asked, she just kept saying that it would work out. I had my doubts. Two flights of steps. No elevator. And two people who couldn't possibly climb those stairs.

Mom liked to sit outside on the patio and gaze over the chain-link fence behind her toward the mobile home park.

"Aren't those trailers nice? Some of them even have decks by the front door. They call them manufactured homes now, you know?"

Oh no! Mom was looking at those double-wides with interest. This could be bad.

Before they could run out of clean underwear, the apartment plan fell apart.

Remember when I was receiving all those distress e-mails on Okinawa? When Julia kept looking over my shoulder? When she wanted me to stop logging onto my laptop? When Mom had called the police for the second time and informed them that she didn't feel "safe" around Dad? Well, this was then. That was now.

Mom's "better half" was once again spending a few weeks in the geriatric/psychiatric evaluation unit of a local hospital (a/k/a "senior-citizen lockup") so Mom had no choice but to move in with my brother. She couldn't live alone in the apartment. She was getting stuck in kitchen chairs and couldn't get up! In social worker terminology, this was my mother's "precipitating incident."

One more time, I found myself wrapping and packing the platinum-edged, Made in Japan, Seyei Fine China, Majesty Pattern, service for twelve (still Mom's most treasured possession!) I was beginning to hate those dishes. Each time they were wrapped, I seemed to be the one who had to unwrap them in another location and try to remember how they all fit into Great-Aunt Margaret's china cabinet. You'd think I'd have had it configured, but there were always just one or two pieces that didn't seem to fit anywhere.

It was sad to stand in that little apartment and look around at what remained of my parents' life. A life that had deteriorated to this: kitchen clutter, stacks of boxes and items of furniture that had to be quickly disposed of because there was no room to store it.

Our son Paul came by with his friends and tried to haul some of the kitchen items and small appliances off to an old house where he was living. Everything needed to be cleared out quickly. At one point, my sister-in-law Paula went running after Paul, trying to convince him how much he *really* needed an ironing board! She tossed it onto the truck and the boys drove away.

Mom was off to live in my brother's house for a second time—whether or not she liked it.

And she didn't. When I visited her after I returned from the big reunion trip to Okinawa, she whispered to me, "This isn't working. This place is dirty, there are too many barking dogs, and I can't stand all the cigarette smoke."

"What did you expect, Mom? Now there are double the people and double the dogs living here. At least you have the back bedroom with your TV, and you can close the door."

And Dad finally had been released from that geriatric evaluation program and insisted on sleeping in the living room recliner with the TV on all night long.

It was around this time that Mom made her decision to die. I'm certain now that it was her frame of reference from that point forward.

My brother and sister-in-law had reconciled once more, and Paula was back in the house. One day, Paula took Mom for a doctor's appointment when she was complaining about leg pain. The doctor agreed to admit her to the hospital to check on a possible blood clot in her leg. Mom never walked again.

Physical therapy sessions were recommended, so she was moved to a nursing home. She refused to participate in most of those therapy sessions, became dehydrated, and was readmitted to the hospital once again. Then she was sent to another nursing home for more physical therapy that didn't work out. Once more she was hospitalized, and eventually was herself admitted to the geriatric/psychiatric unit for evaluation.

While all this was taking place, I contacted some of the nurses from the past, names that I knew from her years at Euclid General, trying to find someone who could perhaps talk some sense into her, but to no avail.

Mom was where she needed to be. She was still considered legally competent though, and was making decisions. The situation was ludicrous. The issue of legal competency had never been explored. Mom's doctors never brought it up, and what was the point now? I knew from my days working as a legal secretary that competency was a complex issue and obtaining a guardianship was extremely difficult. Social workers, doctors and hospital personnel continued to ask Mom what her wishes were. It was pretty clear to me. Mom had given up and this was going to be her exit strategy.

Paula kept waiting for Mom to experience a lucid moment so

that she could snag a witness from the nurses' station to get Mom's signature on a health care power of attorney and a living will. Paula kept dragging around the documents in her tote bag. For all of Mom's medical experience and awareness, she never had executed these basic documents. She was still in control.

Hospital personnel were raising questions about inserting a feeding tube because Mom had stopped eating. We all tried to coax her to take a swallow or a bite of anything...but a swallow was not going to do much to help Mom. At one point, she insisted that she wanted a feeding tube inserted, and when they were ready to roll her into the operating room, she announced that she had changed her mind and everything screeched to a halt.

One day, in an attempt to confront her with some harsh reality, I took on a tough approach and demanded, "What *are* your funeral plans? Since you're not doing a thing to help yourself, I need to know what you want done when you die."

She kept her eyes closed tight and whispered, "Just leave me alone."

When her doctors could do nothing more, Mom was moved to a room where she could simply wait to die. Amazingly, she was gone within a few hours while Paula and I sat beside her bed, trying to figure out a schedule so that one of us could remain at her bedside. Paula and I sat together, whispering, when Mom, propped up on pillows, took one last breath and died.

Mom had accomplished what she set out to do and she had done it in less than three months. Her cause of death was listed as "extreme depression and failure to thrive." It didn't have to happen.

And though she's not really ill, there's a little yellow pill...she goes running for the shelter of a mother's little helper...and it helps her on her way, gets her through her busy day...

Remember that song by the Stones? *Mother's Little Helper?* For

Mom, and many other women like her in the sixties, it was just that.

Some army doc on Okinawa had prescribed Valium for Mom. She began taking it whenever she needed it. The problem was, she needed it for the next fifty years.

Mom always had a little yellow pill nearby to get her through the day. She developed a serious dependency on that drug. And I'm even more convinced now that when each of her doctors realized how long she had been taking it, they backed off and decided that withdrawal was not a viable option. Mom always had a Valium at hand.

You probably could say that Mom was one of those people who always saw the glass as "half empty" and had a negative outlook on life. Now I understand that her use of Valium probably had something to do with her failed ability to remember things.

Whenever something from the past was brought up, Mom never failed to respond, "I don't remember. When did that happen? Are you sure?"

Julia recalled the time when we all spent a weekend at Yaka Beach. She and Bay, and Mom and Dad were all sitting around after a wonderful cookout when out of the blue, my mother sighed deeply and said, "I'm sooooo bored."

Julia told me, "Honey, I just remember your mother always saying things like that. It didn't seem like she enjoyed being there. She used to say how she was so bored and then exclaim 'Oh *my* God!'"

I'm convinced it was just Mom's way of filling "dead" time during conversations. Many of us do that. Awkward silences obviously bothered both of my parents. I told Julia that she should have been around Dad in the evenings, while we kids were lying on the floor in our pajamas, watching TV. Out of nowhere, Dad would be sitting in his recliner, smoking a cigarette, and he would sigh deeply and exclaim to no one in particular, "Oh, shit."

That was Dad's way of filling uncomfortable silences. Army guys were always swearing. Cussing was as natural as breathing to my father.

I like to think Dad was simply perfecting his comedic timing.

Flubber

Everything comes down to teeth in our family. Trust me.

I remember how my brothers and I liked to go to the dental lab with Dad. Sometimes he went back to the lab after supper, to take ceramic cases out of the small ovens. Mom was usually working second-shift at the hospital, and we kids were fascinated with the idea of a laboratory where Dad had his own key. The place was dark, and even when Dad turned on all of the fluorescent lights, the lab still seemed like a place of mystery. Worn linoleum floors were waxed to a high gloss. There were tall work stools in front of even taller metal-edged counters. Set into the tops of the counters were miniature sinks with curved faucets. Sharp and dangerous-looking, strange tools and drills lay about, with rubber mixing bowls, and, of course, mysterious containers of "flubber."

After warning us "not to touch a damn thing, or he'd slap the shit out of us," Dad would let us have little globs of pink acrylic to play with, a substance that he inventively referred to as "flubber." (The hot Disney movie at the time was *The Absent-Minded Professor*. Dad wasn't *that* original.)

"Flubber" was the acrylic compound used to make the gums for dentures. Before it hardened, flubber was soft and rubbery and we rolled it around in our palms. Flubber had a strong chemical odor to it that I'll never ever forget.

We were the only people in the lab while Dad put things in order. There were plaster models of false teeth that were held together with giant clamps. There were cabinets with pullout drawers that held rows of "fake teeth" lined up for selection. These were in various shades that were matched to each patient's teeth. Dad said you had to pick the right shade so it would appear natural. We climbed onto the high work stools to watch what Dad was up to. As long as we didn't touch anything, we were free to explore the place. That was no fun. Exploring without touching!

Inevitably, one of us kids needed to use the latrine—and the stalls that divided the latrines had no doors on them. You just sat right down on the toilet and could look around the bathroom. I knew then that I would never, ever join the army: there was absolutely no privacy.

Dad must have been pretty good at what he did. It amazes me now to think that he found a career in the military. He found a trade that he could make a living at after he retired from the army.

Dad made his own teeth—and wore them until the day he died. Not many people can claim that. And they must have been the best-fitting teeth ever—because Dad made them.

"Soaking dentures overnight is for sissies," Dad always used to say. "When your dentures fit, you just keep them in." He never took his teeth out except to clean them, and he never, ever, soaked them in a glass overnight.

I remember standing by the bathroom sink as a kid, watching with fascination as Dad slid his teeth out of his mouth, scrubbed them vigorously with a regular toothbrush and toothpaste, rinsed them off and then shoved them back into his mouth. I didn't understand then that simple suction kept them in place. I thought it was magic.

I often wondered how it was decided that Dad should train in the army's dental detachment as a lab technician. Was there some kind of an aptitude test? Who decided that Dad had a special talent for making teeth?

Many years later, I learned from Dad's sister Mary that he was in an accident at the age of fifteen—he crashed a home-made scooter called a "scrambola" that you pedaled with one foot—and ended up knocking out all of his front teeth.

"He was a bloody mess when his friends brought him home. Grandma always had to patch up her boys," said Mary. "She took Joe off to a dentist who suggested just pulling the rest of the teeth and getting an upper plate. So your father began wearing false teeth when he was just a teenager."

All my teeth got pulled when I was around five years old.

It's a story that was told so many times, that it must be true. I'll never solve the mystery about *why* my teeth were pulled. Through the years, when family folklore turned to the time when I was in the hospital and got "knocked out" to have my teeth extracted, and we would get to the part where I would inevitably ask "why?" Dad would just growl, "Because they were rotten."

How could my teeth have become rotten? Who was raising me? We were living on an army base in Germany—not in the hills of Appalachia! I'm sure I couldn't have been drinking Mountain Dew. How did I survive my early childhood? I never got any real answers when I asked questions. We always knew when not to ask any more questions from the look on Dad's face.

The first time I mentioned this to my husband, Don looked at me in disbelief and said, "I always figured your family was pretty strange, but that's unbelievable."

And when I filled him in on the rest of the story, he claimed that it was "bordering on negligence."

Obviously there wasn't a strong emphasis on preventive dental care back then. Apparently no one thought kids really needed to brush their baby teeth. They weren't going to last. They were going to fall out. Maybe that's why my teeth must have rotted by the age of five.

I know I didn't dream this. I know I didn't make this up. Family folklore proves it to be true. Through the years, when I heard Mom list my medical background, she would always start with the total tooth extraction at age five and then move on to the appendectomy. When I was old enough to provide a doctor with my own medical history, I dropped the tooth extraction and started with the appendectomy. After all, the scar was there to prove the appendectomy. My teeth had all grown back.

While I was in the hospital getting my teeth yanked, baby brother Danny was born in the same hospital, on the other side of a courtyard that linked the buildings. I've been told that Mom and I were waving to one another as she held up my new baby brother, to the hospital window—across that courtyard.

A new baby brother was not something I had asked for. I already had one other brother, Raymond. More important to me, I had missed the Easter Bunny while in the hospital. Family folklore continues with Dad constantly re-telling the story about how, soon after he brought me home from the hospital, he discovered me toothlessly "gumming" the chocolate bunnies waiting in my Easter basket. I guess maybe it was my fondness for sweets that contributed to the demise of my baby teeth.

Anyway, back to the amazing tale of my lost teeth. When my permanent teeth were starting to emerge, someone must have suggested using a toothbrush.

The new teeth were coming in crooked though, and I was seeing an army orthodontist. I remember having a few front teeth, with some missing on each side and a couple of back molars.

I wasn't in danger of starving. I could gnaw.

We were home from Germany and living in Washington State. Dad was making dentures at the Fort Lewis Dental Lab, so he made me a kid-sized partial plate—with two teeth on each side—enough to fill in the gaps on either side of my front teeth. Suddenly I had a mouthful of teeth! I could smile!

I proudly showed off my new smile in Miss Reid's second grade class at Park Avenue Elementary School. Removing my child-sized upper plate, I would hold it out and let everyone take a good look at it, and then shove it back in my mouth! I wonder how many second-graders remember the girl with the false teeth! I certainly was not invisible in second grade. I was a second-grade celebrity.

No teeth was strike one for me. Strike two was wearing glasses—rose-colored glasses in plaid frames!

I got my very first pair of glasses back when I was in first grade. Someone at Park Avenue Elementary School apparently waved an eye chart in front of me to determine that I was visually-challenged. I was moved to the front of the classroom and my parents were called.

I remember being sensitive to bright lights and the doctor suggesting tinted lenses. I wore pinkish-tinted lenses all the way through high school. And Mom picked out my first frames since I couldn't see anything. Mom was definitely into her "plaid phase" back then, sewing and matching plaids for skirts and jumpers. That's how I ended up with a pair of plaid frames! They clearly matched my little plaid school dresses with the tie backs.

Dad gave my brothers "buzz-cuts" and Mom was trimming my hair in a "Buster Brown" style. To save time, and not have to trim my bangs too often, she liked to cut them to a length of about two inches, showing off most of my forehead. Real cute.

Let's just say that my popularity certainly must have peaked in second grade. I proudly showed off those glasses with a toothless closed-mouth smile in the back yard of our house in Tacoma, Washington. I have the picture to prove it.

SOS

Just mention "SOS" to any military man and it will bring what Dad calls a "shit-eating grin" to his face. I've seen it happen.

Dad cooked a lot of suppers for us kids when Mom worked evenings at the hospital. His specialty was "SOS"—a pasty mess of ground beef, a can of Carnation evaporated milk and flour—blended into just the right consistency to ladle onto toast. We sprinkled it with salt and pepper—and shoveled it in quick, because if "SOS" wasn't consumed immediately, it cooled down and congealed. We kids loved Dad's "SOS" and he made it for us only when Mom was at work—because she couldn't stand it.

It did resemble something that had been eaten once already. Mom couldn't have been the only one who saw it that way.

"SOS" was standard army slang for "shit on a shingle." I even found a recipe—the way Dad cooked it—and from what I can recall, Dad didn't even pour off the grease from the browned hamburger. It added something to the overall consistency. I can still picture Dad standing over the stove with a cigarette dangling from his mouth, wearing his white undershirt…looking like he should be slinging SOS in some roadside diner along Route 66.

Actually, Dad wasn't a bad cook as far as we kids were concerned.

Fried foods were the norm and salt and ketchup made anything tasty. I remember our favorite meal—when Dad would peel potatoes and we kids took turns pushing each potato through the french fry cutter with the red wooden handle. Then Dad would drop those long strips of raw potato into a pot of hot bubbling Crisco. Sometimes that was all we ate for supper—an entire plate full of hot salty french fries that would literally melt in our mouths! What a pleasant pile of pure artery-clogging fat!

Another signature creation of Dad's was his "fluffer-nutter" sandwich—marshmallow fluff and peanut butter. We thought Dad invented that sandwich!

We never did figure out the origin of "stew-gats and sauerkraut," but every time we asked, "What's for supper?" that's the answer we got from Dad. Translation: "Don't ask stupid questions."

Nothing irritated Dad more than when we kids would get the giggles at the dinner table. It didn't take much. Ray would just look at Danny. And then Danny would look at me. Then we would all giggle over nothing. It would set us off. As far as Dad was concerned, laughing was not allowed. Silence was all he wanted.

He would bark, "Wipe those shit-eating grins off your faces." That only made us grin more because we all knew that Dad's threats meant nothing and he rarely hit us. And the more we tried not to laugh, the more we did. He wanted peace and quiet at the dinner table. No talking. No laughing. No eyeballing each other!

When we lived on Okinawa, my job was to mix milk each evening. The milk that was sold in the commissary came in large plastic bags that were packed inside cardboard boxes. There was a little spigot on the outside of the box so that you could dispense the milk. But it had a strange taste that you had to get used to. We didn't like it—or maybe my parents were just being thrifty.

We bought large boxes of Carnation Instant powdered milk that I mixed up in plastic pitchers. It tasted best when it was icy cold.

So my task every night before going to bed was to mix two pitchers of instant milk so that it would be cold and ready to drink in the morning. I hated mixing milk.

Not everything we had for dinner was wonderful. For some reason, Mom and Dad both loved fried liver and onions! The smell was nauseating. All I know is that we three kids didn't appreciate it and employed some creative disposal techniques. We were supposed to eat what was on our plate. Fortunately, one or more of the family dogs was waiting beneath the table, eager to gulp down whatever feral food we could sneak off our plates.

After we had been fed and the dishes were done, Dad sometimes performed one of his inspection procedures—though it was more like a ritual.

He would layer the kitchen table with newspapers, pop open a beer, light up a Raleigh and set to work with cans of Parade Gloss Kiwi Shoe Polish, cotton balls and brushes. I can still remember the strong smell of shoe polish.

I just don't get the "spit" part though. What was that all about anyway? How could Parade Gloss Kiwi and some plain old spit, put such a high-gloss shine on someone's shoes?

One thing I knew was that inspections were very important.

Dad took each shoe in hand and spent a lot of time creating that high-gloss shine. With a cigarette dangling from his lips and appearing to be lost in thought, he spent the entire evening on his shoes. I wonder what Dad thought about.

We three kids were sprawled across the living room floor, with our floor-pillows, watching TV. Mom was working second-shift.

Dad devoted an entire evening to his shoes. Another evening was for brass—more newspapers, a can of Brasso and a "Blitz-Cloth" rounded out that procedure.

All these years later, it seems so silly to me now, but military inspections were of the utmost importance. Dad's preparation must have paid off, because I never heard him complain once about not "passing."

The best thing about smoking all those Raleighs through the years was the coupons. Each pack came with one coupon on the back, and every carton had four bonus coupons tucked inside. Dad shoved all the coupons into a small white baby-shoe box; when the box was full, he spent another evening at the kitchen table, counting out coupons and rubber-banding them into packets of one hundred.

When he had enough coupons to redeem, he'd pack them up in a box and mail them off to the redemption center. We kids liked to page through the catalog to pick out interesting items, like a microscope or a badminton set; but it always ended up being small appliances that Dad sent away for—not what we wanted. A new can-opener or toaster for the kitchen would arrive in the mail. A lifelong smoker, my father eventually switched from unfiltered to filtered Raleighs. And finally, in a concession to healthier smoking, he switched to Belair Menthols. They were advertised as "the light menthol cigarette that gives you true tobacco taste." And of course, he still got to collect coupons because they were manufactured by Brown & Williamson Tobacco.

Army Slang

"Your ass is grass! What in the hell did I tell you? Are you listening? You got your head up your ass?"

Just Dad...yelling at one of my brothers from the back window of one of our houses someplace...somewhere. We were raised on my father's swear-words. Dad was the "king of the cussers" and we kids grew up with some rather creative swearing that was unique to the military. We weren't allowed to swear—only adults could do that. I remember something about little brother Danny, and Mom, and Lifebuoy soap. You get the picture.

I crack up now, thinking of some of Dad's more colorful expressions—"shitting bricks" and "going ape-shit" were among those I heard often. Dad was always grumbling about something... and his grumbling included a lot of swearing.

Army guys swore a lot. At least I figured they all did—especially when they hung out together. I looked at it this way: if you spent an entire day cussing and swearing with your buddies, how could you stop when you walked in the door of your quarters?

Whenever Dad met up with someone, I would hear, "You shittin' me?" Other times I would hear him say, "No shit, Sherlock!" in exclamation and disbelief as a story unfolded. As far as I was concerned, it took absolutely no imagination or vocabulary to come up with the word "shit" in all forms—noun, verb, adjective, adverb, etc.

I listened to Dad's constant cussing and thought about the swear words—and took them literally when I was younger. I could pretty much picture an ape shitting or even a bull…but when it came to a "shit-eating grin" that one really puzzled me. And how could anyone possibly have his head up his ass?

Shit was dad's most frequently-used word. It was so overused that it didn't have any meaning. It was just background noise. Now "fuck" was totally different. Somehow we kids knew that that was the worst word ever. When Dad used that word, Mom got really mad at him. But he still used it.

I tuned out most of Dad's racial epithets and amazing expletives. In my mind, they weren't words. They were asterisks and ampersands.

When Dad called us a "bunch of *Weisenheimers*" it was like a term of endearment. And it sounded more exotic than just calling us "smart-alecks."

And when Dad wanted us to get a move-on, he said, "*cuta-chogie.*" We had no idea what it meant. We just knew what to do when he said it. (According to *War Slang, Second Edition*, the term dates back to the Korean War and means "to fall out" or "break ranks.")

When he got mad at someone's stupidity, he would suddenly blurt out, "He doesn't know shit from Shinola!"

Dad had his own language, and we understood it perfectly.

Dad was much better at being a grandfather than he was at being a father. He cleaned up his act and had more time to spend with a little boy then.

One day, Paul came running up to me with a wide, toothy grin on his face.

"Do you know what this is?" he grinned. "Papa said this is my 'shit-eating grin.'"

My father just stood in the background, laughing. I reminded him that he was supposed to clean up his act. I was never going to change him.

Dad nicknamed his only grandson "Porky" and proved to be pretty patient, letting Porky "monkey around" in the garage and workshop, pretending to let him help fix things.

Dad would come over to our house to watch cartoons with Paul, and after a while, he would just be sitting there in the recliner, lost in thought, and suddenly let out a deep sigh and say, "Oh, shit."

That's my dad.

So when I trip over something around the house, or stub my toe?

I just hop around and say, "Shit, shit, fuck, fuck. Shitty shitty, fuck fuck." I'm not as talented as Dad, but swearing really does seem to make it all feel better.

Last Days

I stared down at the Newfoundland snuffling its head into my crotch while I sat on the sofa at my brother's house.

"This is why I wore yesterday's pants over here today—and this old turtleneck," I mumbled to myself.

I could never wear any decent clothes over to Dan's house. "Considerate" dog-owners, Dan kept the big dogs out in the back yard until I came in through the garage, through the laundry room, through the kitchen and made it into the living room. The little dogs—Emma the Chihuahua and Sadie the dachshund—would squeal and jump all over me, and then Jerry, the Springer spaniel and Bailey, the Newfoundland, would charge in from the back yard. I was their target and they made a beeline for me.

It was always a smart move to stand up quick when the big dogs came running in because they went right for my face. By standing, I avoided that face-licking, and they could only place their damp paws against me. Eventually, they would settle down and just try to crawl into my lap—or like tonight, snuffle into my crotch.

A devoted dog-lover, my brother Dan would come home from work and immediately lie down on the living room floor, while the herd of dogs greeted him with a total face-licking. I never quite understood the need to get that intimate with dogs—after all, they licked their butts and several dogs in our family had a documented history of "pooh-eating."

I was here to "Dad-sit" because Dan and his new wife were headed downtown to the Rock And Roll Hall of Fame for "Guitar God" Ted Nugent's big concert. Dan's band, "Burnt River" was opening for Nugent, and they wanted to stay for the show after "Burnt River" played. They needed to get away for a while, so I offered to stay with Dad. I was working on my story and this probably would be my last chance to get some information out of my father.

Except Dad wasn't talking.

It had been almost two years since Mom had died. Since then, Dad got to live peacefully with my brother, smoking countless cigarettes, drinking bottomless cups of instant coffee, clicking the TV remote and cussing at the dogs while they barked at every sound they heard.

So here we were, together in the same room, watching *All in the Family* on TV Land. This was my chance to get some answers, but how could I ask the questions? I never had been able to talk to Dad before, so what made me think I was going to do it now?

For one thing, Dad was deteriorating and could barely speak. When he did, it was with a grimace. He had to concentrate really hard to bark out a few words. I tried to ask a few questions, but he just turned his head and glared at me. I realized it was pointless. Nothing was important now and nothing was going to come out of this visit. We sat together in silence the rest of the evening, watching episodes of *All in the Family* and then *The Andy Griffith Show*, until Dad fell asleep, snoring lightly.

That was the last time I saw my father alive.

Bedridden in a hospital bed, with hospice nurses checking on him, one week later Dad finally took his last breath and simply died on a Saturday morning. Dan was at home with him. It had been coming for a long time and was no surprise. Dad's life was finally over.

Addicted

Right where he needed to be at the end of life, Dad shared common interests with his two sons: smoking, swearing and drinking. I had nothing in common with my father or my brothers. I don't even have a tattoo.

Clearly Dad was an alcoholic. A beer alcoholic. Somehow my father only got drunk while drinking beer. He was one of those "functional" alcoholics who would come home after stopping off for a few beers with his buddies, and continue drinking into the evening. I don't know how many cans of beer he consumed, because I was only a kid and so used to the sound of the opener…I was happy to fetch cans of Olympia and Hamms. I remember the TV commercials and jingles and would sing, "from the land of sky-blue waters," while I fetched cans of beer from the refrigerator. Dad kept his beer opener right by the chair.

Mom made Dad swear to consume only mixed drinks when they went to someone's wedding or a party and she didn't want him to make a fool of himself. Mom and Dad would have long talks before they went out for the evening. Mom didn't drink. She was always the sober one, the one who could be counted upon to drive home. And this was back when people drove often, while "buzzed."

It scares me to think how many times we were in the car with Dad when he must have been "buzzed."

Mom dreaded each visit to Oshkosh because as she said, "There's a bar on every corner, and your father makes a spectacle of himself up there!"

That pretty much was true.

Dad couldn't wait to visit his old buddies and hang out in his old haunts. We kids loved going to Oshkosh because Main Street was within walking distance from Grandma Kriha's house—and Menominee Park on Lake Winnebago was within walking distance in the other direction. It was so "small-town" that we loved visiting the relatives. Mom unfortunately had to try to keep Dad in line.

When drinking and driving became a social issue, Dad was charged with a DUI at least once that I can remember. He had a tendency to drive slow, real slow, when he'd been drinking. That only called attention to him. I remember going with Mom to pick up the car from the impound lot the next day. Dad had to appear in court and started attending Alcoholics Anonymous meetings. I don't know if it did him much good. Once he fulfilled his requirement, he stopped going.

Dad would sneak beers while out in the garage. He would deposit the empties in a space behind the workbench. Years later, when my parents moved from the house in Willowick, they all came clattering down from behind that bench. Dad's secret stash was uncovered, and we all had a good laugh about it.

My brothers followed the family tradition of alcoholism. They've been pulled over for drunk driving and have made their share of court appearances and served their time in jail.

Always "bailing out" my brothers for one thing or another became my parents' mission. The boys never really grew up. Once I moved out of the house and got my own apartment, I was removed from the daily drama of the brotherhood.

One day, Mom and Dad drove off to the groundbreaking of a new Veterans Cemetery in Rittman, Ohio. She read about it in *The Plain Dealer* and wanted that to be their final resting place. Mom told us kids that they were entitled to it because they were both veterans. And it was free. Mom said that they didn't want any funeral services. They just wanted to be cremated and their ashes taken to the cemetery.

After Mom's passing, I took an antique ginger jar urn over to Dan's house so that her ashes could be preserved in it. Dan and I talked about how all three of us kids would one day take our parents' ashes to the cemetery.

After Dad died of lung cancer and was cremated, I took another covered urn over—a large blue and white porcelain-lidded jar with the word *TOBACCO* lettered in blue across the front.

Only I could appreciate the irony. At least Mom and Dad were out of those crematorium containers.

The Mess Kit

I still have Dad's aluminum mess kit. It's one of the things I managed to save from being trashed when he and Mom first moved in with my brother. I don't know what got into Dad, but he just started filling a big black garbage bag with things from his closet! When I realized what he was doing, I rescued some of those items, including his certificate of retirement.

Military brats got to "play army" with real GI gear—stuff that was around the house. Ray and Danny wore helmets and ammo belts, drank water from canteens, and dug foxholes with Dad's folding shovel. It was pretty cool. My brothers spent their time after school digging trenches amidst the spiky green iceplant that served as ground cover on the sandy hills behind our quarters at Fort Ord. They played with those eight-inch green plastic soldiers, that every little boy had back then, making battlegrounds for them and at times even lighting them on fire to melt them down.

The sound effects my brothers made were pretty realistic. Simulated explosions, air attacks, gunnery fusillades, you get the idea. It included lots of screaming and yelling, expertly-improvised sounds that could come only from the mouths of little boys in backyard combat in the sixties. It continued until Mom dispatched me out into the battlefield to bring my brothers home for supper.

On a reconnaissance mission to get my brothers to come in for supper, I had to work my way through the dug-out foxholes and booby-traps and try to get them to hold their fire.

Yelling, *"Mach Schnell, Mach Schnell"* like they did on *Combat!*, I got their attention and told them that Mom had supper ready, but they pretty much ignored me. They usually came home only because they were getting hungry.

I didn't care about any of that army gear—except for the army-issue wool blanket. Years later, I snatched it to keep for my emergency car blanket. Mom had washed it and dried it often through the years. That olive-drab army wool was indestructible, and it is one thing that reminds me of my former brat life.

Dad used to value his old army gear, and when Paul was a teenager, he decided to give him some of the things he had stashed in his closet. Dad presented Paul with a sixteen-inch rifle bayonet with a scabbard. Not quite the thing for a teen-aged boy to have around. I was unaware of this gift until I heard Paul talking about it and showing it off to his friends.

I decided it was time for a Mom-intervention. It disappeared. I'm not saying where it went, but it's in a safe place of my choice. Paul still hasn't asked where his bayonet from Grampa is.

I certainly wasn't into playing "battle." Ray and Danny could dig around in the back yard in California all day long, but I stayed inside most of the time. The only time I hung out with my brothers was when we buried "treasure."

We would take plastic Corona cigar boxes that Grampa gave us and turn them into "time-capsules" by placing amazing artifacts that included toy cars, empty cigarette packs and Mom's old lipstick tubes. By including a newspaper page from that particular day in

1962 or 1963, we thought we were leaving our mark on the world. As we buried those cigar boxes, we were convinced that someday, someone would discover them, and wonder about the people who buried them.

Another PCS later, when we lived off-post on Okinawa, my brothers played in the hills right behind our house. One day they pushed the entrance stone away from the opening to a turtleback tomb—and went inside to explore. When Mom found out what they did, she was furious and told them never to go near the tombs again. She warned them that they were invading the private burial space of an Okinawan family. Actually, she probably told them that the ghosts in the tomb would haunt them forever. It worked well. You scared kids back then.

Hotei

"Why on earth would a good Catholic girl suddenly become infatuated with Buddha?"

I'm sure that's what Grandma must have wondered as she gazed down at the black-and-white snapshot that my mother mailed to her in Oregon. Letters crossed back and forth from the small Pacific island to Klamath Falls on a weekly basis.

We had just become comfortable exploring the shopping alleys off Highway One when Mom and I wandered into a little shop that specialized in wooden carvings. A *papasan* showed off the hand carved items displayed on the shelves. Smelling strongly of camphor and expertly-carved, the shelves contained standing Buddhas, sitting Buddhas, happy, dancing Buddhas and serious contemplative Buddhas, along with the seven lucky gods, fishermen with bamboo poles and tiny carved fish dangling from a nylon line. And to attract the American shoppers, carvings now included popular breeds of dogs. Mom simply had to have that teak dachshund to go along with Buddha.

Mom liked the sitting Buddha best, the one with the big round belly, the one that everyone called "*Hotei.*" It was carved from camphor wood and was about fifteen inches high. She probably paid only a few dollars for it back in 1964. *Papasan* wrapped it well and Mom carried it home like an armload of bundled baby.

In Buddhism, *Hotei* is one of the seven lucky gods and is based upon a real person. With his cheerful face and big belly, *Hotei* represents the god of contentment and happiness. Tradition has it that *Hotei* carries a large cloth bag, which never empties, from which he feeds the poor and needy. Well, at least Mom fell for a pleasant Buddha.

She didn't know any of this history back then. All Mom knew was that she liked the look of *Hotei* and when people came over to our house, it seemed that everyone talked about how rubbing his big round belly would bring you good luck.

I know Mom cringed every time someone brought up that Buddhist belief and approached her Buddha with their hand outstretched. She didn't want any scratches from people's rings on Buddha's big round belly!

Hotei had a place of honor upon a buffet in our dining room. I was still in charge of dusting and liked to sniff the camphor odor from the bottom when I picked up the heavy wooden piece. It was a strong pleasant scent that brings back memories.

We sent a heavily-carved camphor wood trunk to Grandma. I remember how Mom told everyone that it cost only thirty dollars back then. I have that trunk now and every time I raise the lid, I get a whiff of camphor. Many items were carved from teak wood and Mom fell for an intricately-carved trunk, as well as a bar that featured a raised lid, swing-out side doors to hold glasses and a drop-down front. It was magnificent. She gave it to a relative soon after we retired in Ohio. I wish it was still around.

With Mom now gone, we three kids divided the family artifacts. My brother Dan claimed *Hotei*. He has no specific taste in home décor, so my mother's happy *Hotei* now rests serenely on top of the microwave in his kitchen!

Closing Ceremony

We gathered in the hotel lobby to board the bus to take us to the closing ceremony of the Uchinanchu Festival. It was raining. Just a sprinkle, but nonetheless raining. Larry Number Two was concerned about the festivities that were scheduled for outdoors and whether rain would cancel some of the performances.

We collected our farewell gifts at the Convention Center, and received a *bingata*-cloth tote bag, with a gift pack of *awamori*, as well as festival posters—all three of the designs that we'd seen plastered around the island throughout the four-day event. We rolled them up carefully and tried not to crease them.

Julia and I serendipitously followed the crowd and wandered into the Convention Center Theater. The most amazing performance by the Ryukyu Symphony Orchestra was about to begin. Julia found a seat with Anna and Patti and the Colonel. I stood quietly in the back, leaning against a railing, training my video camera on the performance.

I had no idea that there was a Ryukyu Symphony Orchestra. Women wearing evening gowns in pastel shades, and men in tuxedos were playing instruments, and there was a massive *taiko* drum positioned at the back of the stage. I knew we were in for something big when that drum kicked in.

The 70-member orchestra played several light classical pieces, and then things happened.

The twang of three *sanshins*, the high, shrieking voices of accompaniment, and the soft, yet loud beat by the drummer against the *taiko*...and then primal frenzy...whistling and pounding as dancers took over the stage, moving up and down the aisles, waving flags and tambourines.

More shrieks, more *taiko*, wild *shisa* shaking their heads back and forth, moving down into the aisles. In no time dancers were pulling people from their seats up to the stage. More *taiko*.

I was glad that I was standing at the back of the theater, positioned against the wall. With those dancers grabbing people out of their seats, I was safe. A "happening" was under way.

Somehow, Julia and I had wandered into the best part of the closing ceremony.

As we filed out of the Convention Center Theater, into the Event Hall for the Closing Ceremony, people gathered along the walkway. Soon Julia and I found ourselves clasping hands and greeting people we'd never ever met before in our lives. Many of them were just kids. It was wonderful. Everyone was caught up in the spirit of "*uchinanchu*." We *were* all friends.

After more performances and more speeches, the crowd moved behind the convention center where an outdoor stage was ready for performers. Byron Jones was playing the sanshin and Julia stood with the crowd in front of the stage, while I headed over to the food tents to try to find something to eat—we were starving! I can't even remember what I found. Vendors were running out of food and the lines were long. I brought something back to the table for Julia and me. I don't think I found anything at all for us to drink.

The Colonel leaned over to see what we had to eat, approved of it, and whispered, "Fried tofu! That's what Patti got for us."

Clearly, he wanted what we had.

We all nodded and began to laugh.

As the performances drew to a close, people began to pack up their belongings and we all walked to the parking area where we boarded a bus back to the hotel.

The festival had ended.

Drawing Down

We joined Patti and the Colonel for dinner at the Plaza House Restaurant, in the shopping center with the same name, where Tuttle's Book Store was located. The menu featured Chinese cuisine so we ordered several dishes—and shared. Julia remembered how dinner at this restaurant was such a treat, when she and Bay and the kids would dine out "on the economy."

A Hong Kong businessman opened the Plaza House department store in 1954. And it was still in the same location. Alongside the Plaza House was Roger's Store for Men, and Tuttle's Book Store.

Eighty-eight years old and charming, Retired Lt. Colonel Roderick T. French was a sparkling conversationalist and quite the old-fashioned gentleman. We compared notes about what we'd seen and done in the last ten days. Colonel French managed to get in a few rounds of golf at the Awase Golf Course. Local media interviewed him about his connection to the design and construction of the golf course right after the war, when American occupation started.

Julia and the Colonel talked about their failed attempts to stop their snoring with the same spray product, something they called

"Snore-No-More" and both came to the same conclusion: Nothing really works.

Patti and I agreed.

I stood by my tried-and-true method and said, "When it gets too bad, I just shake Julia by the shoulder and roll her over toward the Pacific Ocean."

We got to talking about shopping, and Julia described the little porcelain dish that she had carried across the ocean as a sample of what she was searching for. Julia told how she saw a set of exquisite dinnerware with grains of rice "baked" into the porcelain when they lived here, back in the sixties. They were made by Noritake and way beyond the family budget. When "fired," the grains of rice disappeared, leaving behind tiny transparent openings beneath the glaze.

The Colonel knew just what we were talking about and described a large dinner service of platinum-edged rice china back home in Illinois. By Noritake!

I could read Julia's mind. She was already thinking about making him an offer he couldn't refuse. She *did* have his e-mail address, phone number and she knew where he lived. But would Mrs. French ever part with her dishes? Probably *not*. What are you thinking, Julia?

She had carried that little rice china bowl around in her purse, because we fully expected to wander into numerous little shops, show the bowl to the proprietor, and somehow put together an entire set of dishes like she remembered. Another thing that didn't happen.

We shared a taxi back to the hotel. Julia and I picked our way through piles of luggage and sports equipment scattered all over the lobby. The Dai-Ichi had just been invaded with hundreds of Japanese teenagers, unloading all their gear for some type of big tournament.

Patti affectionately called her octogenarian father a "geezer-geek."

It was appropriate, because he was off to the second-floor computer area, to check his e-mail.

The Colonel was busy talking with a Japanese teenager who was showing off his digital camera and demonstrating how he uploaded his photos to the web. Later we learned that the boy took a photo of "Geezer-Geek" and added it to his site. "Geezer-Geek" was now famous somewhere in cyber-space among an elite circle of Japanese teenagers.

Back in our room, we continued to sort and pack. Things were winding down quickly, and I had to figure out how to transport all my treasures home. Julia was the smart one and brought two large rolling suitcases. I brought two medium cases. They rolled, but could spontaneously erupt when stuffed. I planned to mail a package home to myself, but I could see now that it was going to be more like two—possibly three. KC gave me some Priority Mail boxes and a roll of packing tape from her supply, so I was busy trying to tape up boxes while Julia hit the shower. The only scissors I had with me were cuticle scissors—rather slow going, but it was better than using my teeth.

The most difficult item to pack was my faux snakeskin *sanshin*, so I made a larger box out of two regular-sized priority boxes and wrapped a lot of dirty laundry around the *sanshin*. I stacked three boxes by the door, ready for tomorrow's Camp Foster Post Office run.

The phone rang and it was Patti, offering us an unused phone card in case we wanted to phone home. Sure!

Julia was already wearing her robe, but that didn't bother her. Who cared? We headed down to the alcove by the elevator, where the telephones were located. Finally! We got to use those bright green pay phones that I thought were so unique!

Julia's son Jim was celebrating his birthday back in South Carolina.

She wanted to surprise him with a call and I decided to phone Don at his office. It was approximately nine p.m. on Okinawa and at the other end of the line in the States, it was yesterday morning!

All we needed to do was to key in 88, the country code 010 for the United States, the phone number, and then enter the 14-digit card number. Somewhere in that procedure, we used the # key, which in Japan is quaintly referred to as the "sharp" key. I liked that so much better than calling it the "pound" key.

We could handle it. The directions were simple. We wrote them all down and then tried at least five times to make it happen. A recorded message in both Japanese and English told us five times that our call could not be completed because the phone card was not valid.

We took turns trying to complete those calls because we just could not possibly be so incompetent that we couldn't follow simple directions!

After about thirty minutes of trying to figure out how to work that damn green phone, we concluded that Jim would just have to enjoy his birthday without an overseas phone call from Mom, and that Don didn't really need to know what we were up to after all.

Admitting defeat—and mumbling to ourselves, we finally knocked on Patti's door and explained to her that we were having a problem with the card. I'm sure she figured we were incompetent, because she accompanied us downstairs to place the call for us! She had no success. Vindicated, we were pleased that we were not idiots after all! There really was something wrong with the activation code.

After breakfast on our last day on Okinawa, Julia and I hitched a ride to Camp Foster with Larry Kelly, who had rented a car for the day. He was positively thrilled to be driving around his island—on the "wrong damn side of the road." We were not as thrilled, but Larry insisted on driving us. Some of those turns were scary, especially when approaching them from the left side of the road and with Larry behind the wheel.

Full of stories about his high school years on Okinawa, he talked about all the girls he dated when he was a teenager. He really seemed to be stuck in the past.

Later, I told Julia about how many celebrities had origins as military brats and that one celebrity with a tie to Kubasaki was Victoria Principal.

"Well, if Larry had dated *her*, we would have all heard all about it by now!" exclaimed Julia.

Using KC's return address, I mailed my packages home, and then we walked over to the PX for our last military shopping experience. Shopping in the PX now was like wandering through a Target store or Kohl's—nothing like the sixties when I can remember rushing to buy whatever hot item showed up on the shelves.

I remembered a small area of the PX where I bought my first record album—*The Beatles Second Album*. The first one, *Meet the Beatles*, didn't come in until a few months later, when it finally arrived by a slow ship. When you bought an album back then, the clerk would slit it open, inspect the LP for damage or warping, and then stamp the cover with a "PAID—Ryukyus Exchange" rubber stamp before you could carry it away.

In sharp contrast, the Camp Foster PX was huge, stocked with Estee Lauder cosmetics and top-name designer perfumes, Dooney & Bourke handbags, fine jewelry, trendy clothing and an enormous electronics department. The latest hardcover books were on display, as well as the latest CDs and DVDs.

"There were never clothes like this to choose from," I remarked. "I was so excited to find one of those ribbed knit body-hugging "poor boy" tops that were popular back then. Color wasn't important. You bought what showed up and were thrilled to have it."

Mom relied on Grandma and the Sears catalog back then. Grandma mailed packages with husky-sized jeans for Danny because Mom could never find pants to fit him.

When Mom wrote Grandma to tell her how most of the cookies and crackers that we found in the commissary were stale by the time they arrived on Okinawa, she arranged for shipments of cookies to be mailed to us from a specialty store in Portland. Now I realize how special those cookies were—fine English biscuits packed in decorated tins. She probably spent a small fortune arranging to have those biscuit tins mailed to us. They arrived fresh, and we wolfed them down. We should have taken time to savor them. I still have one large square tin—dented and with a bit of rust on it—from Peek-Frean & Co. Along the side, it says "By Appointment to Her Majesty the Queen, Biscuit Manufacturers." It now contains my leftover scraps of *bunka* embroidery thread.

Julia and I decided to take a break and split one of those huge Cinn-A-Bon rolls over coffee—which Julia managed to spill all over our table—while deciding what to do next with our final hours.

We decided to go back to Oyama for one more attempt to find my old house. We hailed a cab and hopped out by Frank's Toys and Jiro's Bakery. The toy store was a disappointment—with toy models in dusty old boxes upon the shelves. It wasn't the toy store I remembered, with brightly-colored Japanese toys, dolls and stuffed animals. But Jiro's Bakery was still a bakery. For old times' sake, Julia and I bought small loaves of bread and cookies! How silly! Could we even bring baked goods back with us? Or would we have to shove bread and cookies into our mouths, while standing in front of a scowling airport security guard?

Julia and I continued on foot, heading down the familiar hill, pausing to take photographs and shoot video. At the intersection of old Highway One at the bottom of the hill was the only real landmark left from memory—a small building that looked like some type of roadside shrine. I remembered staring at it from the back seat of our old Plymouth every time Dad drove up the hill toward Fort Buckner.

We crossed the street and once again wandered through the alleys and streets of Oyama. There were so many dead ends and private driveways. We walked and walked, and then it started to drizzle. I was sure Julia's feet were hurting. We had to give up. It really wasn't going to happen. We returned to the main highway and hailed a cab back to the hotel. It was time to go home.

Over breakfast on our final morning, we determined which airport shuttle we were going to take for the flight to Osaka. One final entry into the "bottom-of-our-closet-safe" for our plane tickets home—and it wouldn't open! Julia was sprawled on the floor in a panic!

One phone call down to the front desk and a hotel employee came up, used a master key and simply opened our safe. So much for security—good thing we kept our rare jewels in our bras!

Despite the "no-tipping" policy in Japan, we left some *yen* for our maids as a tip and gathered up all of our belongings. We looked out upon our island and the Pacific Ocean from the ninth-floor balcony and still found being there on Okinawa pretty astounding. Now it was time to go home.

The Naha International Airport was so modern—we located our gate and deposited our carry-on bags with the Kellys while I went to shoot more video of an upscale Duty-Free Shop featuring Gucci, Chanel and Estee Lauder. I waited in line at Starbucks and snagged a menu in Japanese, as well as an Okinawa Starbucks commuter mug for souvenirs. We boarded our plane to Osaka and were all deep in thought. I looked over at Julia and she had her eyes closed.

I wondered what she was thinking. We were all pretty quiet on this flight.

It was when we got to the Osaka Kansai Airport that Julia stirred up trouble. She insisted that the little *shisa* dog cigarette lighter that she had bought for her son Gary was something that she could not give up!

She was getting feisty and people were starting to look our way—toward the source of the raised voices. Julia packed the lighter in her carry-on bag and of course, airport security considered it potentially dangerous. She tried to explain that it had no fluid in it and that it was just a gift. Finally, the matter was resolved when she agreed to pack it in her checked luggage.

"I was ready to cause an incident," she whispered. "I am bringing that lighter home for Gary."

I know. I know. And now my final purchase from the Okinawa Starbucks was causing concern among security personnel—a simple plastic commuter cup that was empty and inside a Starbucks gift bag—was definitely raising red flags about the "no liquids" rule. Finally, a consensus among security personnel determined that it was indeed empty and could be allowed on the airplane! I felt much safer.

While waiting to board our flight, we wandered into the little shops at the Osaka Kansai Airport where I spent my last few *yen* on Japanese crackers and *origami* paper! I must have mentioned that I wanted to fill a large glass vase with colorful cranes, because Anna offered to make them for me, to keep busy on the flight home, so I bought several packages of *origami* paper.

This flight was much more comfortable. Somehow Julia and I ended up sitting in the very first row in the middle section. We had leg room—and a seat between us for our clutter! And this time, we were winding down and didn't have as much to talk about.

We were quiet. We tuned out and tuned in to a movie—something unremarkable that I can't even remember now. Both Julia and I were finally relaxed and this time we managed to doze off.

Our adventure was wrapping up. We accomplished a lot, but the things we thought we would do, didn't happen. Nothing would sever our ties to Okinawa. We were tied to that island and our shared experience forever.

When we landed in Chicago, Anna gave me a plastic bag full of origami cranes. I did fill a huge glass vase with them when I got home.

When we finally made it through the customs area in Chicago, Julia and I went our separate ways—me back to Cleveland and Julia heading off to Columbia, South Carolina.

But before I headed to my terminal, I bumped into Betty Kelly. She said she was looking for a place to check something that security wouldn't let her carry onto the flight to Washington. I wondered what that was all about.

The trip of our lifetime was over. Getting there and back had been exhausting. My husband collected me in Cleveland at the airport—waiting for my luggage at the wrong baggage carousel—and dragged me home. I had regained my memories from the past—and now I had so many new experiences to add to my story. I was determined to preserve them. Within a few days I began to write.

Back Where We Started

When we left Okinawa in February of 1967, it was a very different trip. Dad was leading us this time—and we had been ordered to make a PCS to Fort Campbell, Kentucky. Because my mother had claustrophobia and refused to travel in an airplane, the army made arrangements for surface travel to San Francisco. Someone arranged an itinerary from Naha to Kagoshima by ship, train to Yokohama and then passage was booked aboard the SS President Wilson from Yokohama to San Francisco. I still have the ticket for that voyage. It cost the army more than $4000 to put us on that liner, instead of on a navy transport ship.

Arrangements had been made to fly our dachshund to San Francisco where an old friend from Germany picked her up and cared for her in Pacific Grove until we could claim her.

Our other dog, Maggie the mutt, was given away, the Plymouth was sold, and our household goods were packed, and on their way to Kentucky.

At the end of February, we boarded a small Japanese ship—the Otomi maru—in Naha Port and marveled at the big smelly bulls tied outside on deck. We were on that little ship overnight. Our stateroom was quite small, with bunks and a breakfast-nook by a window. The voyage was rough and

Dad was the only one who wasn't seasick. We took the bunks and Dad sat up through the night by the window, smoking cigarettes and passing basins to us when we needed them.

There was a communal washroom down the hall and I can still remember Mom's shock when she brushed her teeth the next morning. A Japanese man walked in and washed up in the sink next to her!

She had a look of horror on her face, when she told us about it.

At least the toilets were private, but they were Japanese squat-style. If you wanted a Western-style toilet, there was a toilet seat hanging from a hook on the wall that you could place over the hole in the floor—something to squat upon!

When the Otomi maru finally docked in Kagoshima Bay, the southernmost port city of Kyushu, we made our way to a train station. I don't know how Dad managed all of this, but the next part of the trip involved a long train ride to Yokohama. That train took us through an underwater tunnel that connected the island of Kyushu to the main island of Honshu (definitely claustrophobic, Mom certainly must have been sleeping while the train made its way through that tunnel. Maybe Dad never let her know.)

Each time the train slowed down to enter a station, vendors approached the train, shouting "bento, bento" offering little wooden box lunches for purchase. All you had to do was lower the train window. Of course, we didn't buy any bento lunches. I do remember eating lots of tangerines and sandwiches while on the train—obviously safe selections purchased from the dining car.

While traveling through the Japanese countryside on our way to Yokohama, we did see the famous "bullet-train"—the shinkansen—pass by, several times in each direction. Traveling at speeds up to 210 km/hour or 131 mph, bullet train service started in 1964. The first train line was between Tokyo and Shin-Osaka. Those trains have been flying faster and faster—and now travel up to 186 mph along certain lines.

Arriving at the train station in Yokohama, Dad located two "sukoshi cabs" and because they were *sukoshi* Bluebirds, Dad got into one with all the suitcases as we squeezed into the other one. Those *sukoshi* cabs were also called *kamikaze-cabs* because of the way the drivers zipped in and out of traffic. We were supposed to stay the night in the Silk Hotel—a moderately-priced Western-style hotel located on the top floors of the Silk Building near the main passenger liner pier in Yokohama, but when we arrived, something went wrong with our reservation and all I can remember is that we needed to stay somewhere for the night and Mom and Dad didn't know what to do.

We went to the pier where the American President Lines' President Wilson was docked. Somehow Dad convinced someone to allow us to board the ship and spend the night there.

The SS President Wilson, part of the American President Lines fleet, was a 535-foot long luxury ocean liner that could carry up to 550 passengers with a crew of 352 on an ongoing Asia-Pacific route. The APL fleet was advertised as "your American hotel abroad."

The ship was built in 1948 and completed her final voyage in 1973 when she was renamed the Oriental Empress, and sold and operated under the Panamanian flag.

Sadly, when the wonderful era of passenger travel upon ocean liners faded, the President Wilson was sold for scrap and dismantled in 1984. I remember reading about her demise in the newspaper. Her sister ships lasted a bit longer and were retrofitted for freight.

Maybe this "hotel" would be big enough that we wouldn't get seasick. Dad kept reassuring us that really large ocean liners had stabilizers to keep the ship from pitching and rolling. It must have been true, because on this crossing we really didn't get sick. Another bonus: no bulls.

We were ticketed as "first-class" passengers and were shown to two staterooms—one with four berths for Mom, Dad, Ray and Danny—and another two-berth room adjacent to it. I was to share the two-berth-room with a Japanese lady named Miss Setsu Yoshida. She lived in Long

Beach, California and was traveling home from visiting her family in Yokohama.

I took the upper berth. Miss Yoshida didn't speak much English and I still didn't speak much Japanese. We were only in our stateroom to sleep. I spent most of the time with my family. We got along pretty well, considering our lack of communication.

When the President Wilson set sail from Yokohama on March 1, 1967—my mother's birthday—we stood outside on deck as passengers tossed rolls of colored paper streamers to those left behind on the dock. We didn't know anyone down on the dock, but had great fun tossing those paper streamers. Many people held onto the ends of the streamers until the ship pulled away and they stretched out, finally tearing apart, breaking the last link, and "severing the ties that bound them." That maritime tradition took place to the tune "Now Is The Hour," played by the ship's band, that traditional farewell song competing with several blasts of the ship's horn to announce departure from port.

Mom's birthday was the day we sailed and a day or so later, a cake decorated with candles was delivered to the stateroom. Someone in charge of things like that apparently caught up with the date of her birthday. It was a nice touch.

Sailing aboard the President Wilson was indeed luxurious, with two sittings for dinner—informal and formal. As a family, we attended the earlier sitting with other families and children. We sat at the same large round table with the same people. The second sitting was designated as "formal attire." Those guests dressed up and some dined with the ship's captain at his table.

There were shipboard activities, parties and entertainment, organized by a social director. I remember watching reruns of "The Gale Storm Show" back on Okinawa and I thought working on an ocean liner, like the character Susanna did, would be an exciting, glamorous job, full of fun and adventure. I would have needed a zany sidekick though to make it that much fun. ("Nugie" was to Susanna what Ethel was to Lucy.) I discovered recently that the 1950s TV series had been filmed aboard one of the sister ships belonging to the American President Lines. The fictional SS Ocean Queen was in fact, the APL's President Cleveland. "Oh! Susanna."

Each day at sea, a ship's newspaper and the day's menus were printed. Each menu listed our voyage and the date and location in the Pacific Ocean. One in particular, No. 146, stated "At Sea, En Route Honolulu, Hawaii, Monday, March 6, 1967" and on that evening the menu offered, "UNE SOIREE PARISIENNE."

There was quite an elaborate selection of appetizers, including Bouillabaise Marseillaise and Grenouilles Sautees Provencale (Frogs Legs), with entrees that included a breast of duckling and sautéed veal chops! Desserts included a Grand Marnier Souffle and an ever-popular "Plateau de Fromages" for those fond of cheese. I would eat it all now! But back then, those gourmet meals were wasted on us. We saved the decorative menus from the voyage, and as I look at them now, I can appreciate what I didn't select back then!

I remember when someone at our table discovered that items could be special-ordered "off-the-menu," the children at our table soon were enjoying peanut butter and jelly sandwiches—served with trimmed crusts and potato chips! The chef must have been horrified at what was taking place. Our Filipino waiter was a good sport and put up with all of us kids. He folded origami cranes out of dollar bills to keep us amused during the sittings.

And when the sea was rough, I remember how the crew wet down the tablecloths so that the plates and glasses would stick to the surface.

Food was plentiful and the waiters walked around the decks in the afternoon, carrying trays of exotic mango and papaya sherbet for treats.

There was even a kennel on board, and some passengers spent time walking their dogs on deck. There also was a swimming pool, tennis courts, and even a driving range. Shuffleboard grids were painted on the decks and there were teak deck chairs to rest in.

The thing that most impressed me, was that each night, passengers could place their shoes outside the door to their stateroom. Someone mysteriously took them away and shined them during the night and in the morning those shoes were back outside the door.

We never put our shoes outside our door.

There was a gift shop, a library, a barber shop, a beauty shop and even a ship's doctor. I remember taking bridge and galley tours. The President Wilson was indeed a luxury liner. There was nothing "battleship gray" about this ship, with its red, white and blue smokestacks and the APL white eagle logo painted along each side. How lucky could we get?

Artwork decorated the walls along the main staircase, with brass railings to hold onto. Crew members polished those railings early each morning. How many hands held those railings each day?

Crew members walked the decks throughout the day, carrying a xylophone in one arm, striking three tones to announce that it was time for breakfast, lunch or dinner. We thought they were the ones with the best job of all—next to polishing those brass railings!

Below deck, a labyrinth of passageways led to the staterooms—and when you saw the long carpeted corridors stretched out before you, they appeared to twist while the ship rolled back and forth with the waves.

Our crossing was uneventful this time, with no typhoons to avoid; and eight days later, we docked in Honolulu for one full day. We drew close to the Aloha Tower, with its four-sided clock, and we were welcomed by a band and hula dancers, wearing grass skirts! (I'm not making any of this up!) Two dozen passengers bound for Hawaii disembarked.

The ship remained for the entire day and many shore excursions were available. Some people talked about hitting the beach at Waikiki, and others planned to tour the USS Arizona Memorial in Pearl Harbor. There were a lot of possibilities.

When we disembarked, we walked past the lei vendors lining the pier, and piled into a taxi that took us all to Fort Shafter. Dad went into a building to take care of some military business, and then into the PX for cigarettes, while we sat on a lawn beneath some towering palm trees. When Dad came back, we took another taxi to the Ala Moana Shopping Center so that we could wander around. The ship was not scheduled to leave until that evening, so we had several hours.

Mom was so excited by the stores! She especially missed Sears. We spent a lot of time at the Sears store in Salinas, California before going overseas. Dad always used to say, "If you buy something from Sears, you can always take it back and get it replaced. They stand behind everything they sell." (As you can imagine, Dad did a lot of arguing through the years with Sears.)

We wandered through Sears and then discovered that the shopping center also had a Woolworth's—with a luncheonette counter—where we sat in a booth and ate strawberry shortcake! At Ala Moana I bought an olivine pendant necklace as a souvenir. Olivine is a volcanic gem, and it is also known as peridot, which is my birthstone. The large olivine piece I bought came from lava that had once flowed out of a Hawaiian volcano.

Before re-boarding the ship, we walked around the streets, past the Iolani Palace and some government buildings—the Supreme Court building, where a bronze statue of Hawaiian ruler King Kamehameha stands upon a large pedestal.

Once back on the ship, I phoned my school friend, Nancy Miyahira, who came with her mother to visit. Nancy's dad had retired from the army the year before, so she left Okinawa. Nancy brought a Hawaiian flower lei for me and a bag of "see-moi," a salty, dried plum treat that Nancy's mother used to offer us when I would go over to her house after school. Soon, the final call came— "All ashore that's going ashore!"

We took pictures in our stateroom and I promised to write to Nancy when we got settled in Kentucky. We exchanged Christmas letters for many years after that before finally losing track of one another.

The President Wilson left Honolulu around sunset. This time, flower leis were tossed from the ship as it passed Diamond Head. Legend was that if your lei floated back to shore, you would one day return to Hawaii. I tossed my lei from Nancy, and crossed my fingers.

When we departed Honolulu, there was a luau-themed dinner planned. According to the menu I found, that luau dinner featured Suckling Pig, Island Yams and Baked Bananas, as well as Maui Spring Chicken sautéed in Coconut Milk. I'm pretty sure we ate the Macadamia nuts and possibly picked at the pineapple, but undoubtedly all the children at our table said "no" to the Suckling Pig.

Once more, we found ouselves at sea. Several days later, we sailed back into San Francisco Bay, beneath the Golden Gate Bridge, where our overseas odyssey began almost four years earlier

Years later, I mentioned to one of the lawyers I worked with that we had been in Honolulu for an entire day while returning from the Far East. He wanted to know what we saw, and what we did . . but the expression on his face turned to disbelief as I told him about Ala Moana and Sears… and then strawberry shortcake at Woolworths!

I quickly realized that this was not a story I would keep telling. How could someone spend a day in Honolulu and not see anything noteworthy? How was that possible?

Years later, I did tell my husband all about my family's one-day sojourn to Hawaii. He reacted with little surprise. Don already knew what my family was like.

Docking in San Francisco on March 13, 1967, the first person to greet us was Uncle Ray. He sent us on our way in 1963 and here he was to meet our ship at the Oakland Terminal. He was driving the 1967 Chevy Bel-Air station wagon that we ordered from Okinawa—to be picked up at a dealership in San Francisco. We all drove away in our brand- new car. On the way to his apartment right across from Golden Gate Park, I remember gawking at the real live "hippies" who hung out in the park and around the Haight-Ashbury area. There were literally hundreds and thousands of flower children flocking to San Francisco during that "summer of love."

Aunt Nell complained about all those "flower-children" with their "free love" and how they spent all their time in the park smoking marijuana and doing "God knows what!"

Little did she know that the movement would get even larger.

A few months later, the hit song "San Francisco" written by John Phillips of The Mamas & the Papas, hit the airwaves. "If you're going to San Francisco, be sure to wear some flowers in your hair . . ."

I was there. I saw those "gentle people with the flowers in their hair." And many more were on their way.

Aunt Nell had boxes of rocky road candy waiting for us while we watched TV shows that we'd never seen before in living color.

"It's almost time for our favorite show," she announced. "We never miss it. You've got to see it. It's called 'Hogan's Heroes.'" Aunt Nell raved about it. We had a lot to catch up on. How could there be a comedy about a German prisoner-of-war camp?

Before taking off cross-country, we zipped up the Pacific Coast Highway heading north to Klamath Falls, Oregon. We needed one last visit with Grandma and Grampa Jepson before reporting to Fort Campbell. Who knew when we'd see them again?

Grandma had spent hours preserving every newspaper clipping about the Kennedy assassination for me. She had carefully clipped and pasted all the stories into a large scrapbook from Woolworths. She knew that we were pretty isolated back then and had missed the detailed coverage. Grandma was interested in history and I was thrilled to have the scrapbook.

More television to catch up with. There was a new game show in town—and my grandparents never missed it. We saw it and didn't understand. How could people win all those prizes for just showing up in a costume? How could that be a game show? You didn't have to know anything or do anything, but pick a curtain or a door and find out what was behind it. I wanted to be on that game show.

In no time, Dad was back behind the wheel of our new station wagon, and we headed down the Pacific Coast Highway for the Monterey Bay area where the Margadonnas, those old friends from Germany, were taking care of our dachshund Gretchen. As we pulled into their driveway, Gretchen wiggled and squealed to greet us all. Gretchen undoubtedly thought she would never see us again and was settling into her life in California when we suddenly showed up. She jumped into our station wagon and never looked back, ready to go for a very long ride.

We drove south to the Los Angeles area and then followed Route 66, "The Mother Road" across Arizona, New Mexico, Oklahoma and Texas before heading north to Fort Campbell, Kentucky, home of the Screaming Eagles, the 101st Airborne Division.

It was while we were filling up at a gas station in Needles, California that I bought my first souvenir postcard and kept buying them all along Route 66. Many were just from the motels we stayed in—real "mom and pop" motels. No chains back then. Holiday Inns were just emerging.

Before we got very far, we were searching for Chevy dealerships! Most people back then bought a new car and had time to drive it around, make a list of problems, and get it back to the dealership for corrections. But we got our new car in San Francisco—and started to drive across the country! I remember being in towns and cities where Dad would locate a Chevy dealership in the Yellow Pages, take the car in for service, and Mom would try to keep us kids and the dog occupied while Dad waited with the car. What a way to break in a new vehicle.

The most outrageous defect with the new car was when we were somewhere in Arizona, and the roof rack started to come loose! Dad was furious and now he was swearing cross-country.

We started across the Arizona desert at night so it would be cooler for travel. We were heading toward New Mexico. Back then, people venturing out across the desert hung canvas bags filled with water from the front of the car, known as "desert-bags." Several times, we saw warning signs—NO service stations for the next fifty or hundred or more miles as we entered the desert ahead of us. It was scary. What if we had car trouble? Try traveling about a thousand miles with three kids, one dog, NO air-conditioning and at least one kid known for getting carsick. To top it off, our dachshund had developed a problem with her anal gland. I won't go into detail, but whenever Gretchen got nervous (usually while riding for long periods of time in a car on my lap) she would suddenly release an extremely offensive skunky-smelling discharge from her butt.

I just wanted to burn my pants!

A classic Kriha family folk tale related to our cross-country family excursion involved driving right past the Grand Canyon. I can remember reading signs for exits for the Grand Canyon—and begging Dad to stop.

"Are you crazy? We've got to make time," was Dad's predictable response. And after much pleading, it deteriorated into some serious cussing. We were on a deadline—Dad's self-imposed deadline.

I don't know how real those deadlines were. I thought it was just Dad. But forty years later, while reminiscing with Cathy Gillion down in South Carolina, I learned that her dad also drove right past those same exit signs while on the way to Texas, offering similar excuses.

Stopping for motels was another thing that usually provoked an argument between Mom and Dad. He always wanted to just wait just a little longer, and then one more hour, before stopping. Finally, Dad would lose and Mom would win. We'd pull up in front of the office and Mom would run inside to see what they had left and if they would allow our dog Gretchen to stay. I can remember sleeping on the floor one night, with our dachshund, wrapped in an army blanket. When you wait too long to find a place, you take what you can find.

Reconnecting

Dub Bauer was supposed to go on the trip, and I promised to stay in touch with him.

I caught up by phone with Dub in Texas to tell him about the trip. He had a yearbook—and apparently I *am* in it! Dub photocopied the pages for my sophomore year from his '67 *TORII*. Finally, I was able to verify my existence!

Bauer graduated from Kubasaki in 1968 and went on to college Stateside in Texas while his family traded sweltering summers on Okinawa for wild winters in Minot, North Dakota! And you know the old joke— "Why not Minot? Freezin's the reason!"

I kept my promise to travel to Julia's home town of West Columbia, South Carolina the next spring. She lived about ten minutes away from the Columbia airport and I called her when I arrived. Once again, we were hugging one another in an airport. As she drove me to her home, she pointed out all the nearby houses as we drove past, and told me all about her neighbors. We zoomed down something she laughingly called "Thrill Hill" and then she made a sharp left turn into the driveway of her house, perched upon a steep hillside, covered with a fantasia of blooming azaleas and brilliantly-hued rhododendrons. I remarked about the middle-aged man leaning against the truck parked in the driveway—"Who's that guy?"—and soon I was greeting the twelve-year-old boy who had evolved into the half-century Jim Gillion!

And next Cathy—also middle-aged, and a mom and a grandmother—was hugging me, as well as little brother Gary, who was now also approaching his own big "five-oh."

As I reacquainted myself with the three Gillions, I could see traces of those 1960s faces in these suddenly middle-aged kids.

Julia's family was so very different from mine. They were very "huggie" people. It was so obvious that Julia's kids all loved her and cared about her! They kept an eye on her. I was amazed to learn that the three siblings also spent time socializing with one another. They had things in common that I never did with my two brothers. Cathy, Jim and Gary went out to dinner together. It appeared that they really enjoyed each other's company. I envied that.

Gary was the jokester of the family. He couldn't stop telling jokes, especially off-color jokes. Obviously, everyone else had heard all of Gary's stories several times over, but with me there, he had a fresh audience. I kept on laughing.

So why is it that the youngest kid is usually the one looking for the most fun? The oldest is the most responsible and the middle kid often gets lost and overshadowed by the other two. I had a feeling that Gary and Dan would definitely hit it off.

Julia and I sat outside on her back terrace one morning and I remarked about the loveliness of the hundreds of azalea and rhododendron bushes that she had spent years planting along the hillside surrounding her house.

She laughed and told me that when she and Bay bought the house, her daddy came over to see it, and stood up there on that hillside, quietly surveying the terrain and finally proclaimed, "Nobody would live up here, but a damn mountain goat!"

Julia laughed and said, "Daddy was right, but it took us a lot of years to realize it."

Back when we were kids on Okinawa, I can remember talking about the year 2000 with my brothers, and how exciting it would be to live long enough to move into the next century! I did the math and I would be forty-nine, Ray would be forty-six and Danny would be forty-three. We thought that was so old. And as kids, it seemed so far away. It was so hard to imagine ever being that old. Now we've all gone beyond that milestone.

We spent the next ten days reminiscing. Fate had brought two families together on Okinawa; I had come to know these people from the past once more, and it was now up to Cathy and me to keep the connection.

We sorted through many of Julia's artifacts from Okinawa, and while going through boxes of photos, it was inevitable—she found Yoshiko—that picture just jumped right out at her!

Finally, she held in her hand the missing snapshot of the two women standing side-by-side, outside the quarters in the Chatan Housing area.

We continued to flip through photographs, and there were quite a few of Blackie, the dog that was the brother to our best-mutt-ever, Maggie.

I remember how determined Dad was to get a puppy for the Gillions when he found out that Maggie's mother had another litter of puppies. Forty years later, I discovered that Julia was not even fond of dogs. Dad persisted though, and Julia was outnumbered when he showed up with Maggie's puppy brother. What could she say? The Gillions named him "Blackie" and ended up loving that dog forever. He flew home to the States two years later when they returned by ship on the USS General Mann, and couldn't take him along.

"That ship was in horrible shape," said Julia. "We couldn't even latch the portholes."

I did some research and apparently the ship *was* in pretty bad shape. The Gillions came home from Okinawa in 1965 and the Mann was decommissioned in December of that year.

The Gillions were a devoted "one-dog" family and Blackie lived to be 105 in dog years. From Julia I also discovered that our little black-and-tan mutt Maggie was in reality a genuine Japanese breed known as "*Shiba Inu.*"

"After Blackie flew home to the States, we took him to a vet to get him checked over and the vet wanted to know what kind of dog he was. We said he was just a mutt and explained that he came from Okinawa, but the vet said that he really looked like a breed of Japanese dog called a *Shiba Inu*. Didn't ya'll know that?"

Of course not! All those years I had dismissed our Maggie as just a "black and tan mutt." So she was special after all!

Later, while shoe-shopping with Julia, I discovered that her feet really had been *killing* her while on our Okinawa trek. No way should she have been wandering around in those molded plastic "Crocs"! She needed some serious orthotics and supportive sneakers for that trip. I don't know how she kept up with all that walking. I told her to find a foot doctor.

Julia and I had another fun time. The two of us *do* make good girlfriends and Cathy probably wouldn't understand it because she knows Julia as her mother and I know Julia as a friend. There's a big difference when you don't have the mother/daughter dynamic to deal with.

My mother really would have appreciated what has developed between these two families who were serendipitously tossed together aboard the Barrett.

The Gillion kids all live near one another in South Carolina and we three Kriha kids all live near one another here in Ohio. But beyond that, there are no similarities. We don't share the same closeness. What happened to us in our childhoods, to make us what we are today?

My husband often compared our family dynamic to the "Balkanization" of hostile family "member/republics" when Mom pulled everyone together for holiday dinners down in the basement in Ohio after retirement.

Behind Mom's back, Don joked that she was like "Marshal Tito" unifying Yugoslavia's antagonistic groups. Even Don's mother was a party to those dinners. They were preserved for posterity when Dad positioned his full-size VHS Panasonic video cam-corder on a tripod down in a corner of the basement, pushed the "record" button, and let it go until the tape ran out. Dad was the master of the "family-holiday surveillance video."

No one except Dad ever sat and watched those endless hours of videotape.

For each holiday feast, Dad fired up the massive chrome coffee urn in the basement and perked about thirty cups of strong coffee. Scooping coffee from the giant can of Maxwell House that he dipped into only for special occasions, Dad always felt he had to make the coffee well in advance of dinner, while waiting for the guests to arrive.

He and Don were usually the only ones in the group drinking the coffee. Don always pointed out that Dad's coffee was very bitter—but somebody had to drink it!

As the next holiday approaches, my brothers and I will exchange greeting cards. We seem to be strangers as adults. We're losing touch. I know Mom wanted to pass the torch to me, but I just don't wield her "dictatorial panache."

After another year passed and I continued my writing, I visited the Gillions again. But this time, husband Don drove with me to South Carolina. Julia came up with the most amazing idea—and suggested that we visit with the Halls! I had forgotten about them. Mom had exchanged Christmas cards with them through the years. Of course! We needed to visit Leroy and Elinor Hall. She had been aboard the Barrett with us—another army wife taking her two children, Monica and Larry, across the Pacific to Okinawa.

Julia said the Halls lived only fifty miles away in Covington, Georgia, near Augusta. Julia gave them a call. After that, it was all set. I just knew I would get some more interesting stories out of them for my book.

We took off mid-morning—targeting our arrival for 1 p.m., so we'd have the afternoon to visit. I could remember the Halls as a quiet couple sitting in their living room on the sofa—but not much more. We didn't visit them as often as the Gillions did. I remembered Monica and Larry, but it wasn't like Monica and I traded movie magazines and went shopping together like I did with Cathy. The Halls lived on our side of the island, up the hill, just off Highway One.

Julia tried to refresh my memory, but there wasn't a whole lot to go on. Our family wasn't as close to the Halls as we were to the Gillions. I remembered that the Halls were the family who saw us off at Naha Port when we boarded the *Otomi maru*.

Farewells were an inevitable part of military life. I said goodbye to many friends through the years. Mom and I drove to Kadena Air Base to see my friend Sherry Ahl return home to the States with her family. And then Nancy Miyahira moved to Honolulu when her father retired. The Gillions left Okinawa before we did, so that's how the Halls ended up taking us to Naha Port. I wonder who saw them off when it was their turn to go?

When the door opened, there was Elinor, still petite—but not with the shoulder-length coal-black hair that I remembered. She had the same hairstyle, but all grey. Barrel-chested Leroy stood beside her.

I hoped to get some information from the Halls that I could use somewhere in my book. I expected them to be full of stories about Okinawa. I hoped to hear them say, "Do you remember when we… or do you remember the time that…"

But there was none of that. We all sat politely in the living room—a living room that closely resembled their living room on Okinawa in the 1960s. The Halls were still that quiet couple, sitting on the sofa. It was like we were right back in their house up on the hill from Highway One in Oyama. The Halls were frozen in time, along with their living room.

A deeply-carved Asian coffee table with matching end tables stood on either side of the sofa. On each end table was an Asian brass lamp with a coordinating silk shade, still covered in protective plastic…it *was* just like being back in the house that I remembered.

It was becoming awkward. Conversation was so formal, so polite. I was getting nothing out of them.

Leroy did recall driving us to Naha Port. He talked about the paper streamers being tossed from passengers on deck at the railings down to those who remained on shore…and he even remembered that there were bulls tied out on deck.

"We could see them from down on the dock," he said.

Amazing.

Leroy showed off his prized, custom-made teak entertainment center to Don. With a push of the "touch-to-open" cabinet doors, his old-school two-channel receiver, turntable and cassette tape deck were all revealed. Leroy said that it cost $185 to have it built by Okinawan craftsmen, and here it was—still the centerpiece of their living room after more than forty years, and still something to talk about. I wondered how many times he had told his story.

Also on display inside the center was Monica's Japanese doll—the one she made in a doll-making class on Okinawa, along with all of Leroy's bowling trophies.

Through the years, Mom had rearranged our treasured acquisitions, even moving some of them up to the attic. After retirement, the background stories about how we acquired our worldly items lost significance on civilians.

I inquired about Monica and Larry, as I pointed at the framed photos lined up on top of the teak entertainment center. The framed eight-by-ten studio photographs captured the Hall family pretty close to how Julia and I remembered them from many years ago.

We learned that Monica was a nurse and lived with her family in North Carolina. Larry was also married and was a pilot for American Airlines, based in South Carolina.

We learned that the Halls had left Okinawa a year after we did, ended up in Georgia and moved into this house. It was supposed to be temporary, until they found another, but they stayed. They've lived here in this house since 1968, when Leroy retired.

I tried to pull some information out of Elinor about our 1963 voyage to Okinawa on the Barrett and that stopover in Yokohama. Did she and the kids leave the ship to go to the PX with us?

"No way!" said Elinor, shocked at even the idea of leaving the safety of the ship. "We were afraid of getting lost."

Well now I have to give up. I haven't a clue about who led that excursion—how we boldly followed someone into uncharted foreign territory—a major metropolis known as Yokohama.

One thing I learned was that the Halls found us the same way that the Gillions did—a chance encounter in the PX. It was a small island and everyone ended up shopping for something over at the PX.

Finally, Julia said it was time to get on the road.

Elinor pulled Julia aside and whispered to her, "You're *not* driving, are you?"

"Of *course* I'm driving. I don't let any grass grow under my feet," responded Julia.

"And she's kinda fast too," I added.

We climbed back into the Toyota, and as we backed out of the driveway, waving our goodbyes, Julia commented that the Halls always had seemed a bit peculiar.

"The strong connection with military families is never broken," she said. "You're separated, but once you get back together, it's like you never were apart; but with them, I think it's broken."

We left Georgia, on a northerly route toward Columbia, with Julia behind the wheel once more. Don was positioned in the back seat of the Toyota, manning the Tom-Tom GPS system and clocking Julia's occasional eighty mile-per-hour bursts of speed.

Dad's Military Records

Could Uncle Ollie have been right?

I needed to find out. For years, he and Dad had been at odds over whether or not my father had spent time in the stockade, sometime during his army career. Ollie insisted. Dad denied. But based on past history, it just might have been possible.

The two brothers shared a bedroom in the old family home on the south side of Oshkosh on 11th Street. That was the beginning of their rivalry.

Dad certainly didn't have the best reputation around Oshkosh when he went off to Fort Knox, Kentucky for basic training, and then shipped overseas to Japan and Korea. Dad couldn't have undergone a total transformation. GIs were known to get drunk and rowdy...and into bar fights. Dad must have been in some kind of trouble.

Maybe Ollie *was* right.

I learned that I could request Dad's military service records from the National Personnel Records Center (NPRC) in St. Louis. When I located the records request website, the first thing I discovered was that the NPRC receives approximately 4,900 requests daily! Okay. The average response time was stated at four-and-one-half weeks.

Still okay. But then they referenced the Great Fire of 1973, and how many records had been totally destroyed. Not okay.

It was like someone was warning me not to expect results.

But I had all the time in the world. I'm an old secretary, efficient and persistent. I mailed off the request form and a certified copy of Dad's death certificate. And despite the Great Fire that is probably the best excuse ever for governmental delay and red tape, I eventually managed to get photocopies of my father's records after about a year.

Emboldened, I went one step beyond, and requested replacement medals.

Another year passed, and I was just about to send off an inquiry, when those medals suddenly showed up in the mail.

I needed the records to piece together dates and places for my book—and to see for myself if Dad ever got into trouble during his twenty-one years in the army.

When I finally had seventy-nine photocopied pages in hand, I saw my father's familiar printing—with details about his next-of-kin, his health history and work history in Oshkosh—how Dad drove delivery trucks for Elmer Retzloff and worked in his father's shoe repair shop.

There was Dad's familiar signature, the one that I remembered seeing scrawled upon my report cards, and even Dad's fingerprints! The pages contained information about how he had completed only the ninth grade when he enlisted; but later pages documented how he attained his GED through correspondence courses while we were stationed on Okinawa. I could remember Dad doing homework on the kitchen table, and Dad telling me about tests that he mailed away to the University of Maryland for grading.

Dad enlisted in 1947, with the recommendation that he be "permitted to wear low-quarter shoes, no prolonged standing or marching, permitted to wear white socks." That proviso followed my father throughout his entire military career, appearing again and again in his records. At one point, there was even a notation about a steel shank being inserted into his shoes.

Aunt Mary told me all about it.

It all came down to Dad's club feet.

Dad had legs that could only be described as "chicken legs." They tapered down to his ankles, with no shaped calf. They bowed toward each other slightly, as though he was "bowlegged" and "pigeon-toed." Dad's legs were unusual, that's for sure. I remember when I finally asked about his feet one day, especially his "monkey toes," and he just said, "This is the way they've been since I was a kid."

Dad was born with congenital bilateral club feet. And Aunt Mary should know, because Grandma told her all about it. I guess it was pretty serious back in 1929 because Grandma packed up her baby Joe, and took him off to a special hospital, The McLain Orthopedic Sanitarium in St. Louis, a hospital that advertised cures for crippled children back in the 1920s. The hospital ran ads in magazines like *McClure's* and *Popular Science*.

Grandma was determined to find a cure. She rented a room in a boarding house with a little gas burner so she could cook their meals. She had to rent a buggy to wheel her little boy down the street to the hospital every day for treatments. Dad was fitted with metal leg braces that he wore constantly. Grandma squeezed into a single bed with her baby boy—where he proceeded to kick her black-and-blue while tossing and turning throughout the night. Eventually Grandma learned to tighten the braces herself and was able to bring him home to Oshkosh.

Aunt Mary didn't remember how long Dad wore the braces, but eventually he could walk without crutches and didn't end up in a wheelchair when he started school.

Mary said, "Joe didn't appreciate the sacrifice his mother made for him. Not until someone knocked some sense into him many years later, in a bar."

"Joe had been drinking and was bad-mouthing his mother. An old neighbor went up to him and told him to his face that he was so spoiled, and if it hadn't been for his mother taking him to that hospital in St. Louis, he would be drinking in a wheelchair."

"He shut up in a hurry and left."

Dad dropped out of Sacred Heart School in the ninth grade.

"He was always getting into trouble," said Mary. "The police were constantly bringing him home to Ma and Pa."

Dad was twenty years old when Oshkosh Police Chief Goltz issued him an ultimatum: "Join the army or go to jail."

Mary added, "For some reason, this time the army overlooked Joe's club foot history, because Joe tried to join on his own back in 1945 and had been turned down." Under the chief's influence, Dad got out of trouble in Oshkosh and got into the army. It was just what he needed. I wonder if Chief Goltz ever learned about Dad's success in the army. Dad turned things around, kept his nose clean for the next twenty-one years, and was a good soldier.

According to his service records, Dad completed basic training at Fort Knox and drove a heavy-duty truck for a while, before heading to Fort Sam Houston, Texas in 1950 for sixteen weeks of dental mechanics lab training that put him on a path to a career as a dental lab specialist. That training was good for Dad, and perfect for his foot problem, because he sat upon a high stool at a lab bench.

After Texas, Dad was ordered to Camp Cooke, California, where he worked in the medical detachment and met my mother, a licensed practical nurse who was also stationed there.

On March 15, 1951 Dad PCS'd to Sakai, Japan for a few months at the 171ˢᵗ Evac Hospital before heading to Korea, again working in a dental lab.

Returning from Korea, Dad was promoted to Sergeant and PCS'd back to the States, picked up Mom and me in Cleveland, visited with all the relatives, and finally settled in Camp Crowder, Missouri.

Every three years, Dad could choose to be honorably discharged or "re-up" for another hitch. He never got into any trouble. He didn't screw up.

Dad rose through the ranks, earning his stripes, to Sergeant First Class (E-7) before retirement. The pages showed his progression from a single enlisted man, adding a dependent wife and child, to make a family of three and then a family of five.

More pages detailed various security clearances, coursework, annual physicals...more than I could imagine! Dad had qualified in arms training, including an M-1 rifle, a carbine and something referred to as an LMG (light machine gun?). His scores were there. I don't know if they were good numbers or not, but the notation SS (sharpshooter?) was marked in beside the first two weapons. Dad never talked about any of this.

I remember a time when he told his grandson Paul that he had been an MP while in the army. I didn't really believe it when Paul told me later, but there it was! While out at Camp Cooke, Dad had served for a short time with the military police!

Medical records revealed how he was given a shot of penicillin in the hospital in Germany and ended up with a severe allergic reaction. Dad wore one of those medical alert bracelets to advise of his allergy to penicillin. I remember Dad telling us how he had almost died.

There were copies of records from the time he showed up at the Sukiran Dispensary on Okinawa because of an outbreak of foot fungus! Foot fungus plagued him through the years. I can remember Dad sitting in his recliner, with his feet soaking in something dissolved in a tub of warm water.

Dad had been remarkably healthy throughout his twenty-one year career. And there was absolutely no mention of any time spent in the stockade.

Uncle Ollie was wrong, and Chief Goltz was right.

The army had made a man out of my father.

Mom's story was very different. Like I said, one of the first things you hear…is about how many service records were lost or destroyed in the fire…how it might have included the records you are seeking. But don't give up or go away discouraged. Be persistent. You will eventually receive the records, if they still exist. I followed through with what little information I could provide for my mother, and several months later, I received twenty-six photocopied pages about her service, with a cover letter, stating that Mom's record was located in the area that suffered the most damage in the fire that occurred on July 12, 1973. The pages appeared to have smudges, water stains and scorch marks. So there really *was* a fire. I'm convinced. I do believe the fire story.

When 134,000 North Korean troops crossed the thirty-eighth parallel and invaded South Korea on June 25, 1950, things got serious.

The army needed female soldiers and decided to recruit former WACs who had served during World War II. In August of 1950, a headline in *The New York Times* read, "Army Issues Call for 1,644 Women." For the first time, the U.S. Army had ordered the involuntary call-up of women reservists for active duty. Nurses were needed. Recruiting posters appeared on bulletin boards in hospitals. There must have been something on the wall at Huron Road Hospital. Mom answered Uncle Sam's call.

I peered through the water stains and smudges, and learned a lot. I discovered that Mom weighed in at 106 pounds (including her chain) when she enlisted on March 27, 1950. And she was five feet ten inches tall. She really was a skeleton!

Mom's basic training was at Camp Lee, Virginia, and then she went off to Fort Sam Houston for ten weeks of training as a medical technician.

She was ordered to Camp Cooke, California in October of 1950. There, she met my father.

I was amazed to learn that her total time in the WACs amounted to only one year, one month and eight days. And when she was honorably discharged on May 4, 1951, the details of her final medical exam documented that she was fourteen weeks pregnant. Her weight at that time was 118 pounds. She was a nineteen-year-old girl on her way home to Cleveland.

Epilogue

It's hard to believe that both Mom and Dad are gone now, and that we three siblings have become middle-aged orphans.

I think about my parents a lot. Sometimes I hear Mom's voice in my own voice—when I clear my throat, when I laugh and even the inflection in tone when I pronounce certain words.

It was always a family joke about how many people would think I was her when I answered the phone. People would just start talking to "Grace." And then when I explained, they always said, "But you sound exactly like your mother! I can't tell you two apart."

I never understood it then and we used to laugh about it. But now I do. I hear Mom in my own voice.

I would call my mother almost every night just to "touch base" for a few minutes. It was our way of checking in with each other. By 11:30 p.m., we had both finished everything we had to do to wrap up our busy days and could finally catch up by phone. The dogs had been let out for the night and they were settling down in their snug little beds. Dad was usually asleep and snoring in his recliner and didn't even pay attention to the ringing telephone.

I find myself thinking about Mom around this time each night. She would fill me on what was happening and I would do the same.

My newspaper assignments were completed and I had e-mailed my stories and police blotters. I was ready to wind down and watch some late night TV to unwind.

As I go through my days now, I sometimes find myself exclaiming aloud, *"Mom! You're not gonna believe what Danny's done now."*

I drive down the road and think about things to tell her...but then it hits me that she doesn't have a phone number any longer.

She would be shocked that shortly after she died...Dan and Paula "dissolved" their marriage for the second time around...that Dan found a new woman immediately and married her out in his back yard. That the "preacher-man" who was licensed to perform the ceremony, did double-duty as a caterer...that her doggies were still around and still annoyingly ecstatic...that Dad held on for one more year before he died...and that Dan's new wife devotedly took care of Dad at home in a hospital bed in their living room.

She would not be pleased to know that both she and Dad are still waiting in their urns on the top shelf of Great-Aunt Margaret's mahogany Duncan Phyfe corner china cabinet. That's right. Mom and Dad are still keeping an eye on Danny. (At least I got them out of the crematorium containers and into antique ginger jars.)

I'm waiting for Dan to follow through with plans for their interment in the Veteran's Cemetery. Aunt Mary told me that there's a spare plot in the family cemetery in Oshkosh that was intended for my father. I may have to drive Mom and Dad up there one day. Mom would not be pleased to end up in Oshkosh forever. I can just hear her...screaming.

I spent some time at Euclid General Hospital recently, visiting a friend. I hardly recognized the place. I walked around the hospital, noting how it had been drastically remodeled. The gift shop was still where it used to be, and I remembered when Mom once had an "account" and bought some really unique gifts for me. The wall where the pay phones once were located was now just an empty alcove. That was where I called my husband to tell him that our baby was going to be a boy, back in the early days of ultrasound—and pay phones.

When the fifth-floor elevator was slow to arrive, without hesitation, I turned the corner to take the stairs. I found myself in "Mom's stairwell." Mom always took the stairs, because of her claustrophobia.

It was the one area of the building that had remained unchanged. Surrounded by clay-tile walls and "hospital-green" painted metal trim, I felt as though Mom's spirit was in that stairwell…and she was descending the stairs along with me.

She'd spent so many hours climbing up and down the steps to the ICU and Coronary Care and the other nine floors to avoid taking elevators. I'm certain that I'm not imagining how she told me that she would actually wheel a patient onto the elevator, push the button and then run down the stairs in time to meet it. Probably no one but the patient ever knew about that.

Mom wouldn't understand why I was writing this book, but she would be pleased that I have tracked down several of her old friends to gather details for my story. She would have liked that.

I would be excited to tell her all about this. And I would point out that everything I wrote was the truth as I knew it, no matter how much she would have disagreed and not wanted me to tell people about my brothers. I would just keep telling her, "I've got to tell the truth. It must be the truth as I know and remember it."

And thank you Mom, for keeping me, for *not* putting me up for adoption. With some other family, I would never have had all this rich material. And in some way, I feel like Mom is looking over my shoulder, and hopefully at peace with the truth that I am writing.

There's talk on the Internet about the next Uchinanchu Festival scheduled for October of 2011. I mentioned it to Don. He said, "Anything's possible."

In my book, that's definitely a yes! (Translation: We're going. We're *both* going.)

And I just might have to pack Mom and Dad in my carry-on. They could come along. Dan probably won't have gotten around to interring them, so perhaps I should scatter their ashes somewhere along the East China Sea, down in Oyama, the place where we all once seemed happy.

The only person who can help me find my old house is the same person who wasn't all that thrilled about the trip—the same guy who rolled over and mumbled when I told him about going back to Okinawa! But I'll bring him around. I'll drag Don across the ocean with me for the Fifth Worldwide Uchinanchu Festival. We will take an entire day or more, if necessary, to walk Oyama on foot, and we'll find that little cement house.

Don's a "detail guy"—and that's a good thing. Don will help me find my home. He'll make a grid...we'll cover quadrants...he'll configure it...

When you move around constantly as a brat, you learn early that your address and phone number are very important. They are your "life-lines." These are the places I've called home, most of which I committed to memory.

1953	206 Patterson Homes, Fort Crowder, Missouri
1954	299 Patterson Homes, Fort Crowder, Missouri
1954	519 Delaware Street, Neosho, Missouri
1954	1205 Murphy Street, Joplin, Missouri
1955	Building 354, Perlocher Forst, Munich, Germany
1955	Building 348, Perlocher Forst, Munich, Germany
1958	6708 South C Street, Tacoma, Washington
1961	606 Broadway Avenue, Seaside, California
1961	351 Carentan Road, Fort Ord, California
1962	301 3rd Avenue, Fort Ord, California
1963	3018 Kings Circle, Marina, California
1963	1498 Oyama, Okinawa
1964	886 Futenma Housing Area, Okinawa
1967	5025-A Hammond Heights, Fort Campbell, Kentucky
1968	28920 Foxboro Drive, Willowick, Ohio

Acknowledgments:

Thanks and appreciation goes to my family—living and dead—for providing such rich material for this book. I'm glad I didn't climb out of the gene pool after all.

Thanks to Mike Johnson for helping me to "see the light" and venture into the world of "indie" publishing.

And thanks to my early readers for encouragement and helpful comments: Mary Connors, Debbie Scotese, Yvette Slusarki, Linda Vencel and Sandy Walker.

And special thanks to husband Don, my in-house technology guy.

References:

Bumiller, Elisabeth, *The Secrets of Mariko, A Year in the Life of a Japanese Woman and Her Family*, 1995, Times Books.

Dickson, Paul, *War Slang, American Fighting Words and Phrases Since the Civil War*, 2004, Brassey's Inc.

Feiffer, George, *TENNOZAN, The Battle of Okinawa and the Atomic Bomb*, 1992, Ticknor & Fields.

Grahn, Elna Hilliard, *In the Company of WACS*, 1993, Sunflower University Press, Manhattan, Kansas.

Fuller, Louise Lawrence, *Army Wives, Veterans Without Glory, A Memoir*, 2001, 1st Books Library.

Kennedy, Robert F., *Thirteen Days, A Memoir of the Cuban Missile Crisis*, 1969, W. W. Norton & Company, Inc.

Keyso, Ruth Ann, *Women of Okinawa*, 2000, Cornell University Press.

Truscott, Mary R., *BRATS, Children of the American Military Speak Out*, 1989, Penguin Books.

Wertsch, Mary Edwards, *MILITARY BRATS, Legacies of Childhood Inside the Fortress*, 1991, Harmony Books.